THE COMPLETE WORKS OF BRANN THE ICONOCLAST
(VOLUME X)

LECTOR HOUSE PUBLIC DOMAIN WORKS

THE COMPLETE WORKS OF BRANN THE ICONOCLAST (VOLUME X)

WILLIAM COWPER BRANN

ISBN: 978-93-5614-384-5

Published: -

© 2022
LECTOR HOUSE LLP

LECTOR HOUSE

LECTOR HOUSE LLP
E-MAIL: lectorpublishing@gmail.com

THE COMPLETE WORKS OF BRANN THE ICONOCLAST
(VOLUME X)

BY

WILLIAM COWPER BRANN

CONTENTS

THE COMPLETE WORKS OF BRANN THE ICONOCLAST

DOLCE FAR NIENTE AND DOLLARS.

The dispatches state that during the three weeks George Gould was lazing and luxuriating in a foreign land "the business revival added at least $15,000,000 to the value of the Gold securities." Gadzooks! how sweet idleness must be when sugared with more than $714,000 per day! I'm willing to loaf for half the lucre. How refreshing it is to contemplate our plutocrats lying beside their nectar like a job lot of Olympian gods—"careless of mankind"—while

> "—they smile in secret, looking over wasted lands,
> Blight and famine, plague and earthquake, roaring deeps and fiery
> sands,
> Clanging fights and flaming towns, and sinking ships and praying
> hands."

One of Mr. Gould's employees, who was toiling at risk of life and limb for about $2 a day while his imperial master was doing the *dolce far niente* act for $714,000 per diem and his board, comments as follows in a letter to the ICONOCLAST:

> "W. C. BRANN: It might be pertinent for you to find out how the festive George, of yacht-racing, Waler-hob-nobbing fame, has managed to reap such pronounced benefits from the revival in business. It is notorious among railroad men that one of the first moves of Superintendent Trice, who succeeded Tim Campbell as manager of the I. & G. N., was to inaugurate a series of 'reforms,' the chief feature of which was the cutting salaries of from 20 to 40 per cent, especially among the office men, and at the same time covering it by swapping the men around as much as possible. Forces were reduced by compelling the half-starved employees to do overtime at less pay, and the poor devils can only grin and bear it. Suppose you write down, and get the true data from the various places where the I. & G. N. touches, and then show the true source, or the real 'revival' that has given the festive George such a boost in his cash box."

In the first place, "the business revival" has not "added $15,000,000 to the value of the Gould securities"—it is a political falsehood which George can be depended upon to promptly repudiate when the tax assessor calls around to tender congratulations. It is eleven to seven that Georgie assures him that the Gould estate is in a very bad way, that only by the most heroic self-sacrifices in this period of business depression can he succeed in remaining solvent; that there was a slight advance in railway values while crops were moving, only to be succeeded by a doleful slump, caused by the high tariff, which cuts so dreadfully into tonnage. If he refrains from putting up some such game of talk as that I'll take up a collection among the boot-blacks of Texas to help pay his taxes. Fifteen millions in three weeks! Oh my! Since "Count" Castellane pulled one leg off the estate it is no larger than it was when old Jay went to He-aven. Now Jay was an honorable man—at least he wouldn't steal the buttons off your undershirt while you had it on, and hotel keepers; did not take the precaution to chain his knife and fork to the table; but in his palmiest days he paid taxes on but $75,000 worth of personal property—railway securities and "sich." Heavy crops, for which Providence and the industry of the American people are alone responsible, have added somewhat to the present earning power of railway properties, but it is doubtful, if the total mileage and equipment owned by the Goulds would sell for as much actual cash as before the election of McKinley. The great bulk of the boasted advance in Gould securities consists of wind pumped in by the "pulls"; but just the same the American people will be bled to pay dividends on this speculative boodle—both patrons and employees will suffer that interest may be collected on "invested capital" which never had an existence. But even were the dispatches true, what must be said of a "business revival" that reduces wages, that adds enormously to the wealth of the plutocrats while making economic conditions harder for the great mass of the American people? The general trend of wages is downward, while the cost of living is enhanced by the Dingley tariff and the advance in flour caused by foreign crop failures. Why? Because, despite the pumping of the Republican press about the "return of prosperity," the country is full of idle men, and the inevitable tendency of the gold standard and high tariff is to increase their number and further lower wages by the pressure of these people for employment. Railway securities have advanced a little despite the repressive effect of Republican policy, have beaten up somewhat against the adverse winds, impelled by speculators whose *vis vitalis* was the crops of the country—the great bulk of which were produced by men who voted for Bryan. The necessary sequence of an appreciating standard of value is depreciation in the selling price of property, whether such property be Gould securities or Irish potatoes; while a high tariff inevitably reduces tonnage below what it would otherwise be—chisels a yawning hiatus into the revenues of every American railroad. This fact is so self-evident that it may seem unnecessary to say more on the subject—that arguing the matter were like wasting time proving that water is wet; but as a number of Republican papers are having a serious of violent epeliptoid convulsions because I recently asserted that a nation can only be paid for its exports with its imports, it may not be amiss to make a few remarks adapted to the understanding of the kindergarten class. Trade, whether between the people of this republic, or those of Europe and America, is, when reduced to the last analysis, nothing more than an exchange of commodities. It may happen that we sell largely to a country of which we buy but little; but the nations that purchase of our debtor pay for our products. Our exports usually exceed our imports, and for the simple reason that we owe vast sums abroad, the surplus being employed in the payment of interest and the discharge of our foreign indebtedness. When we become a great creditor nation like England, our imports will exceed our exports—we will begin to absorb the labor products of foreign lands. If America received foreign gold for all her exports it would be nothing more than a commodity weighed to her at so much per ounce and which she might exchange at her good pleasure for foreign goods, just as she does her cotton and corn. Some gold crosses the sea; but it goes and comes just as go other commodities—seeks the most advantageous market. A tariff wall, by keeping foreign products *out* keep American products *in*, thereby narrowing our market and limiting production. If the workman does not produce he cannot consume, and production and consumption are the basis of railway business. But why, it may be asked, would the railway corporations cut their own throats by helping elect McKinley? Surely they understand their business much better than does a Texas maverick-brander who writes economic editorials while astride a mustang. Possibly so; but it were well to remember that while it is evidently to the interests of the stockholders of such a corporation that it should prosper, the bond-owner, who is a kind of wholesale pawnbroker and flourishes best during periods of business depression, also has something to say. Whether the former receives any dividends or not the latter must have his interest, and the more of labor products required to pay it the more he is enriched. The railway bondholder is usually the party who holds a $500 mortgage on a $10,000 farm. Crops may fail, the hogs get the cholera and the poultry die of the pips; cotton may go down and cloth go up; but the sorrows of others cause him to lose no sleep. As I have hitherto pointed out, we have it on the authority of Mark Hanna's newspaper organ "lower wages are certainly a feature of the new prosperity"—that the American workman need not hope for permanent employment until willing to accept the same wages paid "the pauper labor of Europe," from whose disastrous competition the Republicans solemnly promised him protection. If Supt. Trice is reducing wages and overworking his men it may be accepted as certain that he is compelled thereto by a higher power—that the edict has gone forth that the employees of the I. & G. N. must work longer hours for less money that interest be paid on the $15,000,000 which the blessed "business revival" added to the value of Mr. Gould's securities while he was idling about Europe.

*   *   *   *   *

SALMAGUNDI.

The daily press announces that there is to be another Cleveland baby. It is to make its debut some time this month. "Mrs. Cleveland has been sewing dainty garments all summer." "Presents of beautiful baby clothes are arriving from friends and relatives." Same old gush, gush, gush! slop, slop, slop! that has set the nation retching three times already. Good Lord! will it never end? The fecundity of that family is becoming an American nightmare. Will the time ever come when a married woman of social prominence can get into "a delicate condition" without having the fact heralded over the country as brazenly as though she had committed a crime? There being little hope that the daily press—"public educator," "guardian of morality," etc.—will suffer a renascence of decency, we can only appeal to Grover not to let it happen again. He certainly owes it to the nation to apply the soft pedal to himself. In no other way can he protect a long-suffering nation from seasickness, or his estimable wife from the unclean harpies of the press. I do not believe that Mrs. Cleveland is *particeps criminis* in these pre-natal proclamations to which the h'upper suckkles of New York are so shockingly addicted. I do not believe that she cares to have the public contemplating her profile portrait just previous to a confinement. Of course it will be urged that a woman of much native delicacy could never have married so crass an animal as Grover Cleveland, have taken him fresh from the embraces of an old harlot like Widow Halpin; but these forget that he held the most exalted position of any man on earth, and his $50,000 per annum had been touched by the genie-wand jobbery—forget that

> "—pomp and power alone are woman's care
> And where these are light Eros finds a feere;
> Maidens like moths, are eer caught by glare,
> And Mammon wins his way where Seraphs might despair."

Probably she has regretted a thousand times that she bartered her youth and beauty for life companionship with a tub of tallow, mistaken at the time for a god by a purblind public, but even though it be true, as often asserted, that the old boor gets drunk and beats her, a woman could scarce apply for divorce from a man who has twice been president. Furthermore, association with such a man will lower the noblest woman to his level. Every physiognomist who saw Frances Folsom's bright face, its spirituelle beauty, and who looks upon it now and notes it stolid, almost sodden expression, must recall those lines of Tennyson's:

> "As the husband is the wife is; thou art mated with a clown,
> And the grossness of his nature will have weight to drag thee down.
> Cursed be the sickly forms that err from honest Nature's rule,
> Cursed be the gold that gilds the straiten'd forehead of the fool."

Last month it was announced with typographical and pictorial trumpet blasts that Mrs. Harry Payne Whitney was about to present her gilded dudelet with a family *edition de luxe*, and the Duchess of Marlborough to find an heir to that proud title whose foundation was laid with a sister's shame, the capstone placed by the pander's betrayal of his rightful prince; and now before the world can recover from its nausea, flaming headlines announce that the Clevelands are about to re-fill the family cradle. Hold our head, please, until we puke! Lord, Lord, is there nothing sacred about motherhood any more? Is a married woman no better than a brood-mare, her condition fair subject for comment by vulgar stable-boys? We thank thee, O God, that the South has not kept pace with New York's super-estheticism—that when our women find themselves in an "interesting condition" they seek the seclusion of the home instead of telephoning for a reporter and a chalk artist and exploiting their intumescence in the public prints.

* * *

Thomas M. Harris, who claims to be 84 years old, has writ a little yellow pamphlet entitled, "Rome's Responsibility for the Assassination of Abraham Lincoln." I have expended almost 5 minutes glancing over Mr. Harris labored lucubrations, and must confess that I have in that time acquired more information—of its kind—

than I ever did in 5 hours before. Of the reliability of his statements there can be no question, as most of them are grounded on the testimony of "Father" Chiniquy—conceded to be the most accomplished liar since Ananias gave up the ghost. It was Chiniquy who first started the story that the Pope was responsible for the assassination of President Lincoln, and I am expecting him to prove that Guiteau who gave the death-wound to Garfield, was a Jesuit in disguise and acted on orders received from Rome. Harris says that agents of the Confederacy in Canada—whom he admits were not Catholics—employed Booth and his accomplices to do the bloody business; that John Wilkes Booth was a Catholic; that the priests were all Southern sympathizers; that but 144,000 Irishmen enlisted in the Federal army, of whom 104,000 deserted; that the cellars of Catholic cathedrals are filled with munitions of war to be used against the government, that Catholics hold the bulk of the offices and dominate the American press. Harris says other things equally awful and interesting. I much fear that he got to thinking how many of his A. P. Apes have broken into the penitentiary, and dreamed a bad dream.

* * *

I once mentioned a little saweiety sheet, published in New York, under the title of *Town Topics*, because it afforded me a kind of languid pleasure to kick the feculent sewer-rat back into the foul cloaca from which it had crawled to beslime the ICONOCLAST. I must beg the patient reader's pardon for again soiling my sandal-shoon with what should only be touched with a shovel. I have been receiving through the mails for some time past, both from disgusted Northerners and indignant Southerners, a paragraph clipped from its epecine columns where in some mental misfit eager to do the Smart Alex act begs to be informed what right Mrs. Jefferson Davis had "to address a peculiar letter to the Queen Regent of Spain, demanding the release of a party accused of a serious crime," then adds: "If Miss Cisneros is released it will be because she is innocent, and not because her case has been meddled with by a party of irresponsible old freaks." I sometimes wish the ICONOCLAST had no lady readers, that I might freely express my opinion of such pestiferous pole-cats. I dearly love the ladies, but they are awfully in the way when only full-grown adjectives will do a subject justice. If the *Tee-Tee* editor had half the gumption of a Kansas Gopher he would know that neither Mrs. Davis nor any other American woman made such "demand." Perhaps he did not know it,—if it be possible for the editor of such a quintessential extract of utter idiocy to know anything—but couldn't resist the boorish impulse to insult an aged woman, because he's built that way. The case of Senorita Cisneros appealed to the sympathy of every manly man and noble woman throughout the world—to every living creature within whose hide there pulses one drop of human blood unblended with that of unclean breasts. Mrs. John A. Logan, Mrs. Jefferson Davis and other magnificent types of American womanhood, *humbly petitioned* the Queen Regent of Spain in behalf of the Cuban heroine. And these noble women, whose names are respected in the very brothels and boozing kens of Boiler Avenue, are referred to by this foul parody on God's masterpiece as "a party of irresponsible old freaks." Christ! is it possible that aught born of woman—that any animal that can learn to walk on its hinder legs—should sink to such infamous depths of degradation! Yet this is the fellow who was so concerned for the feelings of certain sawciety she-males who personated French prostitutes at the Bradley-Martin debauch, that when I criticized their brazen bid for "business" he came near having hydrophobia. Did the *Tee-Tee* trogolodyte contain within his anthropodial diaphragm a single diatom of decency he would have applauded Mrs. Davis' womanly act, else blocked the yawning hole in his prognathic head with a flat-car load of compost. If Mrs. Davis is permitted to petition the King of Kings to have mercy on the miserable journalistic piano-pounder for Gotham's high-toned honk-a-tonks, certainly she may with propriety appeal to the substitute sovereign of a nation of bankrupt assassins to spare Senorita Cisneros.

* * *

Lawd Chelmsfold, now inspecting the Canadian border to ascertain what resistance it could offer in case of a brush with Uncle Sam, is out with an interview in which he says one great element of John Bull's strength is to be found in the fact that our Anglomaniacs could never be convinced "of the justice of any war that might spring up between America and Britain." Lawd Chelmsford, like most Englishmen, is a large, juicy chump. Of course our Anglomaniacs are all traitors in *posse*, as their Tory forbears were in *esse*, and would sympathize with "deah old England, dontcherknow," should war be precipitated by her burning all our coast cities without provocation; but as Chimmie Fadden would say, "Dat cuts no ice." They are but a few thousand in number, and in the whole caboodle there's not a chappie who would fight should a Digger Indian fill his ear with a bushel of buffalo chips, squirt tobacco juice on his twousahs and throw alkali dust in his optics. Lawd Chelmsford has suffered himself to be deceived by the bloodless hermaphrodites employed on such papers as Josef Phewlitzer's *Verrult* and Belo's double-barreled *Benedict Arnold*. Still it is just as well to know that John Bull considers that he can depend upon the sympathy and assistance of our Anglomaniacs in case of war with this country. While these fellows are slobbering over "the mother country," the leading papers of London are sneering at the United States as "a fourth-class power" and proclaiming that if it doesn't conduct itself more to John Bull's liking, "it will soon feel the iron hand beneath the velvet glove." Turn loose your "iron hand," you old he-bawd—and you'll soon stick it further under your own coat-tails than you did at Yorktown.

* * *

The New York *Wail* and *Distress* approves the scheme of Spain, Italy and Germany, to establish a penal colony for anarchists. Yes, yes, granny dear; but would it not be much better to alter those conditions that produce anarchists. Anarchy is simply a protest against oppression. When enough people in a revolt against tyranny it becomes a successful revolution and its promoters are enshrined in history as worthy patriots. When a few men strike blindly but desperately at the hydra and are over-powered, they are traitors or anarchists, rebels or rioters. The *Wail and Distress* was once edited by a party who, according to his father-in-law, "could be more kinds of a d—n fool than any other man in the country," and it is evidently maintaining its old-time reputation.

* * *

It is reported that a British company is about to secure control of the Panama Canal. If it does so, John Bull will practically have Uncle Sam surrounded, and it is worthy of remark that, despite his tearful protestations of friendship, he fortifies every strategical point regardless of expense. What does he want with such Gibraltars as those at Van Couver, Halifax, Bermuda, St. Lucia and half a dozen other points if he loves us so dearly as Anglomaniacs would have us imagine? It costs hundreds of millions to construct and equip these fortifications, yet they are not worth a dollar to him except in case of war with this country. The fact is that he expects another tussle with the Western Titan—intends to precipitate it in his own good time—when India is quieted and he has naught to fear from the continental powers of Europe. Arbitration is the soothing lullaby which Anglomaniacs are to sing to his unsuspecting "cousin" until he gets his "iron hand" in order— weaves about him an anaconda-coil of cannon. Despite all the milk-sick drivel anent "ties of blood, language and literature," "community of interest of the gerate and gal-orious Anglo-Saxon race, *ad infinitum, ad nauseam,* the cold facts of history prove that for more than a century, England has been our implacable enemy. Why? Wounded pride in the first place, commercial rivalry in the second; but the chief reason is that England desires to perpetuate its supremacy as a world power, and sees growing up here a giant who will sooner or later, as Napoleon said, "clip the lion's claws." The best thing this nation can do is to quietly "fix" itself, and then at the first provocation compel J. B. to pull his freight completely out of the Western world. Uncle Sam is an idiot to go practically unarmed while British guns are pointing at his head from all directions. Arbitration the devil! Dismantle that cordon of forts which you have built for our benefit, and we may take some stock in your Pecksniffian professions of friendship. "Actions speak louder than words," says the old adage; and while J. B.'s words are those of Achates, his acts are those of an enemy. The voice is the voice of Jacob, but the hand is the hand of Esau.

* * *

If the dispatches from Hogansville, Ga. be correct, the present federal administration is depriving American citizens of their rights to an extent that suggests the impudence of Germany's swell-head emperor or the petty tyranny of the Turk. It appears that a nigger postmaster was appointed at that place who was *persona non grata,* and the people employed at their own expense the ex-postmaster to receive their mail for them from the moke. Although a man has an inalienable right to appoint what agent he pleases to receive his money or his mail, the ex-p. m. is to be prosecuted for "conducting a post-office." They then ordered their mail to an adjacent town and sent a private messenger for it, but this was prohibited on the plea that a only government has the right to establish a mail route." To crown the infamy the people were not permitted to mail their letters on postal cars. Here are three flagrant violations of the rights of American citizens, and to compel them to patronize a nigger Republican postmaster. The first agent employed by the people was no more "conducting a post-office" than is the Iconoclast, which receives and distributes the mail of a dozen or more people. The messenger sent to the adjacent town was no more running a mail route than is the farmer who brings to town the letters written by his neighbors and carries back those intended for them. The postal department has discharged its entire function when it receives mail, by whosoever presented, and delivers it to those for whom it is intended or to those duly authorized to receive it, and the postmaster-general who permits the department to exceed that simple duty and intermeddle with the rights of the people should not only be impeached and removed from office in one time and two motions, but taken by the slack of the pantalettes and pitched headlong into the penitentiary. It appears that the indignant people assaulted the nigger postmaster. That is indeed to be regretted; still I can but wonder that they do not shoot the whole umbilicus out of every impudent tool of a petty tyranny who attempts to prevent them mailing letters on postal cars while that right is freely accorded to others. The whole affair serves to accentuate the contention of the Iconoclast that postmasters should not be appointed by successful politicians, but elected by the people. If the latter can be trusted to choose presidents, congressmen, etc. they can certainly be trusted to select competent men to lick stamps and shuffle postal cards. As matters now stand the wishes of the people, who "pay the freight," are in no wise respected—the pie is shoveled out to a horde of hungry political heelers, not because of services rendered their country, but as payment for their pernicious activity in promoting the interests of a corrupt and conscienceless party. Thus it happens that in about half the cases federal officials are regarded with aversion by the people they are supposed to serve. It is to be hoped that every Southern white man who hereafter votes the Republican ticket will have his *billets de amour* clapper-clawed and liberally scented by some big fat coon.

* * *

The Buffalo (N.Y.) Distress, commenting on the acquittal of a negro near Barton, Ark., who killed another negro for having criminally assaulted a woman of their own race, wants to know if the law of justification would have held good had the rapist been a white man. Had the *Distress* but paused to reflect that the white men of Arkansas are free silver Democrats, it would not have indulged in a supposition so far-fetched and foolish. Now in Buffalo, which gave Cleveland to the country, and permits a nigger-loving lazar like the editor of the *Distress* to run at large, almost anything in petticoats, from old Sycorax to a malodorous coon, might be in some danger of assault by so-called Caucasians.

* * *

There's every indication that another gigantic prize fight fake will soon make a swipe for the long green of the cibarious sucker. Were it not a violation of the law of the land and the canons of the Baptist church to wager money that we should give to the missionaries, I'd risk six-bits that Corbett and Fitzsimmons get together within a year and that the gamblers who are on the inside "make a killing." For six months or more before their last mill these two worthies chewed the rag, making everybody believe that the battle was to be for berlud. The odds were on Corbett, and he got lost in the shuffle as a matter of course—just as Fitz did when he mixed it with Sharkey. Now the rag-chewing has begun over again, and Bob is doing the lordly contempt act just as Jeems did before the late unpleasantness. He has "retired"—wants Corbett to "go get er repertashun"—says "Corbett quit in the last go like er cowardly cur." It will take time to work the thing up, to resuscitate the old excitement, to set fools to betting wildly on their favorite; but when the pippin's ripe it will be pulled. There's not the slightest reason for the existence of any personal ill will between these pugs—it's all in the play, and being bad actors they overdo the part of Termagant, do protest too much. It is quite noticeable that in the "big fights" nowadays nobody gets seriously bruised. It's easy enough to start the claret, and an ounce o' blood well smeared satisfies the crowd as well as a barrel. The result of the "fight" will be determined beforehand—as soon as the managers learn how they can scoop the most money. The best thing you can do with your ducats is to send them to me with instructions to bet them even that Bill McKinley's job will soon fit Bryan. The man who bets on the result of a prize-fight ought to have a guardian appointed.

* * *

A Los Angeles, Cal., correspondent informs me that the editor of the *Times* of that town, who I trimmed up last month for permitting impudent coons to insult Southern white women through his columns, is named "Col." H. G. Otis, and that during the war he commanded a negro company. He also sends me the following extract from the alleged newspaper published by the ex-captain of the Darktown Paladins:

> In considering the crimes of which some negroes are fre-
> quently guilty it should not be forgotten that these traits of violent
> sensuality are undoubtedly inherited from mothers and grand-
> mothers who were subjected to the lust of their masters under the
> slavery system. In other words, the sins of the fathers are being
> visited upon their children to the third and fourth generation.

That is a vast improvement over the original statement published by Coon-Captain Otis to the effect that Southern white women seek black paramours, and that most lynchings are caused by the guilty parties getting caught. It is a matter of utter indifference to the ex-slaveholders what this calumnious little fice says about them, if he will but refrain from voiding his fetid rheum upon their families. Doubtless some slaveholders were degraded sensualists, but such were exceptions to the rule. Not one yaller nigger in a hundred is the child of its mother's old master. There were comparatively few mulattoes in the South before the war, most of these were the offspring of white overseers—and it is a notorious fact that a majority of our professional "nigger-drivers" were from the North. This is no reflection on the character of the Northern people—these fellows were simply the feculent scum, the excrementitious offscourings of civilization. And now I remember that a second-cousin of mine in Kentucky has an overseer from Ohio named Otis. A very thrifty and choleric man was my cousin, and considering a yaller nigger less valuable than a black one, he threatened to subject his overseer to a surgical operation if another half-breed pickaninny appeared on the place. I do wonder if this "Col." Otis—who knew so much about the management of coons that he was placed in command of a colored company—can be the same fellow; also what was the result of my relative's ultimatum? Can anybody in Los Angeles tell me what state this "Col." Otis came from, or send me a good picture of the ex-commander of coons?

* * *

While the preachers were hustling out of the fever infected districts of Louisiana, the Sisters of Charity were hurrying in from points as far distant as San Francisco. And what were the A. P. Apes doing? They were standing afar off, pointing the finger of scorn at these angels of mercy and calling them "prostitutes of the priesthood." In this land every man has a perfect right to entertain such religious views as he likes; but those who defame women who cheerfully risk their lives for others' sake should be promptly shot. "By their fruits ye shall know them," says the Good Book; and while the Church of Rome is producing Good Samaritans to wrestle with the plague, the A. P. Ape is filling the penitentiaries. I care nothing for the apostolic pretensions of the Pope or the dogmas of the Priesthood; but I'm strongly tempted to make a few off-hand observations with a six-shooter should these papaphobes speak disrespectfully of the Sisters of Charity in my presence.

* * *

Justice Van Fleet of the supreme court of California recently rendered an opinion which indicates the utter emptiness of our boast that in this land all men are equal before the law. Because of the confusion or ignorance of a new motorman, the young child of a plumber, playing upon the track, was killed by an electric car. The parents sued the company and were awarded damages in the sum of six thousand dollars. Defendant took an appeal, which the supreme court sustained, and the cause was remanded on the ground that the damages awarded were excessive—that the boy would probably have followed his father's occupation, and an embryo workman is not, in Justice Van Fleet's opinion, worth so much money! Measured by this standard, what would have been the average "value" of American presidents when they were boys? Now that Justice Van Fleet is measuring human life solely by the gold standard, perhaps he can tell us what a juvenile Shakespeare or Webster is "worth." I have held to the opinion heretofore that blood could not be measured by boodle, that the children of the common people were of as much importance in the eye of the law as the progeny of the plutocrat—that the anguish of parents did not depend on the length of the purse; but Justice Van Fleet seems to agree with Kernan's weeping Canuck, that the more siller one has the more deeply he feels the loss of a son. He seems to need a powerful cardac for his heart and a hot mush poultice for his head, being as fine a combination of knave and fool, as one can easily find. Had the supreme court declared that the plaintiffs in the case were not entitled to a dollar I would heartily approve the opinion; but to measure the "value" of a son by the gain-getting capacity of its sire is simply monstrous. A statute should be enforced impartially, without regard to persons; but I should like to see the law so amended that people could not trade upon their tears, could not coin the blood of their relatives to fill their pockets. A child should not be considered a piece of property for which the accidental destroyer must *pay*, just as a railway company must cough up the cash value of the cow it kills. As not one child in a thousand ever returns to its parents the cost of its rearing it cannot be urged that the plaintiffs in this case were pecuniarily damaged one penny. All they had to sell was "mental anguish," and that should never be made a merchantable commodity. We have criminal courts to deal with those who, through criminal negligence or otherwise occasion death. It may be argued that when the party killed has dependants for whom he or she is providing, the slayer should be compelled to make good the damage in so far as money can do it. I say *no*—that if there be blood guiltiness let the offender be punished in accordance with our criminal code; if there be none then is he blameless, and to deprive a person of his property because of a harmless act is a crime. "But the dependants should be provided for." Certainly they should; but not through rank injustice to others. We are carrying entirely too far the theory that the principal is responsible for the acts of his agents. If the agent is guilty of criminal negligence he is punished by one law and his principal by another; if the agent blunders he is found not guilty and discharged, yet his principal is punished for being a co-partner in his innocence. It should not be forgotten that the agent of a private company is also a representative of that larger and more powerful corporation which we call the state. The private company can do no more than outline his duty and discharge him for dereliction; the public corporation not only prescribes his duty but imprisons or hangs him for neglect; the private company is itself but a creation of the state which exercises over it autocratic power while shirking responsibility. If I loosen a rail on the "Katy" road and cause the destruction of $100,000 worth of property the company must pocket the loss, notwithstanding the fact that it is paying the state for protection. If a dozen people are killed in the wreck the relatives of the last one of them will sue for damages and the state compel it to pay for its own failure to afford that protection to which it is clearly entitled. What then? Let the state issue life insurance at cost and compel every person who has dependants to carry a policy payable on the annual installment plan. For 5 or 6 cents a day it can, without loss, issue a policy to every man in America that will provide his family with the necessaries of life for at least ten years after his death, and the man who cannot pay that premium is worth precious little to anybody considered purely from an economic standpoint. If the state wants to bring damage suits for the slaughter of its citizens, well and good; but for God's sake let us get rid of the degrading spectacle of people hawking the corpses of their relatives through the courts.

*   *   *   *   *

A KANSAS CITY ARISTOCRAT.

I sometimes rejoice with an exceeding great joy and take something on myself that the Iconoclast is read by a million truth-loving Americans, as I am thereby enabled not only to make it uncomfortable for frauds and fakes, but to hold an occasional bypedal puppy up by the subsequent end that Scorn may sight him and stick her cold and clammy finger so far through his miserable carcass that Goliah might hang his helmet on the protruding point. Sometime ago I found America's meanest man in Massachusetts: I have just discovered the most contemptible of all God's creatures in Kansas City. Some may suppose that the first discovery excludes the last; but such forget that there is the same difference between cussedness and contemptibility that exists between the leopard and the louse, between a Cuban hurricane and the crapulous eructations of a chronic hoodlum. I want the world to take an attentive look at one Walter S. Halliwell, to make a labored perscrutation of this priorient social pewee, this *arbiter eligantarium* of corn-fed aristocracy, this Beau Brummel of the border, for though Argus had a compound microscope glued to his every eye he might never look upon the like again. He resembles a pigmy statue of Priapus carved out of a guano bed with a muck rake and smells like a *maison d'joie* after an Orange Society celebration of the Battle of the Boyne. Mr. Halliwell evidently has an idea rumbling round in his otherwise tenantless attic room that he's a Brahmin of the Brahmins, an aristocrat dead right, a goo-goo for your Klondyke galways, a Lady Vere de Vere in plug hat and "pants." He's the Ward McAllister of Kay-See, the model of the chappies, and traces his haughty lineage back in an unbroken line to the primordial anthropoid swinging by his prehensile tail to a limb of the Ash tree Ygdrasyl and playfully scratching the back of the hungry behemoth with the jawbone of an erstwhile ichthyosaurian. Walter S. Halliwell was born when quite young, where or why deponent saith not, and had gotten thus far on life's tow-path, absorbing such provender as he could come at, before I chanced to hear of him. As there be tides in the affairs of men which taken at the flood lead on to fortune, so there be waves which straddled at the proper time will bear a Halliwell on their niveous crest to the dizzy heights of fame, quicker'n the nictitation of a thomas-cat. Walter made connection with the climbing wave, and here he is, bumping the macrencephalic end of himself against the milky-way and affrighting the gibbous moon. His opportunity to make an immortal ass of himself, to earn catasterism and be placed among the stars as an equine udder, thus happened to hap: Kay-See was to have a "Karnival" modeled upon the pinchbeck rake with which Waco worked the gullible country folk once upon a time—when she so far forgot herself as to trade on womanly beauty to make it a bunco-steerer for her stores. The chief attraction wass to be a "Kween Karnation" and her maids of honor, the latter consisting of the most beautiful young ladies of the various Missouri towns. I presume that these fair blossoms were (or will be, for I know not the date of the brummagen blowout) paraded through the streets bedized in royal frippery to make a hoodlum holiday while the megalophanous huckster worked the perspiring mob with peanuts and soda pop, and the thrifty merchant marked his shopworn wares up 60 per cent, and sold them to confiding country men "at a tremendous sacrifice." I infer from the dispatches that Halliwell was made lord high executioner of the "Karnival"—at least accorded ample space in which to wildly wave his asinine ears. Miss Edna Whitney, described as being "one of the most beautiful young ladies of Chillicothe," was put forward by her friends as a candidate for the honor of representing that city at the royal court of "Kween Karnation," the citizens to determine the matter by a voting contest. Now Miss Whitney, while dowered with great beauty, popular and of good repute, is a working girl instead of a fashionable butterfly, being employed in a cigar factory. When it appeared certain that she would bear off the honor, the snobocracy of Chillicothe, furious at being "trun down" by a working girl, appealed to Halliwell to exclude her from the contest, and this miserable parody of God's masterpiece promptly wired that her business occupation was an insuperable barrier. How's that for a country boasting of "Liberty, Equality and Fraternity"—its press and politicians ever prating of "the dignity of labor"! The contest, I'm told, was open to all "respectable young women"; but a working girl, though pure as the lily and fair as the rose, is not considered "respectable" by the would-be patricians of Corncob Corners and the grand panjandrum of the Kay-See Karnival! Working girls must not presume to be pretty or popular or enter into contests for holiday honors with the high-born daughters of successful swindlers, but will be kindly permitted by the lordly Halliwell to stand on the curb and see beauts who are only by the grace of boodle, roll by like triumphant Sylla on Fortune's bike. During the Saturnalia in ancient Rome the master acknowledged the brotherhood of man by ministering to his slave; but Kansas City, thanks to the omnipotent Halliwell, has cut the working class off from mankind—the hewers of wood and drawers of water are no longer considered human! Surely we are making rapid "progress"—are nearing that point in time when the working people will enter a protest against insult added to injury by tying a few bow-knots in the rubber necks of presumptuous parvenues. If it be a disgrace for a woman to work then is this nation in a very bad way, for few of us are the sons or daughters "of an hundred earls"—can go back more than a generation or two without finding a maternal ancestor blithely swinging the useful sad-iron or taking a vigorous fall out of the wash-tub. The parents of some of the wealthiest people of Kansas City, the bon-ton of the town, smelled of laundry soap, the curry-comb or night-soil cart. Some made themselves useful as hash-slingers in cheap boarding houses or chambermaids in livery stables, nursery maids or barbers, while others kept gambling dens, boozing-kens or even run variety dives. There is now a bright young woman working for a wealthy man in Kansas City for six dollars a week. The wife of her employer was once her mother's servant and laundered her infantile linen. The ex-servant, scarce able to read or write, ugly by nature and gross by instinct, is now a glorious star in Fashion's galaxy, while the child whose diapers she used to deodorize, compelled by poverty to accept employment, is socially ostracized. People of gentle blood—those who for many generations back have been educated men and cultured women, do not act as do Halliwell and the snobocrats of Chillicothe. These are giving a very exact imitation of people who lately came up from the social gutter, and it were interesting to know how far we would have to trace their "genealogical tree" before finding something much worse than a working woman. It is said that "three generations make a gentleman"; and if that be true there is some hope of Halliwell's great-grandsons—granting, of course, that the pusillanimous prig is not too epicene to provide himself with posterity. Day by day it becomes more evident that the purse-proud snobocracy of New York's old rat-catchers and sprat peddlers is fast getting a foothold in the West, that the social gulf between the House of Have and that of Have-Not, is steadily widening and deepening—that we have reached that point in national decay where gold suffices to "gild the straitened forehead of the fool," where *wealth* instead of *worth*" makes the man and want of it the fellow." Of course it is not to be expected that working girls, however worthy, will be generally carried on the visiting list of wealthy women, that their society will be sought by the followers of Fashion. None expect this, and few desire it. King Cophetua's beggar maid would have cut a sorry figure at court ere his favor raised her to fortune. For Cinderella to attend the Bradley-Martin ball clothed in rags would be embarrassing both to herself and the company. The woman who must work for a living has little time for the diversions of the wealthy; and is usually too proud to accept costly social courtesies which she cannot repay in kind. Society divides naturally into classes, dilettantism and pococurantism dawdling luxuriously here, labor at hand-grip with Destiny there. "Birds of a feather flock together," say the old copy-books, and Fortune gives to each such plumage as she pleases. Still, boodle does not map out all the social metes and bounds. It was said of old that every door opens to a golden key, but this is not altogether true. The honest working girl shuns the society of the wealthy wanton, and the stupid ignoramus, whatsoever his fortune, is accorded no seat at the symposiac—is blackballed by the brotherhood of brains. Imagine Goethe giving Richter the "marble heart" or Byron snubbing Burns because of his lowly birth! The world would be quick to rebuke their arrogance, would assure them that a singer was not esteemed for his siller, but for his song. In the carnival case it was a question of beauty not of boodle, of popularity instead of purses, and to exclude from the contest a candidate of the working class was to acknowledge her superiority and avenge defeat with brutal insult that would shame the crassest boor. The King of Syracuse was not ashamed to contend with the humblest for Olympian honors, nor the Emperor of Rome to measure swords with Thracian gladiators to prove his skill at arms. Ever does genius sympathize with folly and the truly learned with the unlettered; but Mammon "least erect of all the angelic host that fell from heaven," puts the mark of the beast on the brazen foreheads of all who bow down to his abominations. When working-girls are treated thus, what wonder that some of them become imbittered, discouraged, and go head-long to the devil—affording the wretched pharisees whose brutality wrought their ruin, an opportunity to "rescue" them and pose before the world as Christian philanthropists! What inducement has a young and beautiful woman to toil early and late for an honest livelihood when by so doing she forfeits the right to be called respectable—is flouted by even the paltry plutocracy of a country town and proclaimed a social pariah by such a headless phthirius pubis as Halliwell! If labor be no longer respectable wherein are our thousands of virtuous working girls superior to prostitutes? Clearly if the dictum of Halliwell be correct it were better for the daughter of poverty to regard her face as her fortune and hasten to sell herself—with approval of law and blessings of holy church—to some old duffer with ducats and be welcomed by the "hupper sukkle" as a bright and shining ornament. Or if no beducated old duffer can be come at, she might marry the first shiftless he-thing that offers itself and pick up a luxurious livelihood for her family among her gentlemen friends, as so many enterprising society women now do, and be "respectable" to her heart's content—even a devout church member and prominent in "rescue" work among fallen women. Somehow I cannot help wondering whether Halliwell's respectability be not due to some ancestor who was too lazy to work and too cowardly to steal. To the grand army of working women I would say, Be not discouraged by such gross affronts, prompted by splenetic hearts and spewed forth by empty heads. You may be flouted on the one hand by a few purse-proud parvenues and pitied on the other hand by bedizened prostitutes, but the great world, which learned long ago that the reptile as well as the eagle can reach the apex of the pyramid, estimates you at your true worth and binds upon your pure brows the victor's wreath, while ringing ever in your ears like a heavenly anthem are the words of Israel's wisest—"A good name is more precious than fine gold."

P.S.—Since the foregoing was put in print I have received Kansas City papers giving a fuller account of the affair, and it is in every way more miserable than I had imagined. Halliwell, who is bossee of the whole business, says he sent the telegram at the request of the board of lady managers of the flower parade—in other words, that, at the solicitation of a lot of snobby old females, he made even a greater ass of himself than nature had originally intended. Mrs. J. K. Cravens, chairman of the aforesaid board, denies that the ladies had anything to do with the matter, then flies into a towering passion "cusses out" the newspapers, figuratively speaking, rips her silk lingerie to ribbons, and otherwise conducts herself like a woman educated in a logging camp. I shall not attempt to decide the question of veracity between Halliwell and Mrs. Cravens, but that one is a mental vacuum and the other a ripsnortin' old virago is established beyond the peradventure of a doubt. Everybody connected with the Karnival is doing the Artful Dodger act to escape the withering storm of indignation which the pitiful episode called forth from the American people. The most encouraging feature of the whole affair is the withdrawal of several of Chillicothe's society girls from the contest because of the gratuitous insult tendered Miss Whitney in the Halliwell telegram, thus indicating that the old town's upper ten is not composed exclusively of pudding heads and parvenues.

*   *   *   *   *

A PICTORIAL PAIN KILLER.

Puck is what the erstwhile Artemous Ward would call a "yewmerous" paper, and is published solely for the benefit of bad barbers. When you take your seat in the butcher's shambles he provides you with a copy of Puck because its jokes are so excruciatingly painful that it pulls your piligerous annex out with a stump-extractor and rubbed *aqua fortis* into your face with a bath brick, the physical ill would be forgotten in the mental agony. I never saw anybody but a barber purchase a copy of *Puck* not any son of Adam reading it outside a "tonsorial parlor." Should the Populists carry the country and barbers be tabooed *Puck's* mission on earth would be ended—unless it could persuade dentists to adopts it as an anaesthetic, and sheriffs to read it to condemned criminals to make them yearn for death. The last time I was shaved the razor pulled so dreadfully that I sought refuge in this pictorial pain-killer's editorial page. I there learned, much to my surprise, that the rise in the price of wheat had killed the silver cause; also that W. J. Bryan had "said, in that pose of easy omniscience for which he became remarkable, that 'a bushel of wheat and an ounce of silver were ordained by nature to become equal each to the other'—'wheat cannot rise unless silver rises.' " If W. J. Bryan said that, even in his salad days, he's a hopeless damphool, unfit to be pound-master, much less president; but I'll pay two-bits for incontestable evidence that he ever made such an idiotic remark. My private opinion is that the malice of *Puck's* mendacity is equalled only by its awkwardness. It is possible that its editor mistakes falsehood for fun. Or he may have heard somewhere the statement he parrots and really supposed it true, for a man capable of conducting so *jejune* a journal might easily believe anything. Another article in his paper says that Cardinal Wolsey managed all "Bluff King Hal" divorce business, while the fact is that his hostility to that feculent old tub of tallow's matrimonial crimes was the efficient cause of his downfall. As a historian Puck is about as reliable as Mark Twain's acerbic old sea captain; hence his asservations anent Bryan's utterances should be taken with considerable chloride of sodium. Every man who knows as much about political economy as a terrapin does of the Talmud is well aware that a rise in the price of one commodity simultaneous with the decline in price of another commodity has nothing whatever to do with the currency question. Those who cackle about a rise in wheat synchronously with the fall of silver make a very indecent exposure of their own ignorance. If I had a ten-year old boy who was such a hopeless idiot I'd drown him as not worth honest grub, then seek a surgeon and make sure that I'd never again inflict the world with progeny cursed with cretinism. Wheat went up and silver down, as Mr. Bryan recently explained to the satisfaction of every man possessing an ounce of brains, simply because the demand for the one was increased by foreign crop failures, the demand for the other decreased by Anglo-Cleveland skull-duggery. "Law of supply and demand," bawls *Puck* and all the other journalistic puppets of an impudent plutocracy. You miserable little hiccius doctius, do you expect to deceive an intelligent people with that kind of howl, while the trade in wheat is left untrammeled and the demand for silver arbitrarily limited by law? Suppose that while the world's wheat fields were producing abundantly the leading nations should prohibit their people purchasing any more of that cereal for food production; would any macrocephalous donkey ascribe the decline in the price of wheat to "the immutable law of supply and demand?" When silver is placed on an equality with all other commodities; when the people are permitted to freely employ it as they please, then will the natural law of supply and demand apply to the white metal, and New York editors cease to jabber financial nonsense with the stupid persistence of a poll-parrot praising its own personal pulchritude. The editor of *Puck* should avoid political economy as a subject a trifle too large for the knot on the end of his neck, and confine himself to his threadbare specialty, that of belittling the Jews with his watery wit and atribilarious art. The only funny thing I find in his paper is its solemn "notice to publishers" that all its raccous rot is copyrighted, that infringement will be "promptly and vigorously prosecuted." The editor who would steal from *Puck* would walk through Stringfellow's fruit farm to crib a wilted cabbage leaf from a blind cow. The best things in *Puck* scarce rise to the dignity of Slob Snots' milk-sick drivel in the *Gal-Dal*, while Texas has a hundred country editors pulling a Washington hand press and building stallion poster, who could write brighter things if they were drunk — or dead. "Promptly and vigorously prosecuted" O the devil! Why don't you say that you'll have any fool who attempts to father your hand-made yermer sent to an insane asylum to be treated for prolapsus of the intellect?

*   *   *   *   *

MAN'S GUST FOR GORE.

Hon. Chas. P. Johnson has written for the *Globe-Democrat* an article that will doubtless receive the careful consideration of every sociologist, for he therein assumes that man's instincts are as brutal and bloody to-day as in those far times when, clad only in his "thick natural fell," and armed with a stone, he struggled for food with the wild beasts of the forest—that the prevalence of lynchings is not due to incompetency of our criminal courts, but to an alarming revival of savagery in man himself. He declares that our courts are more effective than ever before, but that Judge Lynch continues active without other cause than the inability of the people to restrain their murderous proclivities. He assures us that the entire suppression of the savage instinct is impossible by any civilization whatever, and adds that "its control and regulation is as difficult to-day as it has been at any period since the historical birth of man." Why this is so he does not directly say, but the following paragraph is significant:

> "Perhaps the statesmanship which looks solely to the development of our material resources and the accumulation of wealth is overlooking the growth and development of many social vices which may yet engulf us in a vortex of anarchical passion or governmental revolution."

Thus Mr. Johnson endorses the position of the ICONOCLAST that the getting of gain should not constitute the sole aim of man; that society cannot long exist with self-interest for "sole nexus," as the French physiocrats would say—that the worship of Mammon is dragging us back to barbarism. It is quite true that man's savage instincts cannot be wholly eradicated; and it is likewise true that could you drain all the Berserker out of his blood he would sink to the level of an emasculated simian. A man in whom there's no latent savagery were equivalent to mint julep in which buttermilk were used as a succedaneum for bourbon. Life, we are told, is "a battle and a march," and an indispensable prerequisite for such stubborn work, call it by what name you will, is but a refinement of the barbaric gust for blood. Whether he be poet or philosopher, priest or prophet, it is the combative man—the man who would find a wild fierce joy in a bayonet charge—who wins new territory from the powers of Darkness and the Devil. Man *is* a savage, and civilization but a cloak with which he covers his ferocity as best he can. If the cloak be scant—as with the Turk—or frayed by time—as with the Spaniard—we may expect to catch frequent and shocking glimpses of the predacious animal. But Mr. Johnson is mistaken in supposing that the lynchings of which he complains evidence an abnormal thirst for blood on the part of the American people. He says:

> "As the masses of ancient Rome enjoyed the carnage of the amphi-theater; as the populace of Paris crowded with eager avidity around the guillotine to see the blood gush from the heads and trunks of the victims of the revolutionary tribunal; as the Spaniard in holiday attire followed over the plaza the procession and rapturously looked upon the execution of the wretches of the *auto da fe*; as in all ages the spirit of savagery has made men to enjoy scenes of suffering, brutality and death—so does the modern mob look with frenzied delight upon like exhibitions to-day."

For a man so erudite and earnest, Mr. Johnson comes painfully near being ridiculous. The evidence is ample that never since the first settlement of this country have the people found *less* pleasure in the effusion of blood and scenes of brutality. Instead of the savage instinct becoming dominant, we are fairly open to the charge of effeminacy, of super-estheticism. Our very sports are becoming namby pamby as those of the Bengalese, the element of danger which gave zest to them in auld lang syne being all but eliminated. Bear-baiting, cocking-mains, shin-kicking, bull-dog-fighting, etc., all greatly enjoyed by the general public a generation or so ago, are now quite generally tabood. Many of us can remember when pugilism was practiced with bare-knuckles and every fight to a finish; it is practiced now with feather pillows "for points," and under police supervision. About the only game left us that is more dangerous than playing Presbyterian billards with an old maid from Boston is college football, and even that will soon be stripped of its vigor on the plea that it is barbarous. When our fathers quarreled they took a pot-shot at each other at ten paces; now disagreements involving even family honor are carried into the courts—the bloody Code Duello has been relegated to "innocuous desuetude." Texas is supposed by our Northern neighbors to be the "wurst ever," the most bloodthirsty place this side the Ottoman Empire; yet the Houston *Post*, leading paper of Harris county, is crying its poor self sick because some peripatetic Ananias intimated to an Eastern reporter that our wildest and wooliest cowboys would even think of shooting the pigtail off a Chinaman bowling along on a bike. Our governor earned the title of "heroic young Christian" by calling a special session of the legislature to prevent Prof. Fitzsimmons giving it to Prof. Corbett "in de slats" with a buggy cushion—was re-elected on the proposition that a boxing-match is "brutal"—which proves that our people are not ahunger and athirst for gore, do not yearn for the sickening scenes of the Roman amphitheatre, where holy virgins by turning their thumbs up or down, decided questions of life and death. "Bloodthirsty?" Good Lord! The average American would grow sick at the stomach if required to slaughter a pullet with which to regale the palate of his favorite preacher. During the past two decades we have practically become Quakers, and now suffer foreign powers to vent their rheum upon us and rub it in, because to maintain our dignity might precipitate a war, and bloodshed is so very brutal. Mr. Johnson seems to imagine that the usual method of procedure in Judge Lynch's court is for the mob to trample its victim to death, bray him in a mortar, kerosene him and set him on fire, then dance the carmagnole around his flaming carcass. This, I am pleased to remark, is simply a mid-day nightmare which should be subjected to hydropathic treatment, reinforced with cracked ice and bromo-seltzer. As a rule lynchings are conducted in quite as orderly and humane a manner as legal esecutions. It is true that cases have occurred, when the public patience had become exhausted by repeated offenses, or the crime committed was peculiarly atrocious, wherein respectable God-fearing men were seized with a murderous frenzy, and whole communities noted for their culture, united in torturing or burning at the state the object of their displeasure; but these were usually instances where failure to enforce the law was notorious, or it did not provide an adequate penalty. The courts imprison the man who steals a mule, or even a loaf of bread to feed a starving family. They hang the man who in a fit of rage of jealousy or drunken frenzy commits a homicide: they can do no more to the brutal buck negro who ravishes and murders a white babe—so Judge Lynch takes cognizance of his case and builds for him a beautiful bonfire; but the average lynching appeals no more strongly to the savage instincts of man than does a hanging by the sheriff.

Then, it may be asked, why do lynchings occur. I have treated this subject at considerable length in former issues of the ICONOCLAST, hence will but recapitulate here and add a few observations suggested by Mr. Johnson's very able but sadly mistaken article. Lynchings occur because, whatsoever be the efficiency of our courts, they are a trifle shy of public confidence; because there are some offenses for which the statutes do not provide adequate penalties; because the people insist that when a heinous crime is committed punishment follow fast upon the offense instead of being delayed by a costly circumlocution office and perhaps altogether defeated by skillful attorneys—men ready to put their eloquence and tears on tap in the interest of worse criminals. I will not take issue with so distinguished an authority as Mr. Johnson regarding the competency of our courts to deal with criminals in accordance with the laws of the land; but the people see that despite the vigilance of officers, the erudition of judges and the industries of juries, murders multiply, rapes increase and portable property remains at the mercy of the marauder. If my memory of statistics does not mislead me, we have in the United States something like 10,000 homicides per annum, while every newspaper teems with accounts of robbery and rape. When we consider this in connection with the further fact that the courts continue to increase in cost—are already a veritable Old Man of the Sea about the neck of the Industrial Sinbad—can we wonder at the impatience of the people? But there is another feature which Mr. Johnson has quite overlooked in his vision of a brutal mob drunk with blood—like most lawyers, he stands too close to his subject to see more than one side, views it from beneath rather than from above. We set a higher value on human life than did our ancestors of the old dueling days. This may be called the Age of Woman—the era of her apothesis. She occupies a higher intellectual, social and political level than ever before in human history, and as she increases in importance crimes against her person assume more gravity. A generation ago such a thing as the criminal assault of a white woman by a negro was almost unknown, but now it is of every day occurrence; thus as womanhood becomes more sacred in our eyes it is subjected to fouler insult. Nor is this all: The American people are becoming every year more mercurial. The whole trend of our civilization—of our education, our business, even our religion—is to make us neurotic, excitable, impatient. In our cooler moments we enact laws expressive of mistaken mercy rather than of unflinching justice. Some of the states have even abolished capital punishment and in but one can a brute be tied up and whipped for the cowardly crime of wife-beating. We establish courts rather to acquit than to convict by disqualifying intelligence for jury service and enforcing the stupid unit rule. We provide convicts with comforts unknown to millions of honest working men and regard them as poor unfortunates to be "reformed rather than as malefactors to be punished. And when our misguided mercy has borne its legitimate fruit we take fire, curse the laws and the courts, seize and hang the offender, and have the satisfaction of knowing that there's one less monster alive in the land. Mr. Johnson suggests no remedy for what he regards as the evil of the age, and is therefore like unto the doctor who volunteers the entirely superfluous information that you "have a misery in your innards," but provides neither pill nor poultice. As Judge Lynch probably makes fewer mistakes than do the courts; as those he hangs usually deserve hemp and he renders no bill of costs to the country; and as the people are the creators and not the creatures of the courts, I am not particularly interested in his suppression, notwithstanding the fact that he seriously interferes with the material welfare of the professional juror and my lawyer friends. But were I duly ordained to perform that duty I would not begin by creating new deputies or calling out local militia companies to shoot down their neighbors and friends, to protect the miserable carcass of a rape-fiend. I would wipe out our entire penal code and frame a new one in which there would be no comfortable penitentiaries. If a man were found guilty of rape or homicide I'd promptly hang him, if of a less heinous offense I'd give him stripes proportionate to his crime and turn him loose to earn a livelihood and thus prevent his family becoming a public burden. For the second offense in crimes like forgery, perjury, theft, arson, etc., I'd resort to the rope. I would abolish fines in misdemeanor cases, thereby putting the rich and poor on a parity, and set the offenders in the stocks. I'd get rid of the costly delays which are the chief cause of lynchings, by elective jurors and the majority rule, by appointing one man well learned in the law to see that all the evidence was properly placed before the court, and advise the rest of the legal fraternity now making heaven and earth resound with their eloquence and weeping crocodile tears at so much per wope, that it were better to make two fat shoats flourish where one hazel-splitter pined in the hitherto, than to employ their talents and energies securing the conviction of the innocent and the aquittal of the guilty. By such a system almost any criminal case could be fairly tried in a couple of hours. If the defendant desired to appeal from the sentence of the court, instead of sending the case up to a higher tribunal thereby entailing heavy cost and vexatious delay, I would empanel a new jury then and there, composed of reputable citizens of the community, retry the case, and if the first verdict was confirmed, the sentence should be executed within the hour. The quicker the courts "get action" on an offender the more terror they inspire in the criminal classes and the better they please the people. If a murderer or rape-fiend captured at daylight could be fairly tried and executed by sundown Judge Lynch would speedily find himself without an occupation.

*   *   *   *   *

A RIGHT ROYAL ROAST.

THE ICONOCLAST MADE HARD TO CATCH.

Galveston, Tex., August 12, 1897.

Mr. W. C. Brann:

In your editorial on the "Henry George Hoodoo," which appears in the August number of the Iconoclast, the following passage occurs: "It seems to me that I have treated the Single Taxers as fairly as they could ask, and if I now proceed to state a few plain truths about them and their faith they will have no just cause to complain." From the tone and tenor of these words it is fair to assume that in the editorial referred to you have discharged against the Single Taxers and their faith the heaviest broadsides of which your ordnance is capable. If, notwithstanding all the time you have wasted "crucifying the economic mooncalf" which has played such sad havoc with the wits of Single Taxers, it should turn out that the monstrous concept, far from being crucified, annihilated, or even "dying of its own accord," only gathers strength, energy, and renewed activity from the healthful exercise with which you provide it, must it not seem the part of prudence for you, even if occasion of regret for us, that you should abandon the war and leave the calf to his fate? Your belated and apparently desperate resolve to "tell some plain truths" about us, Single Taxers, justifies the inquiry, what were you telling before? The fact that it seems to yourself that you have treated Single Taxers fairly is not absolutely irrefragible proof that they have been so treated at least it has not brought conviction of the fact to them. That the offer of your space to Mr. George was courteously declined affords no just ground for refusing it to those "whose matin hymn and vesper prayer reads, there is no God but George," etc. I'll warrant you that if you and the Single Taxers had access on equal terms to a journal which neither controlled, and whose space both were bound to respect, you would not have to go outside the limits of your own state to find a dozen foemen worthy of your steel, and I'd stake my life on it that you'd find not a few to unhorse you. This is not claiming that any one of them, or all of them together, can come anywhere near you in the artistic manipulation of words or the construction of ear-tickling phrases; but it is claiming, and that without any false pretense of modesty, that they have yet seen no reason to fear you in rigidly logical argument when the Single Tax is the question at issue. Their cause is so palpably just, its underlying principle so transparently simple and elementary, its practical application so direct, feasible and efficient that no mere wizardry of words, no thimble-riggery or language, can by any possibility obscure the principle—or confuse the advocates. Of course there are among Single Taxers, as among other enthusiasts, men who indiscreetly use abuse for argument, and of these you may have some reason to complain; but should not your great talents and the immense advantages which the undisputed control of your own journal give you, enable you to rise above their abuse, to ignore it completely, and to grapple with only those who present you with argument? I have no right to expect from you more consideration than has been meted out to better men; still, you can but refuse this rejoinder to your August editorial, which is respectfully offered for publication in your journal. If you are quite sure of your ground, you can only gain strength from exposing my weakness, but even if you are not sure of it, both the requirements of simple justice and the amende honorable to Single Taxers would still plead for the publication of this article.

You say that Mr. George has obtained no standing of consequence in either politics or economics "because his teachings are violative of the public concept of truth." Do you really believe that the fact that he has obtained no standing of consequence in politics is in any way derogatory to his character or his teaching? Do you not know full well that a Bill Sykes, a Jonas Chuzzlewit, or a Mr. Montague Tigg would have a hundred chances to attain that distinction to-day to the one chance that Henry George, Vincent de Paul or even Jesus Christ would have? Don't you know this well, and if you do, why do you use it as an argument against Henry George? As to his standing in economics, that, I submit, is a matter of opinion. You think he has no standing of consequence; I think his teaching is the most active ferment in the economic thought of to-day. We may be both mistaken, but whether we are or not cuts no figure in the truth or falsity of the Single Tax. But it is worth while to point out that the reason you have given for his lack of "standing" lends neither weight nor force to your argument. "Because," you say, "his teachings are violative of the public concept of truth." When did the public concept of truth become the standard by which to test it? The public concept of the best form of money is, and has been for thousands of years, gold and silver coins. I am much mistaken if that be your concept. By the way, why did you not say "violative of truth," instead of "violative of the public concept," etc.? I guess you had an inward consciousness that a thing is not true or false by public concept, but by being inherently so. What Henry George taught was inherently true or false before he ever taught it, and would be so still if he had been never born. The only difference would be that so many of us who now bask in the blessed light of inward, if not of outward, freedom would, in that event, be still barking with the great blind multitude over every false trail along which blinder teachers might be leading them and us.

You admit that Mr. George is a polemic without a peer, and you say that "no other living man could have made so absurd a theory appear so plausible, deceived hundreds of abler men than himself." Surely there is something very faulty in the position you assume here. If what you say be so, how do you know that you are not yourself the victim of deception at the hands of some inferior? Or is it only men who have "gone daft on Single Tax" that possess the extraordinary power of leading abler men than themselves by the nose? Surely that were too much honor for an antagonist to concede to them. More surely still, if a man's intelligence is not proof against deception by inferiors in argument, he can never reach finality in a process of reasoning, and logical proof for him there is none.

"He mistakes the plausible for the actual and by his sophistry deceives himself." O pshaw! We all say things sometimes that just do for talk, but this hasn't even that poor excuse. I might just as well say, "He takes the conceivable for the supposable and by his logic enlightens himself. One statement would be as valuable as the other and neither would be worth a pinch of snuff. Come, let us argue with dignity and composure, like honest men sincerely searching after truth, and eager to lend a hand in abolishing this social Inferno of legalized robbery which fairly threatens to consume us all.

There is, you'll admit, such a thing as land value, i. e. value attaching to land irrespective of improvements made in or on it by private industry. This value arises from the presence of a community and can never actually exist without it. If the exclusive creator or producer of a thing is its rightful owner, land belongs to the community that creates or produces it, and can never, in the first instance, rightly belong to any other owner. The Single Tax is the taking of this value for this community. Is it just? The highest homage, the highest act of faith which the human mind and heart can offer to God is to say that He could not be God and pronounce the Single Tax unjust! Here now is a gage of battle cast at the feet of whoever wishes to take it up, be the same logician, metaphysician or theologian. (Pardon me, Mr. Brann, for momentarily turning aside from you.)

The justice of the Single Tax is beyond all question of refutation. What about its efficiency for the cure of social ills? Here, I think, is where we are widest apart. You say, "the unearned increment is already taken for public use under our present system of taxation." If by "unearned increment" you mean what I have defined as land value (and I think you do) your statement is the wildest and most astounding I ever heard or read from a sane man making an argument. Is it possible you have not learned that where all the land value is taken in taxation there can be no selling value? And where is the land to-day with a community settled upon it that has not selling value? If land value is already absorbed by taxation, what is it that goes to maintain landlordism? Perhaps you'll contend that landlordism doesn't exist. What value is it that a man pays for when he buys an unimproved lot in the heart of a city? What is it that the boomer booms and the land speculator gambles on when he adds acre to acre and lot to lot without any intention of productive use? What, if not the community value which he expects to attach to his land as a result of increase of population? And what advantage to him as a speculator would this community value be if, as you claim, it is now being absorbed in taxation and should continue to be so absorbed as fast as it arises? Do landlords in cities and towns retain for themselves only the rent of buildings and hand over to the government the full amount of their ground rents as tax? I know an old eyesore of a building in this city not worth $150, whose occupant pays $100 a month rent. Do you seriously believe that all of this $1,200 a year which does not go to the city and state in taxes is rent on the old $150 rat-warren? Why, the thing is too childish for serious discussion; and to have discussed it with you without having been driven to it by yourself, I should have regarded as in the nature of a slight on your intelligence. If what you claim as a fact were true, we would have the Single Tax in full swing now and would be fretting ourselves to fiddle-strings, not to bring it about, but to get rid of it for its evil fruit.

As to whether the Single Tax, in full force, would provide enough revenue for municipal, county, state and federal governments, we, Single Taxers, are not greatly concerned. We have our own opinions on that question and can give better reasons for them than our opponents can give for theirs. But the question is not essential to our argument. What we hold to is that until land values fully taxed prove inadequate for the expenses of government economically administered, not one cent should be levied on labor products, no matter in whose possession found. This, however, belongs to the fiscal side of our reform. Of infinitely more importance is the social side. Here our end and aim is to secure to all the sons of Adam an equal right to life, liberty and pursuit of happiness by securing to them an equal right in the bounties of nature—and passing strange it certainly is that men who would not dream of denying this right in the abstract are ever ready to anathematize it in the concrete.

With the Single Tax in force, that is, with the plain behest of nature observed and respected, no man will hold land out of use when, whether he uses it or not, he must pay to the community its annual value for the privilege of monopolizing it. No man will hold land for a rise in community value when that value is taken from him for the use of the community as fast as it arises. No man will need to mortgage his home and the earnings of his most vigorous years to a boomer or speculator for the privilege of living on the earth for there will be no boomer or speculator to sell him the privilege, and the privilege itself will have ceased to be such and become an indefeasible right.

"He (Mr. George) is a well-intentioned man who confidently believes he can make the poverty-stricken millions prosperous by revoking the taxes of the rich and increasing the burthens of the poor." Fie, fie! What is to be gained by such transparent, palpable misrepresentation as this? Do you verily believe that land values, which Mr. George proposes to tax, are mainly in possession of the poor? Did you not see—of course you did—a diagrammatic exhibit made not long ago by the New York Herald of the holdings of twenty New York real estate owners? Let me quote a passage from an article in the New York *Journal* on this exhibit:

> "The reason 170 families own half of Manhattan Island, as stated in the *Herald*, and that 1,800,000 out of the two million residents of Manhattan Island, until very recently, had no interest whatever, except as renters, in this superb property, is because, until the last few years, it required a fortune to own the smallest separate parcel of this great estate. Only the rich could participate in its ownership, its income, its profits."

Now is it your view that all this is but clumsy lying, and that in reality it is the poor people of New York as of other large cities that own the bulk of its land values? Again you say, "He would equalize the conditions of Dives and Lazarus by removing the tax from the palace of the one and laying it upon the potato patch of the other." This statement is much more artistic than the preceding one. It wears a jaunty semblance of truth. Indeed it is true in a sense as far as it goes. But it is vague and incomplete, and for that reason as deceptive and misleading as half truths always are. With your permission I will fill it out in parenthesis and convert it into an honest whole truth: "He would equalize the conditions of (both freedom and justice for) Dives and Lazarus by removing the tax from the palace of the one (and from the labor products of the other) and laying it upon (the community value of the land occupied by the palace and) the potato patch of the other." Now, if the potato patches of the poor occupy, as a rule, more valuable land than the palaces of the rich, there might be some apparent ground for your contention. It would be only apparent, however, for in such a case the potato patch would be as much out of place as a public school on a wharf front. To devote highly valuable land to ordinary potato culture would be about as sensible as to print the Sunday edition of the Galveston *News* on costly linen paper. One of the virtues of the Single Tax is its potency to prevent such stupid waste of opportunity. Your way of stating the case, however, has this virtue that it is a welcome variation of the old wearisome chestnut about the poor widow owning a valuable lot, etc.

You believe Progress and Poverty inspired by the plutocracy, "250,000 of whom own 80 per cent. of the taxable wealth of the country, while the land is largely in possession of the great middle class." Passing over the source of the inspiration, you have come pretty close to the truth here! Unfortunately for you, however, the statement has no value in the argument. Single Taxers do not need to deny that the great middle class largely own the land, but they do claim, and you won't have the hardihood to deny it, that the plutocracy own the vast bulk of the land values. You will perceive the distinction when you reflect that the land is nearly all out in the country, while the land values are nearly all in the cities and towns. To tax land according to area is the bug-a-boo you are putting up your guards to; to tax it according to community value is what we invite you to smash if you can. You "cannot understand how a man possessed of common sense could fail to see that removing taxation from the class of property chiefly in the hands of the rich and placing it altogether on property chiefly in the hands of the comparatively poor, could fail to benefit the millionaire at the expense of the working man." Neither can I, if you tax it according to quantity, but that is not the Single Tax and it is time you knew it. Let me tell you now something that I can't understand — why a man who has the means and the ability to strike giant blows for the cause of the blind, stupid, plundered humanity prefers to waste his time, his talents, his opportunities making himself a straw man and, with that silly-looking thing for antagonist, belaboring all about him like a bull in a china shop. You sincerest well-wishers, of whom I claim to be one, earnestly hope you will soon change your tactics.

You ask some practical questions which it may be well to answer: "How will you prevent the Standard Oil Company forcing weaker concerns to the wall by the simple expedient of selling below cost of production?" The Standard Oil trust is maintained (1) by monopoly of oil lands; (2) by monopoly of pipe lines; (3) by collusion with railroads. The Single Tax and its corollaries would absolutely destroy each of these advantages; (1) by throwing unused oil lands open to all on equal terms; (2) by government ownership or complete control of pipe lines to all distributing points, such lines being open for use to all oil producers on equal terms; (3) by exactly analogous treatment of railroads. With the three-fold monopoly of oil lands, pipe line, and railroad abolished, the Standard Oil trust would find no wall against which to crush weaker concerns. As to the trust, we hope that the abolishment of the thieves' compact, i.e. the protective tariff, will make the trusts sick unto death. Absolute free trade, a necessary concomitant of the Single Tax, will leave 99 per cent. of the trusts stranded. If any survive it will not be the fault of the Single Tax. Be it remembered that the evils which the Single Tax is guaranteed to cure are, primarily, land monopoly, and, secondarily, all the other monopolies based upon it; as those of the coal, iron and lumber trust, the Standard Oil trust, etc.

"With coal fields leased to the operators by Uncle Sam, how would you prevent Hanna organizing a pool, limiting production, raising prices and reducing wages?" Coal fields are included in the economic term, land. When unused land is free for occupancy, unused coal fields will also be free. If Mark sought to limit production by shutting down his mines, one of two things would happen. Either somebody else would start in to mine coal, or Mark's tax would be raised till the wisdom of either letting go or resuming would dawn on his fat wits. Unless he owned or controlled the coal fields he could not limit production, raise prices, or cut down wages. "How will you prevent the Standard Oil company forcing weaker concerns to the wall by the simple expedient of selling below cost of production?" We wouldn't prevent them. But if they afterwards tried to recoup their losses by raising prices as they do now, we might get after them with a tax commensurate with their asinine generosity, and keep after them till other concerns got well on their feet. If they became too refractory, what's to prevent the government from taking hold itself and working the oil wells for the benefit of the whole people? Remember the government is theoretically the people's servant, and it could be actually so if the people only had a little intelligence and moral courage.

You very needlessly tell your Ft. Hamilton friend that land is the primal source of all wealth; that it does not produce wealth, but simply affords man an opportunity to produce it; you forgot to add—provided the landlord doesn't prevent him. You say in another place, "Figure it as you will, adjust it as you may, a tax is a fine on industry and will so remain until you get blood from turnips," etc. This very objection in protean form is continually being raised by a class of shallow-thinking men with whom the editor of the Iconoclast should not be proud to herd. "What difference docs it make," they say, "whether I pay rent to the government or to a landlord when I've got to pay it anyhow? And what difference does it make whether taxes are levied on my land or my improvements, or both, so long as I've got to pay them with the products of my labor?"

Now, it is quite true that all taxes of whatever nature are paid out of the products of labor. But must they be for that reason a tax on labor products. Let us see. I suppose you won't deny that a unit of labor applies to different kinds of land will give very different results. Suppose that a unit of labor produces on A's land 4, on B's 3, on C's 2 and on D's 1. A's land is the most, and D's is the least, productive land in use in the community to which they belong. B's and C's represent intermediate grades. Suppose each occupies the best land that was open to him when he entered into possession. Now, B, and C, and D have just as good a right to the use of the best land as A had. Manifestly then, if this be the whole story, there cannot be equality of opportunity where a unit of labor produces such different results, all other things being equal except the land. How is this equality to be secured? There is but one possible way. Each must surrender for the common use of all, himself included, whatever advantages accrues to him from the possession of land superior to that which falls to the lot of him who occupies the poorest. In the case stated, what the unit of labor produces for D, is what it should produce for A, B and C, if these are not to have an advantage of natural opportunity over D. Hence equity is secured when A pays 3, D, 2 and C, 1 into a common fund for the common use of all—to be expended, say in digging a well, making a road or bridge, building a school, or other public utility. Is it not manifest that here the tax which A, B and C pay into a common fund, and from which D is exempt, is not a tax on their labor products (though paid out of them) but a tax on the superior advantage which they enjoy over D, and to which D has just as good a right as any of them. The result of this arrangement is that each takes up as much of the best land open to him as he can put to gainful use, and what he cannot so use he leaves open for the next. Moreover, he is at no disadvantage with the rest who have come in ahead of him, for they provide for him, in proportion to their respective advantages, those public utilities which invariably arise wherever men live in communities. Of course he will in turn hold to those who come later the same relation that those who came earlier held to him. Suppose now that taxes had been levied on labor products instead of land; all that any land-holder would have to do to avoid the tax is to produce little or nothing. He could just squat on his land, neither using it himself nor letting others use it, but he would not stop at this, for he would grab to the last acre all that he could possibly get hold of. Each of the others would do the same in turn, with the sure result that by and by, E, F and G would find no land left for them on which they might make a living. So they would have to hire their labor to those who had already monopolized the land, or else buy or rent a piece of land from them. Behold now the devil of landlordism getting his hoof on God's handiwork! Exit justice, freedom, social peace and plenty. Enter robbery, slavery, social discontent, consuming grief, riotous but unearned wealth, degrading pauperism, crime breeding, want, the beggar's whine, and the tyrant's iron heel. And how did it all come about? By the simple expedient of taxing labor products in order that precious landlordism might laugh and grow fat on the bovine stupidity of the community that contributes its own land values toward its own enslavement! And yet men vacuously ask, "What difference does it make?" O tempora! O mores! To be as plain as is necessary, it makes this four-fold difference. First, it robs the community of its land values; second, it robs labor of its wages in the name of taxation; third, it sustains and fosters landlordism, a most conspicuously damnable difference; fourth, it exhibits willing workers in enforced idleness; beholding their families in want on the one hand, and unused land that would yield them abundance on the other. This last is a difference that cries to heaven for vengeance, and if it does not always cry in vain, will W. C. Brann be able to draw his robe close around him and with a good conscience exclaim, "It's none of my fault; I am not my brother's keeper."

It will not do, my dear friend; you must think again on the Single Tax, even though, in doing so, you might make men suspect that you are not infallible. The sublimest act it will ever be given you to perform is to candidly confess to your grand and ever-growing constituency that you were mistaken in your estimate of the Single Taxers and their faith. "Government must compel each to pay toll in proportion the amount of wealth it has produced—and this is the only equitable law of taxation." Just reflect for a moment what a monstrous conclusion flows from these premises. Labor applied to land produces all wealth. Landlordism as such produces nothing. Therefore labor should bear the whole burden of taxation, while landlordism and all other forms of monopoly should go scot free. The iniquity of our present system of taxation is that a portion of it is levied on land instead of being all levied on labor products, like the tariff! To be strictly just, we must quit taxing land and exact no royalty from owners of coal mines and oil wells! That your view?

"There is every indication that his cult has had its day and is rapidly going to join the many other isms, political and religious, that have been swallowed up like cast off clothes and other exuviae by the great mother of dead dogs." This is fine, incontestably fine! Also forcible, impressibly forcible—with the force of a squirt of tobacco juice. If "the Single Tax party will not long survive its creator," perhaps it is because it has not as much attraction for the great sovereign voter as the blessed protective tariff, which, to use your own fantastic expression, you should "cosset on your heaving brisket" for its splendid success as a survivor of its primogenitors. Look at the pinnacle of political success to which the McKinley bill has brought Bill McKinley (excuse the paltry little pun) and sound money (saving your presence) brought Grover Cleveland, and then contemplate the ignominy and obscurity has brought George and free silver has brought Bryan. Evidently George isn't a mouse to McKinley, while Bryan is but a brindle pup compared to the great and only Grover. Yes, the "public concept of truth" makes it plain that protection is all right and Single Tax all wrong. "George is a reformer who can't reform because he took issue with the wisdom of the world," just like the man who said that the earth was round and that the sun didn't go round it every twenty-four hours, contrary to what the wisdom of the world had long ago decided.

You are not mistaken in saying that "Mr. George was unable to keep one of these expounders of his doctrine (a S.T. paper) from running on the financial rocks." It is a very logical deduction to draw from this fact that the teachings of the paper were worthless. Why should anybody teach what does not, in the teaching, promote his financial prosperity? See what fools Professors Bemis and Andrews have made of themselves. Because they did not have due regard for the "public concept of the truth" they are cashiered; and it serves them right, for the truth must be vindicated—if it pays. On the other hand, see what splendid financial successes the ICONOCLAST, the Galveston News and the so-called yellow journalism of New York all are. "Deserve, in order to command success," the old copy-book headline used to say, from which it follows as mud does rain, that whatever succeeds deserves it, and whatever doesn't, doesn't. It doesn't take much besides capital to succeed, however, "where the conditions for the propagation of empiricism are more favorable than ever before." All you have to do is to propagate and expound the "public concept of truth" and let the truth itself alone. The Single Taxers respectfully solicit some more plain truths on the "Mumbojumboism of George."

THOMAS FLAVIN.

* * *

Ever since the appearance of my first courteous critique of the Single Tax theory the followers of that faith have been pouring in vigorous "replies"; but as my articles were directed to Mr. George and not to his disciples, I saw no occasion for the latter to intermeddle in the matter, and the tide of economic wisdom went to waste. Although a publisher is supposed to be privileged to select his own contributors, and Mr. George had been requested to make reply at my expense, the Single Taxers raised a terrible hue and cry that the ICONOCLAST was unfair in that it "permitted one side to be presented." In order to cast a little kerosene upon the troubled waters I decided that they should be heard, and selected Dr. Flavin as their spokesman, believing him to be the ablest of those who have followed this particular economic rainbow into the bogs. So much by way of prolegomenon; now for the doctor.

My very dear sir, I shall heed your advice to "rise above" the abuse of those who mistake impudence for argument, and ignore the discourteous remarks with which you have so liberally interlarded your discourse. Doubtless you include yourself among that numerous tribe of Texas titans who can "unhorse" me as easily as turning a hen over; and having accorded you unlimited space in which to acquire momentum, I would certainly dread the shock were I cursed with an atom of polemical pride. Frankly, I wish you success—trust that you can demonstrate beyond a peradventure of a doubt that all my objections to the Single Tax are fallacious, that it is indeed the correct solution of that sphinx riddle which we must soon answer or be destroyed. At a time when the industrial problem is pressing upon us with ever increasing power, it is discouraging to hear grown Americans prattling of "unhorsing" economic adversaries—priding themselves on polemical fence, like shyster lawyers, and seeking victory through sophistry rather than truth by honest inquiry. That is not patriotism, but a picayune partisanship which I profoundly pity.

Regarding "the public concept of truth" which seems to irritate you sorely, I will simply say that the people are slow to accept new and startling truths like those promulgated by Galileo, Newton and Harvey; but a truth, howsoever strange, *grows* year by year and age by age, while a falsehood creates more or less flurry at its birth, then fades into the everlasting night of utter nothingness. That Mr. George's theory, after several years of discussion, is declining in popular favor, and has never made a convert among the careful students of political economy, is strong presumptive evidence that it is not founded on fact. The more you hammer truth the brighter it glows; the more you hammer Georgeism the paler it gets. It is not for me to prove the fallacy of the Single Tax theory—the onus probandi rests with its apostles, and they but saltate from mistaken premises to ridiculous conclusions. Like the German metaphysicians, they are abstract reasoners who do not trouble themselves about conditions. It is not well to sneer at "the great blind multitude" because it fails to see the beauty or wisdom in the Single Tax, for many a great man before Lincoln's time had profound respect for the judgment of the common people. "Truth," say the Italians, "is lost by too much controversy;" and while the Georges and Flavins split hairs and spute and spout themselves into error, the hard-headed farmer and mechanic, exercising their practical common-sense, arrive at correct conclusions. In saying that Mr. George has, by his sophistry, "deceived hundreds of abler men than himself," I simply accredited him with a feat that has been a thousand times performed. Carliostro was an ignoramus and possessed very ordinary intellect, yet for several years he succeeded in deceiving some of the wisest men of his day with his Egyptian Masonry idiocy. Thousands of fairly intelligent people believed poor looney Francis Schlatter a kind of second Messiah, some of the ablest men of Europe were misled by half-crazy Martin Luther—and Dr. Flavin regards Henry George's economic absurdities as omniscience. The latter has "mistaken the plausible for the actual," has deceived himself with his own sophistry, else he and his few score noisy followers are wiser than all the rest of the world, or, for the sake of gain or cheap notoriety, he's peddling what he knows to be arrant nonsense. You may take as many "pinches of snuff" on that proposition as you please.

All your remarks about land values, their origin and rightful ownership—the tiresome old piece de resistance of every Single Tax discourse—I answered fully in my two former articles on this subject, wherein I also explained how the "unearned increment" is at present appropriated by the public, and I cannot afford to rethresh old straw for the benefit of Single Taxers who *will* write and *won't* read. I will remark en passant, however, that by "unearned increment" I mean exactly what I suppose Mr. George to mean—increase in the market value of land for which the proprietor is not responsible. This, I have explained, is already appropriated by the public, because the total annual increase in land values in this country—barring betterments of course—does not exceed the total annual tax levied upon the land. There's always a boom in land values here and there; but hundreds of millions of acres, urban and suburban, have not increased a penny in selling price during the past decade. The owners are reaping no unearned increment, but they are paying taxes regularly into the public till. "The exclusive creator or producer of a thing is the rightful owner," says Dr. Flavin. Quite true; and *as the only thing the community creates for the land owner is the unearned increment, it has no moral right to take anything more*. The Single Taxers persist in ignoring the fact that there is an *earned* as well as an *unearned* increment, and that the former is as much the property of the individual as the barn he builds or the calf he breeds. Of this earned increment more anon.

"The highest homage, the highest act of faith which the human mind and heart can offer to God is to say he could not be God and pronounce the Single Tax to be unjust!" O hell! That's not argument, but simply empty declamation intended to tickle the ears of the groundlings—to raise a whoop among the gallery gods. As you have suggested, "Come, let us argue with dignity and composure," instead of emitting fanatical screeches like fresh converts at a Methodist camp-meeting, let's see about this God of Justice business: About 200 years ago a party whom we will call Brann, as that happened to be his name "cleared" a farm in the wilds of Virginia, enduring all the hardships and dangers of the frontier. He built roads and bridges, drained swamps, exterminated Indians and wild animals. His descendants helped drive out the British butchers, some of them being scalped alive by John Bull's red allies, while their wives and children were tomahawked. They contributed in their humble way to secure the blessings of free government which the present inhabitants of Virginia enjoyed. They helped support schools, churches and charities and otherwise make the district desirable as a place of residence. Finally railways were built and stores opened, not to enrich these people, but to be enriched by them. These conveniences added to the value of the land, but were paid for at a good round price, as such things ever are by the users. The land is now worth about $30.00 an acre, and while this value is unquestionably due to the presence of population, it is fair to assume that in two centuries the estate has yielded that much in the shape of taxes. As the present owner, I ask, has the Old Dominion against that property for unearned increment? I say it has not; that the $30.00 an acre represents the savings of seven generations of my ancestors; that while the community created the land value, said value has been duly purchased and paid for—that it represents *earned* increment. Unearned increment is not what Dr. Elavin is after; he would confiscate the *rent* of my patrimony; he would deprive me of the *values* created by my people—would allow me no larger share therein than he accords to the newly arrived immigrant from that damned island we call England. If our God says *that* is just, then I want no angelic wings—prefer to associate with Satan. Has the son a just right to wealth created and solemnly bequeathed him by his sire? That land is as much mine as the gold would be mine, had my people their savings in that shape, and the rent is mine as justly as the interest on the gold would be. It is quite true that none of my clan *created* that land; it is true that I cannot show a title to it signed by God Almighty and counter-signed by the Savior, any more than I can show a title from the same high source to the watch I hold in my hand; but I have a title to all the rights, conveniences and profits appertaining to control of the land, issued by their creator, the community, for value received. I have the same title to the land that I have to the watch; not to the material made by the Almighty, but to whatsoever has been added of desirability thereto by the action of man. The community has been settled with up-to-date for both the land and the watch, but has a continuing claim against them so long as it enables me to employ them advantageously than I could without its assistance. If I sell my land the purchaser receives in return for his money all those advantages which it required so many years of toil and danger to win—he pays for the sacrifices made by others in preference to going into the wilderness and making them himself. The market value of my land is a "labor product," just as my watch is a labor product, hence all this prattle about relieving industry of governmental burdens by any economic thaumaturgy whatsoever is the merest moonshine.

It is quite true that "the great middle class" does not own the most valuable lots in New York and London; but I have the "chilled steel" hardihood to affirm that not only the bulk of the land but of the land values are in the possession of people who are poor as compared with the occupants of those sumptuous palaces which the George conspiracy for the further enrichment if Dives and the starvation of Lazaras would exempt from taxation. The total wealth of this nation is not far from 75 billions, while all the land, exclusive of improvements, would not sell for more than 20 billion. The naked land of our 5 million farms is estimated at about 10 billion, so that leaves but about 10 billion for urban lands—less than one-seventh of the total value. I have no reliable statistics at hand showing what proportion of urban inhabitants own their homes; but we may safely assume that one-half do so. Now, if this be true, we may also assume that the land values held by the very wealthy—the people whom the Single Taxers profess to be after,—do not exceed one-fourth of all land values, or one-fifteenth of total property values. Hence you see it is quite possible for 250,000 to own 80 per cent of *all* values, while the bulk of the *land* values remain with the common people. And it is these common people that the Single Tax will crush for the benefit of these 250,000 plutocrats, the bulk of whose wealth is in personal property.

Sit down and think it over, doctor; you are really too bright a man to be led astray by the razzle-dazzle of Single Tax sophistry. You do your enviable reputation for intelligence a rank injustice by mistaking poor old George for an economic Messiah, and if you are not careful somebody will try to sell you a gold-brick or stock in a Klondike company. Suppose that you and Hon. Walter Gresham occupy residence lots worth $1,000 each, but that you inhabit a $1,500 cottage and he a $150,000 mansion; and suppose that your income is $2,000 a year while his is

$20,000: Do you think there is any necessity for tearing your balbriggan under-shirt because not compelled to put up as much for the maintenance of government as your wealthy neighbor? Is it at all probable that Gresham will become discouraged, refuse to longer serve the corporations and sit in the woodshed and sulk, even jump off the bridge, because taxed in proportion to the property in his possession rather than according to the land he occupies? If Col. Moody builds a million dollar cotton mill on suburban land worth but $500 why should you refuse to sleep o' nights because not required to pay double the taxes of that old duffer? As a worthy disciple of Aesculapius you should know that too heavy a burden on your own back is liable to make you bow-legged.

I suspected all along that the Single Tax would require several able-bodied "corollaries" to enable it to effect much of a reformation, to usher in the Golden Age. It were very nice to throw unused coal and oil lands "open to all on equal terms," have the government pipe off all their products for equal pay, then compel operators by piling on taxes to maintain high prices to consumers "till other companies got well on their feet"—and a combination was effected. If Rockefeller, Hanna, Carnegie, et id genes omnes tried any of their old tricks "we might get after them"—just as we *have* long been doing. These plutocrats are so afraid of our politicians that there is danger of their dying of neuropathy. If the coal, iron and oil operators advance prices we'll advance their taxes—for the people to pay. And I suppose that when the whiskey trust get gay, the doctor will raise the rent of corn land, when the cotton-seed oil trust becomes too smooth, he'll knock it on the head by adding a dollar an acre to cotton land, and so on until we get the cormorant fairly by the goozle. It's all dead easy when you understand it—works as smoothly as an "iridescent dream" on a toboggan slide! We are continually discovering new coal, iron and oil districts, and these are "open to all on equal terms"—I can acquire them just as cheaply as can Rockefeller or Carnegie. Then what's the matter? I lack the capital to properly develop them, to produce so cheaply as my wealthy competitors. Or if able to become a thorn in the side of the great corporations they either lower prices and freeze me out or make it to my advantage to enter the syndicate. When Rockefeller lowers the price of oil he lowers his rent; when I am either crushed by competition or taken in out of the cold, he advances the price of oil. His rent is regulated by competition for the use of oil lands—you cannot make him pay more than the market price. When you raise his rent you raise that of all the other operators in proportion, and the same is the same as an increase of the excise on whisky—the people get a meaner grade of goods at a higher price. If an ordinary man cooked up such a scheme as that for the benefit of the people, I'd feel justified in calling him a "crank," and I cannot conceive how a man like Dr. Slavin can tack his signature to such tommy-rot. Before we can make the Single Tax "a go" we've got to have government ownership of telegraphs, railways, pipe-lines, etc., etc., and use the taxing power to regulate prices just as the Republicans do the tariff—and for what? To humble the haughty landlord? Oh no; to knock the stuffing out of capital—so long wept over by Single Taxers as a fellow sufferer with toil. Why not call the George system Communism?—"a rose by any other name," etc.

When the doctor get matters arranged it will really make no difference whether a farmer is located in the black-waxy district, or on the arid cactus-cursed lands of the trans-Pecos country, as he will have to surrender to the public all he produces in excess of what the poorest land in use will yield. He will have no incentive to study the capabilities of his land and bring to bear upon it exceptional industry, for he will be deprived of all the increase he can make it yield by such methods. A will be placed on a parity with D because he took the best land he could get instead of the poorest he could find. Intelligence and enterprise are to have no reward under the new regime. You can squat on a sand-bank or pile of rocks in any community and be on a financial parity with the man whose black soil reaches to the axis of the earth—no need to bundle the old woman into a covered wagon, tie the brindled cow to the feed-box and head for a country where better land is to be had. There will be no temptation to carve out a home in the wilderness, for later immigrants will set at naught your toil and sacrifices and deprive your children of their patrimony—the best situated merchant in Waco will have no advantage of the keeper of a tent store on a side street of Yuba Dam or Tombstone. A tax will not longer be "a fine on industry"—it will be a fine on fools.

My Galveston friend should not work himself into a fit of hysteria because I declared that the George doctrine has had its day, it being sheer folly to quarrel with a self-evident fact. When Henry George first flamed forth he made a great deal of money out of his writings, and has thus far shown no more aversion to the silver than has your humble servant. His paper was doubtless launched with a view of promoting his financial and political fortunes, for he did not go broke publishing it "for the good of the cause," but promptly rung off when he found that it did not *pay*, hence I fail to see that he is entitled to any more credit than Col. Belo or myself. I called attention to the failure of his paper, not in a spirit of rejoicing over its downfall, but simply to accentuate the fact, after giving some years to consideration of his rather pretty platitudes, that people condemned them—that his heroic attempt to reclothe with living flesh the bones of the impot unique had proven a dismal failure. Now, my dear doctor, I have not undertaken in this hasty article to fully expose this Single Tax fallacy, having attended to that heretofore, but simply to answer a few of your arguments which I had not hitherto heard. Let's drop the subject—let the dead go bury its dead, while we devote our energies to *living* issues.

*   *   *   *   *

TEXAS TOPICS.

I note with unfeigned pleasure that, according to claims of Baylor University, it opens the present season with a larger contingent of students, male and female, than ever before. This proves that Texas Baptists are determined to support it at any sacrifice—that they believe it better that their daughters should be exposed to its historic dangers and their sons condemned to grow up in ignorance than that this manufactory of ministers and Magdalenes should be permitted to perish. It is to be devoutly hoped that the recent expose of Baylor's criminal carelessness will have a beneficial effort—that hence forth orphan girls will not be ravished on the premises of its president, and that fewer young lady students will be sent home enciente. The ICONOCLAST would like to see Baylor University, so called, become an honor to Texas instead of an educational eye-sore, would like to hear it spoken of with reverence instead of sneeringly referred to by men about town as worse than a harem. Probably Baylor has never been so bad as many imagined, that the joint-keepers in the Reservation have been mistaken in regarding it as a rival, that the number of female students sent away to conceal their shame has been exaggerated; still I imagine that both its morale and educational advantages are susceptible of considerable improvement. The ICONOCLAST desires to see Baylor a veritable pantechnicon of learning—at least a place where the careful student may acquire something really worth remembering—instead of a Dotheboys (and girls) hall, a Squeeritic graft to relieve simple Baptist folk of their hard-earned boodle by beludaling the brains of their bairns with mis-called education. Unfortunately there is more brazen quackery in our sectarian colleges than was every dreamed of by Cagliostro. The faculty of such institutions is usually composed of superficially educated people who know even less than is contained in the text-books. As a rule they are employed because they will serve at a beggarly price, but sometimes because their employers are themselves too ignorant to properly pass upon the qualifications of others. You cannot estimate a man's intellect by the length of his purse, by the amount of money he has made and saved; but it is quite safe to judge a man's skill in his vocation by the salary he can command. I am informed that there has never been a time when the salary of the president of Baylor University exceeded $2,000 per annum—about half that of a good whisky salesman or advertising solicitor for a second-class newspaper. If such be the salary of the president, what must be those of the "professors"? I imagine their salaries run from $40 a month up to that of a second assistant book-keeper in a fashionable livery-stable. Judging by the salaries which they are compelled to accept, I doubt if there be a member of the Baylor faculty, including the president, who could obtain the position of principal of any public high school in the state. People cannot impart information which they do not possess; hence it is that the graduates of Baylor have not been really educated, but rather what the erstwhile Mr. Shakespeare would call "clapper-clawed." There is no reason, however, why the institution should be in the future so intellectually and morally unprofitable as in the past. Change is the order of the universe, and as Baylor cannot very well become worse it must of necessity become better. It will have the unswerving support of the ICONOCLAST in every effort to place itself upon a higher educational plane, to honestly earn the money it pockets as tuition fees. I am even willing to conduct a night school free of charge during three months in the year for the instruction of its faculty if each member thereof will give bond not to seek a better paying situation elsewhere as soon as he learns something. In any event, when Baylor can send me a valedictorian fresh from its walls who is better informed than the average graduate of our public schools, I'll give it a thousand dollars as evidence of my regard, and half as much annually thereafter to encourage it in the pursuit of common sense.

* * *

I greatly regret that my Baptist brethren, Drs. Hayden and Cranfill, Burleson and Carroll, should have gotten into a spiteful and un-Christian snarl over so pitiful a thing as Baylor's $2,000 presidency—that they should give to the world such a flagrant imitation of a lot of cut-throat unregenerates out for the long green. If one-half that Hayden and Cranfill are saying about each other in their respective papers be true—that I presume that it is—then both ought to be in the penitientiary. Brethren, please to remember that ye are posing as guardians of morals, as examples for mankind—as people out of whom the original sin has been soaked in the Baptist pool and whose paps are filled to the bursting point with the milk of human kindness. If you must fight and scratch like a brace of Kilkenny cats, why the hell don't you sneak quietly into the woods and fight it out instead of exhibiting your blatant jackasserie to the simple people of Dallas and McLennan counties and thereby bringing our blessed church into contempt! Gadzooks! if you splenetic-hearted old duffers don't sand your hands and take a fresh grip on your Christian charity I'll resign my position as chief priest of the Baptist church and become a Mormon elder. I'll just be cofferdamned if I propose to remain at the head of a church whose educators, preachers and editors are forever hacking away at each other's goozle with a hand-ax and slinging slime like a lot of colored courtesans.

* * *

Our little boiler-plate contemporary, the Austin Statesman, prints a court docket containing 69 divorce cases—side by side with 12 church notices. Which is cause and which effect I will not assume to say; but Austin is headquarters for camp-meetings—and every neurologists endorsed the ICONOCLAST's theory that emotional religion is a terrible strain on the Seventh Commandment.

* * *

"Our heroic young," etc., etc., announces himself a candidate for the United States Senate to succeed Roger Q. Mills. The young man's modesty is really monumental. Having succeeded by all manner of petty chicanery in capturing the governorship, I am surprised that he isn't seeking the job of Jehovah. Displacing Mills with Culberson were much like substituting a Chinese joss for the Apollo Belvedere or an itch bacillus for a bull-elephant. I really cannot consent that the little fellow be sent to Washington lest some hurdy gurdy man should swipe him. Chawles says: "Next spring and summer I shall canvas the state thoroughly, presenting my views of public questions to the people." Which is to say that while we are paying him a good stiff salary for doing his little best to discharge the duties of one office, he will "canvas the state thoroughly" chasing another. If he attempts to perpetuate such a brazen swindle on the tax-payers of Texas, I'll camp on his trail to some extent, and see that he has a hot time in at least a few old towns. I cannot afford to trail him at my own expense all spring and summer, while he's cavorting around on free passes and drawing $11 a day from the public purse for unrendered services; but I'll trump his card in all the large Texas towns as quick as it strikes the table. I'm getting dead rotten tired of helping pay the salaries of Texas officials for time devoted to fence-building, and it will afford me considerable *satisfaction* to place this cold-blooded little ward on the body politic properly before the people. The duties of the governor's office were supposed to be so onerous that a board of pardons was created at the tax-payers' expense to lighten his labors; yet Mr. Culberson proposed to spend the spring and summer, not in a reasonable effort to earn his salary, but in explaining why he should be sent to the senate. Coming before us thus self-evidently unfaithful over a few things, this "heroic young Christian" poker-player and red-light habitue has the supernal gall to ask us to make him lord over many things,—to accord him political promotion for dereliction of duty! In the name of Balaam's she-ass, does this snub-nosed little snipe suppose that we are all hopeless idiots? You are the state's hired hand, Charlie boy—duly employed to remain at Austin and display your anserine ignorance in the governor's office. The people don't care two whoops in hades what your "opinions" may be on any subject within the purview of the United States Senate. If you want to spend the "spring and summer" rainbow chasing, a proper sense of duty to your employers, even a slight conception of commercial honor, would induce you to resign your present position. If you are destitute of both honor and decency you will probably campaign at our expense as you have promised; but I opine that I can pour enough hot shot under your little shirt-tails in a few engagements to drive you back to your duty, and that you will go in a gallop. What the devil do you suppose that Texans want with a two-faced little icicle like yourself in the United States Senate? What taxpayer has asked you to become a candidate? Despite all your wire-pulling, your trading and self-seeking, and the further fact that you are employing the state machinery to strengthen your pull, you really stand no more show of succeeding Roger Q. Mills than you do of succeeding the Czar of Russia. You have managed to get thus far, not on your own merits, but solely because you are "Old Dave" Culberson's son. Yours is simply a case of magni nominis umbra, and the umbra is getting deuced thin at the edges, is no longer capable of concealing the ass. For many years past we have been paying men fat salaries for gadding about the country exploiting their supposed "opinions." It is high time we put an end to such idiocy, and I have selected you, as probably the worst specimen of these political malefactors, of which to make an example in the interest of honesty.

* * *

A correspondent writes me from Nacogdoches, Texas: "The Baptists of this town have forced your agent to promise to discontinue selling the ICONOCLAST under penalty of expulsion from the church." That's all right; having purchased and paid for a Baptist ticket to the heavenly henceforth, he doesn't want to be bounced from the boat. Being thrown overboard in a canal two feet wide and four feet deep is not so bad by itself considered, but contumacious recalcitrants are invariable boycotted in business by the hydrocephalous sect which boasts that it was the first to establish liberty of conscience and freedom of speech in this country, yet which has been striving desperately for a hundred years to banish the last vestige of individuality and transform this nation into a pharisaical theocracy with some priorient hypocrite as its heierach. The ICONOCLAST is in its seventh volume and has never yet been caught in a falsehood or published an unclean advertisement. I am proud to say that no honest man or virtuous woman was ever its enemy, but that holy hypocrites and sanctified harlots regard it with the same aversion that a pickpocket does a policeman. Yes; the action of the Baptists of Nacogdoches was perfectly natural. What they want is a paper that will afford them a charming mixture of camp-meeting notices and syphilitic nostrums, prayer-meetings and abortion pills, Prohibition rallies and lost manhood restorers. I cheerfully recommend the Baptist Standard to their kindly consideration.

* * *

When J. S. Hogg was governor of Texas he compelled the Southern Pacific road to move a train-load of Coxey-ites, whom it had, carried in from California and side tracked west of San Antonio to starve. As counsel for that impudent corporation—whose officials seem to have been formed of the quintessential extract of the exerementitious matter of the whole earth—he now makes a "compromise" with the Culberson crew whereby it is some $975,000 *in* and the state that much *out*. James Stephen can scarce be blamed for securing every possible advantage for his client, even tho' it be such a notorious criminal as the "Sunset"; but had he been attorney for the state instead of for the corporation there would have been no compounding of a felony "for the good of the people," no sacrifice of both dignity and dollars. It is amusing to see Culberson and Crane making a house of refuge of the coat tails of Reagan. "He approved it! he approved it!" Of course he approved it—Attorney General Crane "not having time during his term of office to prosecute all the cases." But he'll "have time" just as hard to spend half of next year chasing the governorship on time paid for by the people. Reagan was compelled to accept the compromise because the Culbersonian crew were too busy office-chasing to prosecute the corporation. If the Culbersonian crowd lined their pockets by that compromise they are a set of thieves; if they didn't line their pockets they simply suffered the corporation to play 'em for a pack of damphools. As neither a thief nor a fool is fit to hold a public office, I move that we build a large zinc-lined political coffin and bury the whole crowd.

* * *

The St. Louis Mirror, the brightest weekly in the world, recently had a remarkably interesting article on Texas politics; but somehow it suggested to my mind that German metaphysician who, having never seen a lion or read a description of one, undertook to evolve a correct idea of the king of beasts from his own inner consciousness.

* * *

It were interesting to know what kind of a swindle W. L. Moody & Co. have in soak this season for the guileless cotton grower. I have provided this office with a car-load of nickel-plated tear-jugs for the benefit of cotton men who will call later to tell me their troubles. My idea is to build a condenser, start a wholesale salt store and supply Baptist dipping-tanks with water free of wiggletails. Say! There's millions in it. Col. Mulberry Seller's eye-water enterprise were as nothing to my graft when I get it agoing.

* * *

I note that the Wrong-Reverend E. H. Harman, formerly presiding elder of the Methodist church at Brenham, but given the grand bounce for getting too gay at Galveston, where, in company with another sanctified ministerial hypocrite named Wimberly, he had "a hot time in the old town," with hacks, harlots and barrel-house booze, has been converted to the Christian (or Campbellite) faith and proposes to preach. Possibly his conversion is genuine; but it is worthy of remark that he saw nothing attractive in the Christian cult until no longer allowed to occupy a Methodist pulpit—until reduced to the necessity of either seeking a job in a new corner of the Lord's vineyard or taking a fall out of the lowly cotton patch. He ought to make an excellent running mate for the "Rev." Granville Jones, the poorty preacher who puts his picture on his evangelical guttersnipes to show the people how a holy man of God looks after confessing to having forged a letter derogatory to a poor motherless working girl's reputation. As my father is a Christian preacher I feel I have a right to protest against his being placed on a clerical parity with bilkers of hack bills and crapulous associates of two-for-a-penny prostitutes. If Harman attempts to defile the Christian pulpit with his presence, I hope to the good Lord that the decent members of that denomination will tie him across a nine-rail fence and enhance the torridity of his rear elevation with a vigorous application of pine plank.

*   *   *   *   *

THE RETORT COURTEOUS.

F. L. Lewis writes from San Antonio to an obscure sheet called the *Railway Age*, that Brann is not an Englishman as the *Age* editor in one of his elephantine efforts to be humorous seems to have suggested, and that "all Englishmen in this country repudiate his every utterance." Thanks, awfully; that's the highest compliment ever paid an American sovereign by a British subject. When I next visit San Antonio I'll testify my gratitude by giving Lewis 50 cents instead of the usual two-bits for toting my grip from the "Sap" depot to the Menger hotel. I once said, "There are some very decent and brainy Englishmen;" but as all Englishmen in this country repudiate the soft impeachment, I hasten to acknowledge my error. As the editor of the *Age* is quite anxious to ascertain my nationality he probably suspects that I may be his father.

* * *

The *Independent*, which I infer from the date-line of a letter calling attention to its existence, is published at Pomeroy, Wash., proposes, bumbye, to "give a history of the robberies committed by Brann during the war." H— —;! I can do that myself. Attired in a triangular strip of birds-eye linen and emitting savage yells, I repeatedly stormed and captured the most magnificent breast-works ever built in Kentucky and ravenously appropriated whatsoever I found therein without so much as a thankee mum. Yes sirree, I was a robber dead-right in those old days; but the Independent editor is safe: he's got nothing but a shirt-tail full o' pied type and a card of membership in the A.P.A.—Aggregation of Pusillanimous Asses. I have no use for his "plant," and God knows I would not be caught dead in a Chinese opium den with his certificate of infamy concealed in my clothes.

* * *

The St. Louis *Post-Dispatch* of August 20, contains a half-page puff of one John

Morrissey, who seems to be a peripatetic iconoclast who has started out with a Bible in one hand, and a free lunch in the other to abolish preachers. According to Morrissey he was a Roman Catholic until he learned better, a drunkard until "the Spirit of God entered his heart" and caused his reformation, and used to write sermons for St. Louis preachers who palmed them off as their own. I don't know about that; but I know that of the interview he gave the Pee-Dee a column was cribbed without credit from the article on "Charity" in "Brann's Scrap-Book." "The Spirit of God" may have done much for Morrissey, but it hasn't cured him of the thieving habit, and I would advise people to keep a sharp eyes on their portable property until this religious reformer succeeds in breaking into the penitentiary.

* * *

The Texas Republican, which appears semi-occasionally at Greenville, Tex., denounces in what Dorenus was wont to term "livid language," my statement to the effect that a nation pays for its imports with its exports. He says it is all "iconoclastic foolishness," declares that a nation does nothing of the kind, and proceeds to animadvert in an unchristian spirit on the density of my economic ignorance. My contemporary's criticism is clearly unconstitutional in that it is cruel and unusual punishment. Now that its editor has annihilated my poor little theory, it is his duty as a great public educator and charter member of the Markhanna Illuminati, to inform me what the hades a nation *does* pay for its imports with, instead of permitting me, as he seems inclined, to "burst in ignorance." You have the floor, my sweet little man, and the shades of all the standard economists from Smith to Walker are waiting to see you raise one of their favorite dogmas over the ropes. Call Prof. Jevons a jackass, give Ricardo a tremendous rap, have no mercy on John Stuart Mill, make old Adam Smith's bones to rattle, take a terrible fall out of Turgot—then flap your ears and bray until the welkin rings again. That's the way to settle a political adversary who goes galivanting off after false economic gods. In the meantime it might be a good idea to take your brains out, brush the cobwebs off its cogs and apply a little kerosene with a corncob.

* * *

It is seldom indeed that I give any attention to insulting letters, but I cannot refrain from paying my respects to one Byron Jassack Wales, who, with gray goose-quill for Pelian spear, charges down on the Iconoclast as blithely as a gay moss-trooper making an English swine-herd hard to catch. Such insults usually come unsigned—are simply cross insolence which their cowardly authors fear to father; but Byron sets down all the dreaful things he thinks of Brann, boldly signs his name and adds an ornamental flourish of defiance. The possibility of some long-legged, slouch-hatted, wire-moustached cowboy ambling into his august presence armed with a shooting iron carrying iron bullets as big as goose-eggs and hurling him with a flash and whoop into the problematical hitherto, does not shake to its base the heroic fortitude of the man whose mother named him for the most notorious chippy-chaser known to history. Byron proposed to express his opinion, to say what he dad-burned pleases, though the redoubtable Lieutenant-Colonel Rienzi Miltiades Johnsing, of Houston, who does all the Iconoclast's fighting under yearly contract, should swoop down upon him like a double-barreled besom of destruction,

> "With death-shot glowing in his fiery hand
> And eye that scorcheth all it looks upon."

Byron is offended because I saw fit to criticize New York's priorient parvenues for exploiting the pregnancy of their wives in the public-prints, and he lets me know where he can be found in case his remarks offend, by daringly dating his letter "New York." True, he refrains from giving his street and number—even tears the printed headings off the letter paper he employs; but that does not matter, as in a little village like New York a Texan with a hair-trigger temper has only to inquire of the first man he meets to be directed to the one he wants. Byron insists that I print his letter to show people what a desperate dare-devil he is; but I refrain lest it scare all the cattle off the range and cause Bill Fewell and Doc Yandell of El Paso to move over into Mexico. Among other dreadful things he promises to have my paper suppressed by the postal authorities if I speak of him disrespectfully, which proves that he has a tremendous political pull concealed about his person. I guess I'm safe so far as he is concerned for a careful inspection of his letter makes apparent the utter impossibility of speaking of Lord Byron Jassack Wales disrespectfully—indicates that it were fulsome flattery to refer to him as a blind pile on the body politic, a suppurating sore on the hedonistic society of Sodom.

* * *

T. Shelley Sutton, of Boise City, Idaho, has "writ a pome" entitled "That Man Brann," and the proud author sends me an A.P.A. paper containing his production. It is an excellent composition—of its kind; and I am gratified to learn that it has at least gravitated to its proper level. Some six months ago a commercial traveller sent me substantially the same thing, saying that he had copied from the walls of a water closet in a Kentucky hotel. It appears that it was too foul to harmonize with the place in which it was composed, so it was stolen by a thieving yahoo in search of carrion and puked into the putrid columns of an A.P.A. paper. T. Shelley Sutton can probably find more "original poetry" in the same place.

* * *

"Rev." Bill Homan, who conducts a little pecasmman paper somewhere in North Texas for the long green and the misguidance of three or four hundred fork-o'-the-creek Campbellites, devotes two more columns of his raucous tommyrot and brainless balderdash to the Howell-Jones imbroglio. Although he manages to tell at least three deliberate lies in his idiotic eructation, he dares not deny that the trial committee, of which he was a member, permitted Jones to continue belching his fetid bile in the Christian pulpit after being cornered and compelled to confess to a cowardly crime which should be rewarded with a rope. Until this corticiferous little cur explains why he is defending a fourth-class preacher who confesses to having foully insulted, by a base forgery, a motherless young girl committed to his care, the Iconoclast must, for the sake of its own self-respect, decline further controversy.

*   *   *   *   *

BRANN VS. BAYLOR.
REVOLVERS, ROPES AND RELIGION.

I have just been enjoying the first holiday I have had in fifteen years. Owing to circumstances entirely beyond my control, I devoted the major part of the past month to digesting a couple of installments of Saving Grace presented by my Baptist brethren, and carefully rubbed in with revolvers and ropes, loaded canes and miscellaneous cudgels—with almost any old thing calculated to make a sinner reflect upon the status of his soul. That explains the short-comings of the present issue of the ICONOCLAST. One cannot write philosophic essays while dallying with the Baptist faith. It were too much like mixing Websterian dignity with a cataleptoid convulsion, or sitting on a red ant hill and trying to look unconcerned. Here in Waco our religious zeal registers 600 in the shade, and when we hold a love-feast you can hear the unctuous echoes of our hosannahs from Tadmor in the Wilderness to the Pillars of Hercules. We believe with St. Paul that faith without works is dead; hence we gird up our loins with the sweet cestus of love, grab our guns and go whooping forth to "capture the world for Christ." When we find a contumacious sinner we waste no time in theological controversy or moral suasion, but promptly round him up with a rope and bump his head, and we bump it hard. Why consume our energies "agonizing with an emissary of Satan," explaining his error and striving by honeyed phrases to lead him into the light, when it is so much easier to seize him by the pompadour and pantelettes and drag him bodily from the abyss? Some may complain that our Christian charity carries a razor edge, that we skim the cream off our milk of human kindness then put the can under an alkali pump before serving it to our customers as a prime article; but bless God! they can scarce expect to

> "... be carried to the skies
> On flowery beds of ease,
> Whilst others fight to win the prize
> And sail through bloody seas."

My Baptist brethren desired to send me as a missionary to foreign lands, and their invitation was so urgent, their expressions of regard so fervent that I am now wearing my head in a sling and trying to write with my left hand. Although they declared that I had an imperative "call" to go, and would tempt Providence by loitering longer than one short day, I concluded to remain in Waco and preach them a few more of my popular sermons from that favorite text, "If ye forgive not men their trespasses, neither will your Father forgive your trespasses." It is quite possible that a few heathen will go to hell whom I might enable to find the river route to heaven, but I believe in doing the duty that lies next my hand—in first saving the heathen right here at home.

But enough of persiflage; now for cold facts. In all candor, I would cheerfully ignore the recent disgraceful occurrences in this city could I do so in justice to the South in general and to Texas in particular. I have no revenge to gratify, no more feeling in the matter than though the assaults had been made upon an utter stranger. It is quite true that for a time I was eager to call my assailants out one by one and settle the affair after the manner of our fathers; but being creditably informed that instead of honoring a cartel, they would make it the basis of a legal complaint and send me to the penitentiary, and having no desire to enact the role of the street assassin, I became once more a law-abiding citizen. Truth to tell, there's not one of the whole cowardly tribe who's worth a charge of buckshot, who deserves so much honor as being sent to hell by a white man's hand. If Socrates was poisoned and Christ was crucified for telling unpalatable truths to the splenetic-hearted hypocrites of their time, it would ill become me to complain of a milder martyrdom for a like offense. It may be urged that having been twice accused of the heinous crime of slandering young ladies, and twice beset on that pretext by armed thugs, I owe it to myself to make some explanation satisfactory to the public. Not at all; from my youth up noble womanhood has been the very god of my idolatry; and now that I have reached the noon of life, if the reputation which I have honestly earned as a faithful defender of the vestal fires can be blown adown the wind by the rank breath of lying rascals, I would not put forth a hand to check its flight. If old scars received while defending woman's name and fame in paths of peril which my traducers dare not tread, fail to speak for me, then to hell with the world, and let its harlot tongue wag howsoever it will. Never but once did I stoop to refute a cowardly falsehood circulated about myself. I was younger then—had not learned that public opinion is a notorious bawd, that "nailing a lie" but accentuates its circulation. Unfortunately, the recent assaults upon me are not altogether my private concern. They were armed protests against a fundamental principle of this Republic—freedom of the press. They are being citied by ill advised or malicious persons as evidence of "Southern Savagery." They are calculated, if suffered to go unexplained, to cast reproach upon revealed religion. They were futile but brutal attempts in the last decade of the Nineteenth century to suppress truth by terror, to conceal the iniquities of a sectarian college by beating to death the only journalist who dared to raise his voice in protest. They were appeals to Judge Lynch to strangle exposure, hence it is imperative that the blame be placed where it properly belongs; not upon the South, which unqualifiedly condemns it; not upon the Baptist church, which indignantly repudiates it; but upon a little coterie of white-livered black-hearted hypocrites, any of whom could look thro' a keyhole with both eyes at once, a majority of whom are either avowed sympathizers with or active members of that unamerican organization known to infamy as the A.P.A. The same old God-forsaken gang of moral perverts and intellectual misfits who more than two years ago brought a Canadian courtesan and an unfrocked priest to Waco to lecture on A.P.A'ism, and who threatened at one of these buzzard-feasts to mob me for calling the latter a cowardly liar, were responsible for my being dragged with a rope by several hundreds hoodlums up and down a Baptist college campus in this city Oct. 2, and for the brutal assault upon me five days later by a pack of would-be assassins who had waited until my back was unsuspectingly turned before they had the nerve to get out their guns. I can overlook the assault made by the college students, although most of them were grown men, because they were encouraged thereto by their elders. I have positively refused to prosecute them; but the last assault was led by a shyster lawyer of middle-age, a so-called "judge," a member of the board of managers of Baylor. I am seeking no trouble with any of them—they are perfectly safe in so far as I am concerned; still if the latter gang are not satisfied with their cowardly crime, if they regret that they were beaten off ere they quite succeeded in sending me to Kingdom Come, they have only to notify me where and when they can be found alone, and I'll give the whole accursed mob a show for their money. I'm too slight for a slugger—cannot lick a herd of steers with one pair o' hands; but I can make a shot-gun sing Come to Christ. I am credibly informed that "at least half a dozen" of my meek and lowly Baptist brethren are but awaiting an opportunity to assassinate me, and that if successful they will plead in extenuation that I "have slandered Southern women." I walk the streets of Waco day by day, and I walk them alone. Let these cur-ristians shoot me in the back if they dare, then plead that damning lie as excuse for their craven cowardice. If the decent people of this community fail to chase them to their holes and feed their viscera to the dogs, then 'd rather be dead and in hades forever than alive in Waco a single day.

The claim set up by my assailants that I had slandered the female students of Baylor University is a malicious calumny, that was but made a lying pretext for the attacks. That my article in the October ICONOCLAST did *not* impeach the character of the Baylor girls is amply evidenced by the fact that my offer to leave the matter to the decision of a committee of reputable business men, to abjectly apologize and donate $500 to any charity these gentlemen might name in case the decision was against me, was flatly refused. "The honor of young ladies is not a proper subject for arbitration," I was told. Quite true; but the proper construction of an article which is made a pretext for mob violence, *is* a proper matter for cool-headed and disinterested parties to pass upon. The Baylorians insisted upon being judge, jury and executioner—proof positive that they well knew the article would not stand the arbitrary construction they had placed upon it. After the first outbreak the Baylor bullies of the lost manhood stripe and their milk-sick apologists held a windy powwow in a Baptist church, and there bipedal brutes with beards, creatures who have thus far succeeded in dodging the insane asylum, whom an inscrutable Providence has kept out of the penitentiary to ornament the amen-corner— many of whom do not pretend to pay their bills—some of whom owe me for the very meat upon the bones of their scorbutic brats—branded me as a falsifier while solemnly protesting that they had never read a line of my paper. They proclaimed in stentor tones and pigeon-English that would have broken the heart of Lindley Murray, that I was a defamer of womanhood—while confessing that they didn't know whether I had ever mentioned a female. They howled that they "were willing to sign Brann's death-warrant"—on mere hearsay. These intellectual eunuchs, who couldn't father an idea if cast bodily into the womb of the goddess of wisdom, declared positively that I would be permitted to print nothing more about their beloved Baylor—and that without knowing whether I had advertised it over two continents as an oasis in a moral Sahara or a snakehole in the Dismal Swamp. It was a beautiful, a refreshing sight, this practical approval of mob violence by unfledged ministers on the campus of a Baptist college, this raucous tommyrot about death-warrants and ropes, this sawing of the air and chewing of the rag by people so d——d ignorant that they couldn't find either end of themselves in the dark, this chortling over the fact that one desk-emaciated welter-weight had been caught unawares and trampled upon by a sanctified mob—a refreshing sight, I say, in a temple consecrated to that Christ who forgave even his enemies from the cross. But every man at that meeting who said he never read the ICONOCLAST deliberately lied. The Baptists all read it. Some subscribe and pay for it like gentlemen, some buy it, some borrow it, and the rest steal it from the newsstands. The greatest trouble I have is to prevent, Baptist preachers spoiling my local sale by telling everybody in town what the ICONOCLAST contains before the revised proof-sheets are read. It is but fair to say, however, that the Baptists were not alone to blame. Much of the noise was made by a lot of tickey-tailed little politicians who have no more religion than a rabbit, but who were trying to open a popular jack-pot with a jimmy. Some of the brawlers were self-seeking business men, willing to coin blood into boodle, ready to slander Deity for a plugged dime, anxious to avert a Baptist boycott by emitting a deal of stinking breath. These bloated financial ducks in a provincial mud-puddle have had entirely too much to say. When the present lecture season is over; when I get the Baptist mob thoroughly cowed; when I can walk the streets without expecting every moment to get shot from a stairway or double-banked by the meek and lowly followers of the Messiah; when I have time to amuse myself with trifles, I'll sue this brace of Smart Alecs for $20,000 each for deliberate defamation of character, and if I recover the money I'll use it to make a partial payment on the grocery bills of the rest of the gang. Intellectual pigmies who accumulate much cash by trading in cash or tripe in a country town are quite apt to become too big for their britches and require to be taken down a peg or two, to be taught their place. They sometimes have the nickel-plated nerve to play Rhadamanthus to the purveyors of brains—swell up like unclean toads and conceive themselves to be in "select society." Some of them actually imagine themselves of more importance to this community than Judge Gerald and Waller Baker; yet you could scrape enough intellect from under Gerald's toe-nails to build the crew, while Baker forgets more every fifteen minutes than they have learned since they were born. The meeting held at the Baptist church to ratify the outrage was composed of a lot of self-seekers and whining hypocrites, half of whom would sell their souls for a copper cent and throw in their risen Lord as lagniappe. It was a mob that writhed and wriggled in its own putridity like so many maggots, while the local press cowered before its impotent wrath like young skye-terriers before a skunk. If I couldn't beget better men with the help of a digger Indian harem I'd take to the woods and never again look upon the face of woman. It was a glorious sight to see these "pore mizzuble wurrums of the dust" spraining their yarn galluses trying to hurl the writhen bolts of Olympian Jove—and now bellyaching because hit in the umbilicus with their own boomerang. The second assault, more brutal and cowardly than the first, followed as the logical sequence of that powwow of pietists, peddlers and politicians. The utterances of that congregation of unclean adders, the resolutions adopted by that sanctified body of dead-beats in the sanctum sanctorum of the Baptists, was a bid for blood-injected the idea into the warty heads of a trio of thugs that by way-laying and beating me to death they would pass into history as heroes. Then the real manhood of Waco rose en masse and laid down the law in no uncertain language to the hungry hypocrites and their Baylorian hoodlums. They declared that religious intolerance would no longer be permitted to terrorize this town. Fearing just retribution at the hands of the citizens, Baylor called out its three military companies and mounted guard with rifles furnished by the government, while the very girls in whose name they had dragged me around the college campus with a rope, laughed them to scorn and sent me flowers—and the password of the bold sojer boys. One young lady writes: "The password for the night is 'Napoleon.' Our bold soldiers halted a milk wagon at daylight this morning. Probably they thought Brann was concealed in one of the cans with his bowie-knife." Half a dozen men armed with cannon-crackers could have chased the brave mellish into the Brazos and danced with the Baylor girls till daybreak—and I suspect that the latter would have enjoyed the lark. For a third of a century the bigotry of a lot of water moccasins had been the supreme law of this land. To obtain an office the politician had to crawl to it on his marrow bones and slavishly obey its behests. To obtain trade the merchant had to sneeze whenever it took snuff. To obtain patronage the local publisher had to make it the absolute dictator of his policy. Like Jehushran, it "waxed fat and kicked"—until it got its legs tide in a double bow knot about its *own* neck. Its tyranny became insupportable, murderous, there was a new declaration of American independence, and now this J. Caesar that erstwhile did bestride Central Texas like a colossus, is more humble than Uriah Heep. And what were the A.P.Apes of Waco doing while honest men were raising the standard of revolt and chasing the Baptist hierarchy into its hole? Were they in the front rank shouting their war-cry of "no union of church and state"—the "little red school-house" rampant on their orange-colored rag? Not exactly. They had sneaked off to some bat cave to plot against the whites, to protest against the proceedings of their fellow citizens. Had a Baptist editor been mobbed on the campus of a Catholic college they would have howled a lung out about Popish tyrannys stood on their heads and fanned themselves with their own shirt-tails.

The faculty of Baylor protest that they did all in their power to prevent the brutal outbreak. They confess, however, that it had been brewing all day, yet they neglected to notify either myself or the sheriff. Before me is a Lake Charles, La. paper, in which a letter from one of the scabs who participated in the first attack is published. He says: "The faculty did not say do it, or not do it." And that's about the size of it. That the students were encouraged by one or more members of the board of trustees can be demonstrated beyond the peradventure of a doubt. All the stale bath water in all the Baptist tanks this side Perdition cannot wash the conviction from the public mind that the Baylor management was behind that howling mob. The second assault was led by a trustee, a member of the board of managers; and this after I had stated positively in the local press that I meant no disparagement of the young ladies—that it was the administration of the University I was after. In the October ICONOCLAST I expressed the fervent hope that no more young ladies would be debauched at Baylor. That constituted the ostensible casus belli.. Do the trustees of Baylor dare deny that such things *have* occurred at that "storm center of misinformation" and ministerial manufactory? If so, they are a precious long time putting me to the proof in the courts of this country. Texas has an iron-clad criminal libel law, and I suspect that I could pay a judgment for damages in any reasonable sum without spraining my credit or bankrupting the ICONOCLAST. If they have not the chilled-steel hardihood to deny that girls have been debauched at Baylor—if by their resounding silence anent this matter they mean to give assent—what then? Do they hope that more girls *will* be ruined there? They may take either horn of the dilemma they like, but I beg to state that the issue here raised cannot be obscured by dragging me around with a rope. When Jonah was caught in a scheme of vindictive rascality he thought he "did well to be angry." The best thing the Baylorites can do is to 'fess up and reform—it's too late in the century to suppress truth with six-shooters. I have heard of no "deplorable accidents" at Add-Ran, the Christian college, consequently it has no complaints to file against the Iconoclast. The Convent of the Sacred Heart gets along somehow without "mishaps," and even Paul Quinn, the colored college, is graduating no "missionaries" for Hungry Hill. Because some girls go wrong at an institution for the promotion of ignorance, it by no means follows that all, or any considerable number thereof are deficient in morality. I doubt not that a vast number of the female students of Baylor, past and present, are pure as the flowers that bloom above the green glacier; but some have fallen, and the conclusion is inevitable that they were not properly protected from the wiles of the world. I care not how noble-minded, how pure of heart a girl may be, if she is committed when young and inexperienced to a college where both sexes are received, it becomes the imperative duty of the management to render one false step impossible. When the president of a pretentious sectarian institute must plead with the public that he had "wept and prayed over" a 14-year old girl, but was powerless to prevent her rushing headlong to ruin; when at a grand rally of the faithful to condemn a well-meant criticism and encourage mob violence, an old he-goat who couldn't get trusted at the corner grocery for a pound of soap, confesses to more than the Iconoclast had charged, by saying that some *accidents* had occurred at the college, it were well for mothers to look carefully to its management and note its discipline before entrusting it with their young daughters. "Accidents," indeed! Criminal negligence would be a more appropriate name. A university consecrated to the Baptist Christ, whose trustees lead cowardly assaults upon law-abiding citizens and beat them with bludgeons after they are insensible; whose faculty know that mob violence is contemplated yet fail to report it to the police; whose students enter the home of a man for the purpose of dragging him by force and with drawn pistols from the presence of his family (the Baylor thugs had the impudence to invade my home in search of me before finding me in the city)—such an institution, I say, is not a proper guardian for any youth whose father doesn't desire to see him land in the Baptist pulpit or the penitenitary. I have been publicly warned on pain of death, and heaven alone knows what hereafter, not to speak "disrespectful" of Baylor; but I feel in duty bound to caution parents against committing their children to such a pestiferous plague-spot, such a running sore upon the body social.

* * *

Not only has Baylor demonstrated its unworthiness to be the custodian of young people of either sex, but such unworthiness has been proclaimed in the public prints by Dr. Rufus C. Burleson, who served as its president for almost half a century. I insisted that the salaries paid the faculty at Baylor were insufficient to command the services of first class educators, and that those entrusted with the duty of selecting teachers were incapable of correctly estimating the educational qualifications of others Dr. Burleson goes far beyond that, expressly declaring in the Dallas *News* that a majority of the present board of managers are not college educated, that for them to properly administer discipline and make wise selection of teachers "is simply impossible." What, in God's name, can be expected of an institution containing several hundred young people of both sexes, if it be deficient in dissipline? Of what earthly use is a University if it be not provided with a wisely selected faculty? It now remains to be seen whether the Baptist brethren will mob Dr. Burleson—or sneak up behind him with an assortment of clubs and six-shooters! But that is not the worst that Dr. Burleson says. In a published letter of his now before me he denounces Dr. B. H. Carroll, chairman of the board of trustees and present high muck-a-muck of Baylor, as an ingrate, a self-seeker, a mischief maker and an irremediable liar! Now if Burleson is telling the truth—and I am not prepared to dispute his statements—what can we expect of a University managed by such a man? I am frank to confess that I did not suspect Bro. Carroll to be quite so bad. I knew that he was an intellectual dugout spreading the canvas of a seventy-four, that there was precious little to him but gab and gall; but I did not suppose that he was an habitual falsifier and guilty of base ingratitude. I really hope that Dr. Burleson may be mistaken—that the new boss of Baylor has not contracted such a habit of lying that it is utterly impossible for him to tell the truth. I should dislike to believe all that is said about each other by the two factions of my Baptist brethren now struggling for the control of Baylor. According to Carroll, Dr. Burleson, president emeritus, ought to be in the penitentiary; according to Burleson, Carroll is not a fit associate for a brindle cow. "Speak disrespectfully of Baylor and die!" Good Lord! were I to repeat one-half the Baylor factions are saying about each other I'd wreck the state. Time was when the faculty of Baylor was the pride of the South. Those were the days when many of the noblest men and women of Texas were educated within its walls. They love their alma mater, not for what she is, but for what she was. The old professors are gone, have been supplanted in great part by a lot of priorient little preachers, selected by a board of trustees, half of whom couldn't tell a Greek root from a rutabaga, pons asinorum from Balaam's ass. Dr. Burleson seems to be of the opinion that a majority of the Baylorian managers were educated in a mule-pen and dismissed without a diploma—couldn't tell whether a man were construing Catullus into Sanskrit or pronouncing in Piute a panegeric on a baked pup. Were I not persona *non grata* I would like to witness the classroom performances of these young professors— chosen with owlish gravity by men who cannot write *deer sur* without the expenditure of enough nervo-muscular energy to raise a cotton crop, chewing off the tips of their tongues and blotting the paper with their proboscides. Yet for offering to open a night school for the benefit of the Baylorian faculty I was mobbed; for intimating that the hoard of managers had not socked with old Socrates and ripped with old Euripides I was assaulted by one of their number and his brave body guard and beaten with six-shooters and bludgeons until I was insensible.

* * *

It is not my present purpose to drag forth all the grisly skeletons of Baylor and make them dance for the amusement of the multitude. I have yielded to the urgent appeals of my friends to let the institution down easy, to cast a little kerosene on the troubled waters, to hold out the olive branch to Baylor. Besides, I already have more holes in my head than nature intended, and am not particularly anxious to increase the assortment. Let what is hidden from public ken so remain until that great incubator of Christian charity, that ganglion of brotherly love, attempts to redeem its long-standing promise to land me in the penitentiary for criminal libel. It could serve no good purpose at present to trace out here the history of those "accidents" so feelingly referred to at the ratification of the Brann round-up—would but cause cheeks to flame and hearts to break. I would not destroy Baylor; I would make it better. I would deprive the ignorant and vicious of control. I would expel all the hoodlums whose brutality and cowardice have disgraced it. I would place at its head a thorough educator and strict disciplinarian, a man of broad views and who sets a good example by paying his bills. I would make its diplomas badges of honor as in the old days, instead of certificates of illiteracy at which public school children laugh. No, I do not want the presidency—there are enough perspiring Christians for revenue only quarreling and lying about each other because of that beggarly plum already. For months past it has given every Baptist journal in the state a hot-box, has filled every little preacher's head with all the petty intrigues of peanut politics. If one-half that the leaders of the factions, now warring over this $5 per diem bone, say about each other be true—and I have no evidence to the contrary—they would disgrace a boozing ken on Boiler avenue. I do not mean to say that all Texas Baptists are bad; at least 50 per cent. of them are broad-gauge, tolerant, intelligent; the remainder are small-bore bigots upon whom nature put heads, as Dean Swift would say, "Solely for the sake of conformity."

* * *

Baylor and the Baptists complain that the ICONOCLAST has "persecuted them until it has become unbearable." Bless God! who began this thing? Before the ICONOCLAST was three days old it was boycotted by the hydrocephalous sect. As it grew fat on that kind of fodder, ex-Priest Slattery and his ex-nun wife were brought hither to lecture on A.P.Aism, and incidentally make the town too caloric for my comfort. The Baptists took their wives and daughters to listen to Slattery's foul lies about the convents and the confessional, the Pope and "his Waco Apostle," and his most infamous utterances were applauded to the echo. They sent their wives and daughters to hear the Slattery female defame women who had given up the pleasures of the world and were devoting their lives to the reclamation of such unclean creatures as herself. Slattery's last harangue was delivered to men only and the house was packed with Baptists and Baylorites at half-a-dollar a head. The so-called lecture was the foulest thing that ever fell from the lips of mortal man, yet his audience gloated over it and rolled his putrid falsehoods as sweet morsels under its tongue.[1] Unable to restrain my indignation, I arose and denounced his every utterance as a malicious lie. Immediately the audience yelled, "Throw him out! Down with him! Smash him!" I chanced to have my back near the side-wall,

---

[1] Brann's reply to Slattery appears in Vol. XII.

and that's why I wasn't mobbed—the cowardly crew couldn't get *behind* me. They suspected that I'd make an angel of the first sanctified galoot who attempted to place his paws upon me, and none cared to draw on his celestial bank account. That's the identical gang which has the immaculate gall to accuse me of defaming virtuous women—the same gang which applauded Slattery for calling convents priestly harems wants me killed for expressing the hope that no more young girls will be debauched at Baylor.

* * *

Scarce had Baylor's applause of Slattery and his woman died away, scarce had it ceased to gloat over the "iniquities" of convent schools and priestly harems, scarce had it ceased chuckling over the crimes of "the Scarlet Woman," ere the police discovered that the duly ordained "ward of the Baptist church," who was being educated at Baylor University for missionary work among the heathen Catholics of Brazil, was in a dreadfully "delicate condition." She was brought from Brazil at the tender age of 11 years by a returning missionary, she was formally adopted by the Baptist church, she was consecrated to the salvation of souls and placed at Baylor to be educated. She was under the special supervision of the president and was a member of his household—yet at 14 years of age she became enciente. Did Baylor pity and protect her? Did it strive to secure the punishment of her seducer? Not exactly. It fired her out and made no complaint to the police. When the latter discovered her and she was required by the court to account for her condition, she stated that she had been forcibly despoiled by a young man about town on the premises of Baylor's president. It chanced that this young man was brother to the president's son-in-law, and the whole influence of Baylor was brought to bear to clear the accused! The son-in-law, who is a Baptist preacher and editor (as well as other things not necessary to mention) strove to make her confess that her guilty paramour was a pickaninny—wanted the world to believe that orphan girls committed to the care of that great Baptist college might become enciente by coons! Yet the Baylor students didn't mob him—none of its trustees laid in wait for him and slammed him over the head with a six-shooter. The girl soon put a white babe in evidence—a pretty little 2-pound Baylorian diploma. The doctors declared that she had been raped and the case looked ugly for the accused. The child died. The ignorant little mother wanted money to go to Memphis—and first thing we knew she had signed a "retraction" and had a ticket to Mike Conolly's town. Who bought it—and why! Damfino. The defendant was acquitted of the charge of rape—the age of consent in Texas being 12 years at that time; but whether she was raped or seduced, the infamy occurred at Baylor University. That's *one* of the "deplorable accidents"; but it is not the only one you will please not forget to remember. Reads like a fairy story, doesn't it? But the law doesn't permit Texas editors to tell fairy tales of that type. No doubt the man who has the audacity to breathe a hope that no more girls will be debauched at Baylor deserves to die. Dr. Burleson, in the fullness of his Baptist charity, branded the unfortunate girl as a natural bawd. I don't know about that; but I do know that after she got beyond Baylorian influences she married and began leading a respectable life.

* * *

Defamer of womanhood? Get the sawlogs out of your own eyes, brethren, before howling over the micrococci in the optics of others. For three years past Baptist preachers all over the land of Christ have been telling their congregations that the ICONOCLAST is read only by depraved people,—chiefly criminals and courtesans—and that despite the fact that the names of thousands of the noblest men and women of America are on its subscription books. During the past three years the ICONOCLAST has had upon its books the names of more than a thousand ministers, representing every denomination. Are these men criminals and their wives courtesans? Has any busy little Baptist parson been rounded up with a rope for proclaiming them as such from the pulpit? When a deserted babe was found in the street and carried by the Sisters into the convent, was Jehovah Boanerges Cranfill—organ-grinder for the Baylor bosses—mobbed by the Catholics for saying that it probably came *out* of the convent? Now, you people keep down the narrative of your nether garment and apply a hot mush poultice to your impudence. The ICONOCLAST is only tickling you with snipe-shot now; but don't forget for one moment that it has buck a-plenty in its belt.

* * *

A word to the lady students of Baylor: Young ladies, this controversy does not in the least concern you. The ICONOCLAST has never questioned your good character. You are young, however, and mischievous people have led some of you to believe that it has done so. If you so believe, I am as much in duty bound to apologize as though I had really and intentionally wronged you. A gentleman should ever hasten to apologize to ladies who feel aggrieved; hence I sincerely crave your pardon for having printed the article which gave you offense. Upon learning that you read into it a meaning which I did not intend, I stopped the presses and curtailed the circulation of the October number as much as possible, proving my sincerity by a pecuniary sacrifice. I would not for the wealth of this world either do you a wilful injustice, or have you believe me capable of such a crime. May you prosper in your studies, graduate with honor and bestow your hands upon men worthy of noble women.

* * *

P.S. In looking over the foregoing since it was put in type, I suspect that I have been a trifle too hard on some of those who met to ratify the action of the first mob and publicly brand me as a defamer of women. I would not do my deadliest enemy an injustice. Two wrongs do not make a right; hence I concede that perhaps half of those present pay their debts and make a reasonable effort to be decent. If God neglected to bless them with brains that is their misfortune instead of their fault. Let it go at that. They have had their say, I've had mine, and right here I drop the subject until another attempt is made to run me out of town. I make this concession, not that Baylor deserves it, but at the earnest request of the law-abiding element of this city.

*   *   *   *   *

SPEAKING OF SPIRITUALISM.

A correspondent seizes his typewriter (the machine, not the maid) with both hands, and peremptorily demands to be informed why I "don't jump on that fake called Spiritualism." O I don't know, unless it's because more corporeal things than spooks continue to jump on me. It seems a waste of energy to criticize disembodied spirits who do no worse than "revisit the pale glimpses of the moon." I have never heard of a ghost robbing other than its own grave. They are not addicted to despoiling widows and orphans, then putting up long-winded prayers. They do not sing "Jesus lover of my soul" on Sunday, then sell that same soul to the devil for six-bits on Monday. No ghost, so far as I know, was ever accused of lying about his neighbor, fracturing the Seventh Commandment or beating his butcher-bills. They appear to be quite harmless creatures, therefore not legitimate game for the Iconoclast. Furthermore, I am not fully convinced that Spiritualism is a "fake." There appears to be as good biblical and natural reasons for belief in Spiritualism as for belief in the Immaculate Conception or the efficacy of baptism. Doubtless some of the professors are frauds, but as much can be said for the professors of all other faiths. I confess that I haven't much confidence in "mejums," who find employment for the shades of G. Washington, J. Caesar, and others of that ilk, at table-tipping, slate-writing and such unproductive enterprises; nor in the class of spooks who "materialize" in dark rooms, come prancing out of "cabinets" and other uncanny corporeal incubators for no other apparent purpose than to enable their mundane manipulators to realize two dollars in the coin of the realm. I opine that a ghost who must retire to a "cabinet" to pull himself together is no honest ghost; that those who consent to tip tables and indulge in crude telegraphy for the entertainment of a lot of long-haired hemales and credulous females must find time hang very heavy on their hands in the great henceforth, and heartily wish themselves back here wrestling with Republican prosperity, doctor bills and other blessings. It seems to me that were I a ghost I would float about on cloud banks and bathe in the splendors of the morning, instead of hiding in bat-caves all day and snooping about all night seeking an unsalaried situation at some dark-lantern seance. When America's greatest lexicographer writes me an ungrammatical message on a double-barreled slate, signs it "noeh webstur," and instructs his terrestial to deliver it to me on payment of one cart-wheel dollar, I suspect that there's something sphacelated in the psychological Denmark. Of course they may have the phonetic system of orthography in Elysium, but in dealing with mortals I scarce think the old man would discredit his own dictionary. A spook manipulator once solemnly assured me that the spirit of Tecumseh was my guardian angel, that the old Shawnee chief was ever at my elbow. I don't believe it; had he been there on recent occasions he would have hit sundry and various Baptists on the head with his tomahawk. If old Tecum is trailing me around I want to give him a pointer right here that as a guardian angel he's utterly no good in a clime

"Where the rage of the vulture, the love of the turtle,
Now melt into sorrow, now madden to crime,"

and he had best cast his aegis over some Boston editor. It by no means follows, however, that because many professional fakirs and intellectual fuzziewuzzies have "gone in for Spiritualism," it is all a fraud. If the morad floating in a sunbeam be indestructible, existing in some shape from everlasting to everlasting, it is inconceivable that mind, the lord of matter, should perish utterly—should fade like an echo into the great inane. That were a reversal of the law of the survival of the fittest—casting away a priceless jewel while preserving its tawdry setting. That the lesser should survive the greater; that the case of Anaxarchus should continue and Anaxarchus' proud self become nonexistent, were to leave matter without law and wreck the universe, for law itself presupposes prescience. "Natural law," so called, must either be an act of intelligence compelling order, or a freak of nescience entailing chaos; hence if order be eternal mind must necessarily be immortal, for it is an axiom of science that "Nature wastes nothing." What becomes of the mighty life-force of a Milton? If it be utterly extinguished; if it becomes a forceless shade on Acheron's shore, or an "angel" withdrawn from active influence in the universe, it is certainly wasted, in so far as what we call nature is concerned. In his lecture on "Evolution," Henry Ward Beecher said: "I believe there is a universal and imminent constant influence flowing directly from the bosom of God, and that is the inspiration of the human race." Is God continually giving out this "influence," this life-force, this vis vitalis, to the people of this planet, and with each death withdrawing a portion thereof and either casting it into the waste-basket of Perdition or cording it up, like back-number newspapers, in the New Jerusalem, never to be again employed? If it "flows directly from the bosom of God" is it not God? And if Nature waste nothing can Nature's Prince be such a prodigal? Is he not rather the great psychological heart of the universe through which the same life-current, the same intellect flows back and forth forever? But here! We are drifting into metempsychosis—are in a fair way to get ourselves excommunicated. Furthermore, we are actually predicating a probability that the editor of the Chicago Inter-Ocean is a reincarnation of Balaam's ass. I am not prepared to assert that Spiritualism is all brazen charlantry or foolish self-deception. It may be that the "inspiration" of which Beecher speaks as an emanation from God himself, is but a higher wisdom taught the longing heart by those it has loved and lost. The souls of the dead scratch no messages on greasy slates for stupid eyes, shout none across the Styx that can be heard by vulgar ears; but there be men who can hear in the silent watches of the night the music of lips long mute. There be those for whom the veil that separates the two eternities is no black inpenetrable pall, but an Arachne's web, a sacred shadow through which comes sweeping, not the roar of myriad voiced hosannahs and the rustle of countless wings of dazzling white beating the everlasting blue; but the soft incense of love, bringing healing to broken hearts, calm to rebellious souls. These seek no thaumaturgic incantations to secure messages from the other shore, for they are coming continually. They do but listen, and interpret as best they may to their dull-eared brethren, the celestial wisdom. The latter protest that they "inspired," and the trumpet Fame casts upon them her purple robe. It is not the peripatetic "mediums," but the poets and prophets who "call up the spirits" and bid them speak to us; those who find all the dead Past living in the Present; who are themselves so spirituelle that they can understand Nature's finer tones—who realize that

"Life is but a dome of many-colored glass
That stains the white radiance of eternity."

All truly great men are spiritualists—even mystics. A materialist may be a logician, a mathematician, in a limited way; but never an orator nor a poet. He is of the earth earthly; an intellectual Antaeus—the moment his feet leave the sodden clay he is strangled by the gods. For him there is no Fount of Castaly whose sweet waters make men mad. Parnassus is but an Egyptian pyramid to be scaled with ladders, and by the aid of guides who serve for salary. Fancy has no wings to waft him among the stars. He sees in the Bible only its errors, never its wild beauty. For him Villon was only a sot and Anacreon a libertine. In his cosmos there's neither Garden of the God, nor Groves of Daphne. He can understand neither the platonic love of Petrarch nor the psychological ferocity of Rousseau.

"The Apostle of affliction, he who threw
Enchantment over passion, and from
Woe wrung overwhelming eloquence."

For him all, all is clay—even the laughter of childhood is a cunning mechanism, and the Uranian Venus but a lump of animated earth. The flowers bring him messages only from the muck in which their roots are buried, the "concord of sweet sounds" is but a disturbance of the atmosphere. Such men do not live; they merely exist. They do not enjoy life; they do not even suffer its pangs. They know naught of that sweetness "for which Love is indebted to Sorrow." God pity them.

*   *   *   *   *

The gang of mutton-heads whose duty it was to select twelve poets whose names should be commemorated in the new congressional library, excluded that of Tom Moore on the plea that he wasn't much of a poet, and now the Irish-Americans are fairly seething with indignation. Take it easy; Tom Moore doesn't need a memorial tablet. He will be read and honored centuries after the library building with its poet's corner has perished of old age. He is the poet of the people, and has more readers than any ten of those honored by the committee.

*   *   *   *   *

SOME GOLD-BUG GUFF.

If it is gold that has appreciated, as the silverites claim, aren't the farmers now getting two dollars a bushel for their wheat?—*Montgomery* (Ala.) Advertiser.

The foregoing is irrefutable evidence that the fool-killer is enacting the role of cunctator. Only a gold-bug editor could insult the people of Alabama with such an exhibition of idiocy. I am heartily tired of this whole currency question; but the *Advertiser* has been fairly stinking for attention a long time—its Smart Alecism has become simply insupportable. Politically considered, the *Advertiser* has been all things to all men and "nothing to nobody." It is a journalistic George Clark, mistaking political treachery for diplomacy and impudence for intellect. As Clark cannot interview himself to the extent of half a column for the *Morning Bazoo* without getting his goozle entangled in the skein of his own intorted argument, so the

Advertiser cannot grind out an editorial of equal length without getting hoist with its own logical sequence, split from vermiform appendix to occipitofrontalis by the recoil of its own syllogisms. The *Advertiser* is unreliable as Proteus; the base vulpine instinct serves it in lieu of brains; the clink of cash in the counting room is the keeper of its conscience. At least such is the pen-portrait drawn of it by the best men in Alabama. Its allusion to $2 wheat is a trick that would disgrace the sophists who practice in our municipal courts with drunks and courtesans for clients. Such a horse-play for the benefit of the political gallery gods would be contemptuously ignored by the ICONOCLAST were not the *Advertiser's* betters indulging in the same unmitigated bosh. Our Alabama contemporary is but an anile echo of the New York *Tribune*, a faint adumbration of the Chicago *Inter-Ocean*. The bigwigs cut out the work for the journalistic wiggletails. They pitch the tune and all the intellectual eunuchs come in on the chorus. The editorials of all such sheets as the *Advertiser* are but a stale re-hash of Eastern utterances. They pick up these things and "work 'em over," just as the *Herald* of Astoria, Ore., revamps articles from the ICONOCLAST and runs them as original. The farmer *is* now receiving $2 a bushel for his wheat. That is to say, the dollar with which he is paid has double the purchasing power of the dollar two decades ago. He is exactly as well off as though he received two old-time dollars—if he chances to be out of debt. If he is not out of debt, if he must discharge old scores with these 200-cent dollars, he is being deprived of his adventitious good fortune resulting from foreign crop failures. It makes no earthly difference what the measure of value may be if it is immutable. The purchasing power of the dollar might be safely increased or decreased 90 per cent. were the whole business of this country on a cash basis. Under such conditions we might contract our volume of money to a million dollars or expand it to five billions, and harm nobody; but it seems to me that any fool on earth—even the editor of the *Advertiser* could comprehend the following unequivocal facts: (1) that a majority of the American people owe money; (2) that an enhancement of the purchasing power of the dollar must work grievous injury to the debtor; (3) that unless the volume of money keeps pace with the increase in the money work to be done the unit of value must inevitably appreciate. Let us state the case in kindergarten language for the benefit of intellectual infants; while the demand for money is increasing in a ratio of geometrical progression we have eliminated one great source of supply—have cast upon gold alone the money work which from time immemorial had been done by two metals. The gold product has not kept pace with the growth of the world's business; the law of supply and demand is irrevocable; ergo, gold *has* appreciated and the debtor *has* been despoiled. The temporary rise in price of one or two or a score of American products in obedience to the laws of trade cannot obscure these incontrovertible facts. *While the price of wheat has advanced the price of labor has declined.* The wage-worker now receives *less* than formerly, while it costs him *more* to feed his family. And this is what the Republican press and its mugwump echo call prosperity! The wheat-growers, numerically unimportant, are prospering despite the gold standard, just as the placer-miner who washes out ten dollars each day and gives up five of it nightly to cut-throat gamblers; but in this prosperity the great body of the American people have neither lot nor part. Texas is selling middling cotton at 5½ and paying $3 for flour. Adult male operatives are working in Massachusetts cotton mills for 50 cents a day, and their families doing without flour. Pennsylvania miners are braving subterranean dangers for 90 cents a day and living on potatoes and point. Although this is the busiest season of the year—the time when the Republican tidal wave of prosperity is supposed to buss the very clouds—there is scarce a town or city in the United States where able-bodied men are not begging for employment. If you don't think so put a 3-line "ad" in your morning paper that you want to employ a man for any purpose, and offer *one-half* the salary that such service would have commanded before the demonetization of silver, and see how quickly your office will be jammed! Texas has probably suffered less than any other American state from hard times, Waco less than any other Texas city, for here we can subsist on climate and sanctification. Waco is a city of but 30,000 souls—conceding that the Baptists are supplied with that immortal annex; yet when it was reported the other day that the Iconoclast needed another book-keeper applications were filed before night by a score of men competent in the craft. Men apply a month ahead for employment on mailing day, because at that time a dozen or so extras can each earn a dollar. I have in hand an article by one of the brightest journalists of Chicago, who states that reporters are paid $10 to $25, editorial writers $25 to $35 per week, and that a man who offends the newspaper trust can get no further employment in the town. Twenty years ago a scribe who could turn a bright editorial paragraph or manufacture an interesting falsehood was worth $50 to $75 a week in Chicago, and if lost one situation he'd find two more before he got half-sober—but that was before Markhanna and his peon took charge of this country's prosperity. Will the Advertiser or any other mugwump organ, kindly explain why it is, if the gold standard is making this country to flourish like a green-bay horse, the idle money of Europe and New England continues to pour across the state of Texas, ignoring its matchless resources, to find employment in free-silver Mexico! Why wages are slowly but steadily rising in that country and are steadily declining in this? Why is it that when a man cannot obtain employment here he turns his face to "the Land of God and Liberty" if he has the price of passage, feeling assured that there he has but to ask for a job to obtain it? Why is that above all this cackle about prosperity can be heard the stentor tones of Markhanna's organ advising American workmen that they must come squarely down to the European wage level before they can hope for permanent employment? Perhaps I could find answers to these questions myself had not my Baptist brethren lately pounded my head to a pulp. As it is, I humbly ask for information, beseech the *Advertiser* to uncork its omniscience. Will the millions of Americans who can barely make a living of it during the busy season, thank God and the gold-buggers for manifold mercies when the fall trade is over and the crops are all in?

*   *   *   *   *

"THE TYPICAL AMERICAN TOWN."

BY THE COLONEL.

It is worth a man's life in Chicago to state his unbiased opinion of Chicago. The city is filled with dirt and vanity. Its population is the most complex in the world. It has more than 300,000 people who do not speak, read or write the English language. In certain of its west side districts a sound of the mother tongue is not heard from year's end to year's end. The number of bodies within its limits closely approximates 1,500,000. It will be noticed that I do not say "souls." Not a daily paper published in the city has a bonafide circulation of 100,000 copies, which is, in itself, a striking commentary upon the character of the people who live in the largest town of Cook county. A circulation of that size is not thought to be a thing to be bragged about in New York. In Chicago, its attainment is the ambition and heart's desire of every newspaper publisher in the town.

A traveling man who was not from St. Louis, once summarized Chicago as "a big, dirty, noisy roaring bluff." He was a fellow who had a just appreciation of the value of adjectives. That is what it is. It is said of the merchants that in the summer time they load wagons with empty barrels and drive them about the streets to simulate business. I don't doubt it. If they haven't done it, they forgot it. There is no shady trick of commercial competition that they will not stoop to, nothing short of a penitentiary offense that they will balk at. Sometimes they do not stop there.

Chicago has been called "the representative American city." It is. It represents the America of to-day, because more than any other municipality, its life is wrapped in the pursuit of the dollar. A man in Chicago is weighed by dollars. The attractions of his wife and daughters are judged by dollars. His value as a citizen, his worthiness as an American, his fitness for public service, his chances of heaven are measured by the standard of the dollar.

There is a merchant prince in Chicago whose private life contains a scandal that is absolutely unprintable. He is looked up to by men and admired by women. His name is often upon the lips of the good, although I cannot learn that he gives freely to charity, or to the city's advancement. He is held up as a model for young men struggling in the race of life. He is pointed out to girls as an epitome of brainy American manhood. It cost him $500,000 to hush up this scandal, or rather to keep it out of print. It is known to thousands of course, because a matter of this kind can no more be stilled than the winds and the waves can be stilled. But the dollars did the work they were designed to do. Not a paper of the newspaper trust contained a line in reference to it. The man advertises, you see.

There is another man high in Chicago financial circles. Men tip their hats to him on the streets. His name appears on the prospectuses and in the lists of directors in many powerful institutions. He is a prominent figure at many social functions. His hair is white with age, but he still has a lust for tender maidenhood. This man has served a term in the penitentiary for stealing from his government. As a result of that theft he has many dollars.

When a man hears of Chicago he is pretty apt to hear of Yerkes. Yerkes owns all of the north side street railways and is a dictator in a dozen enormous enterprises. It is the fashion to regard Yerkes as an octopus who has Chicago grasped in his strangling arms. It is the custom to hurl abuse at Yerkes and hold Yerkes responsible for all the many ills of the city. In the popular mind Yerkes is the Chicago exemplar of the grasping, soulless, blood-sucking monopolist. This is because the newspaper trust does not like Yerkes. He began fighting it a long time ago, holding war to be cheaper than tribute. Up to date Yerkes has a long way the best of the contest. He has a thick skin. Abuse glides off him like water off an oiled board. Yerkes, too, is a jail bird. He has served, it is said, a term in a Pennsylvania penitentiary. Yerkes went to the penitentiary, it is further said, because he would not betray his fellow robbers. He took his punishment, but he kept his mouth shut. In other words, he "did not peach on his pals." It will be seen that there is a good deal of a man in Yerkes—much more, in fact than is to be found in any one of his newspaper publishing traducers; but even his fondest intimates have never denied that he is a rascal.

There are women high in the society of Chicago who know more about the services of unscrupulous midwives than they would care to tell. There are girls still wearing their maiden names whose white arms and throats flash with the ransoms of princes who will feel no blush stealing over neck, cheek and chin when they lie waiting in the bridal bed. Three are mothers of children—many of them— who have "graduated" from Dwight and whose breaths still reek with the fumes of whiskey. There are wives whose annual flitting to the summer resorts means six weeks of unrestrained lechery. Meanwhile the old man, who is left in the city to wrestle for some more of the dollars, is not overlooking any bets. It is possible that he knows his wife is unchaste. Certainly he makes no pretensions to chastity himself.

Things have reached this pass in "the representative American city": A youth born, reared and educated there believes that it is his mission and his duty to get dollars and has no other idea. A girl born and reared there thinks it her mission and her duty to marry dollars. If her parents are poor, if she is compelled to "work out" as stenographer, typewriter, shop-lady, or whatnot, and if she keeps her virtue, she is a phenomenon. The vaudeville stage is recruited from her ranks. The bawdy houses are recruited from her ranks. The fetid river's yearly burden of corpses is recruited from her ranks.

What is to become of it? What is the natural fruit of such a tree? What is the legitimate of a million and a half of such humanity cooped into one space and boiling and seething with ten million different aims and passions? What part in the drama of the future is to be played by the 300,000 non-English speaking residents, many of whom are voters? Men say that the signs of the times point to revolution. Men behind the scenes say that this country was dangerously near it in 1896. It needs no prophet to foresee trouble when the rich are becoming richer, through scoundrelism, and the poor are becoming poorer, through drunkenness, idleness, dirt and all viciousness. Of that revolution when it comes Chicago will be the fountain and the center. I dare to say that if there are 5,000 open anarchists in Chicago to-day there are 50,000 anarchists unconfessed. The trouble is that their indictment against the wealthy ruling classes contain true counts. They are not worth the powder and lead necessary to their execution, but are those who sit in the high places any better?

Preachers on fat salaries may preach in rich churches, scrolled and cavern and mullion-windowed, then form laisons with choir-singers; hired writers may write of the goodness of the times, then pose in beer-joints and denounce God and the universe. Christian Endeavorers and all the other bands of inane asses may shout their mawkish hymns, but facts are facts. The city of the dollar is in a bad way, and it is the "representative American city."

More men to tell the truth are needed. More men willing to lead clean lives. One object lesson is worth a hundred told from books. More women are wanted who will hold their virtue as God-given and a priceless gem. Such men and such women would be laughed at for a while as oddities in Chicago, but even the modern Gomorrah would be affected by them in time. Missionary boards are spending thousands every year in endeavors to induce highly moral Chinamen to become immoral Christians; but right before their eyes in the county of Cook, state of Illinois, is a more fruitful field than they have ever plowed, a field that is lying fallow, although there are ministers enough camped on it, God knows. It is the fashion of the snug missionary board, however, to see only those things which are far off. It has been so since missionary boards first tortured savages whose chief offense was that they worshipped God in their own way, and it will continue to be so until the last missionary has taken up his last collection and laid in his winter's coal therewith. The ICONOCLAST has done its level best to snatch the Chicago brand from the burning and now and then some Chicago man walks straight for a little way under the influence of its teaching, but one journal cannot do the work of a hundred, nor is the whole of heathendom to be saved by one preacher. Until the great sweeping time comes around and Chicago is purified in the most cleansing of all liquids, though each quart of it means a human life, the money changers will sit in the temple and the bawds and lovers of bawds drink in the sanctuary.

* * *

Not long ago Chicago had a celebration. It placed a statue to "Black Jack Logan" on the lake front. This statue, which is by St. Gaudens, represents a large-moustached man on a slimly-built horse that has his right hoof elevated to his ear, apparently endeavoring to paw a fly therefrom. Of course, it is understood that any natural horse which stood in that way, would fall down and skin his pasterns and hocks and stifles and barrel and withers and other parts of him known to the veterinarians. I am no horse doctor.

The large-moustached man has on cavalry boots which are dug into the stirrups and his legs are very stiff and calm. He holds a flag in his right hand—holds it far up and away and its folds are blown by the wind. Every child knows that a United States flag and staff weigh only two ounces and a man on horse-back can swing it around as if it were a feather. These things do not enter into the rapt dream of St. Gaudens. Nothing enters into his dream save poetry to be expressed in bronze and the dollars that are to come therefrom. The statue is well enough in its way. Let it go at that.

* * *

There was a celebration. Troops came and marched from many states. Veterans of the Grand Army of the Republic tramped along and the people cheered them. I suppose that one quarter of the heroes who are drawing $160,000,000 a year in pensions from the government were on hand. I have been unable to find out anything that "Black Jack" did, other than the fact that he came back from the front in 1863, and legged for Abraham Lincoln, thereby getting into politics and staying in until he died. Also he scoured the country carefully and found everybody that was connected with him by blood or marriage and put him or her into office. At one time Logan and family were drawing enough money from Uncle Sam to draw a respectable navy. As the orators were orating and the cannon were barking and the sweating people on the sidewalks were shouting, they knew not and cared not for what, I thought of some lines which opened a Washington letter in the Boston *Globe* many years ago, when John A. Logan was in the United States Senate. There was a tariff discussion on and he took a part. These were the lines: "Pranced there in, on the arena of the great debate, like a trick mule in a circus or a spavined nightmare on the track of a beautiful dream, Logan of Illinois." They fitted him.

A part of that celebration consisted of fireworks which were given at the Coliseum, a large building which stands in the southern part of the city and is used as a place of entertainment. John T. Dickinson, formerly of Texas, and now of the earth, is the president of the Coliseum Company, and engineered the display. It takes money to have fireworks and the company of "big-bugs" who bossed the entire marksman's contest, told him so. With that hustle which made him a marked man in Austin and other large cities in which he lived before he broke into Chicago, Dickinson rushed out and raised the money. He got subscriptions from prominent merchants, collected the funds and turned them over to William R. Harper, who was chairman of the committee on arrangements and committee on glory and pretty nearly everything else. The fireworks were touched off and fizzed and banked and spluttered, and the people cheered some more.

The fellows who furnished the Catherine wheels and sky rockets and so forth, sent in their bills, which were audited and marked correct and Harper was requested to settle. He refused. The fireworks were not a success, he said. The fireworks men represented to him that whether the display was a success or a heart-breaking failure sawed no frozen water whatever. They were not entrusted with the management of the affair. They had furnished the goods and wanted their money. Harper refused. Dickinson jumped in once more and carried to Harper testimonials from the men who had furnished the money, saying that there never had been any fireworks so good as those fireworks. Harper refused. Harper was then bombarded with orders from the subscribers directing him to pay out the $2,500 which he held to their credit. He refused.

So the matter stands. The fire-cracker men are desolate. Dickinson has lost thirty of his 250 pounds. Harper has the money. Chicago has the scandal of a lot of unpaid workmen and manufacturers who helped to celebrate the unveiling of the pawing horse and big moustache out on the lake front-the bronze memorial of "Black Jack" Logan, who never did anything but wed a smart woman and hold office and beget a son who married money in Ohio.

* * *

These are the components of the Chicago newspaper trust, of which many people have heard: The Tribune, the *Record*, the *Times-Herald*, the *Chronicle*, the *Post*, the *Journal* and the *News*. The object of the trust is to advance the interests of the proprietors and swell their bank accounts at the expense of individuals and the public in general. It is an offensive alliance against decency and fair play. It is powerful. Such enterprises as it elects to boom are boomed. Such as it elects to destroy are destroyed. Such men as it cares to advance are advanced. Such men as it cares to attack are viciously lampooned day after day and week after week and month after month. It does not lampoon anyone who pays it. In each of these papers the editorial room is utterly and thoroughly dominated by the counting room. It gets its order day by day from the business counter and it obeys them with a slavish servility. The merchant with a display advertisement in their columns is safe from attack, no matter what his crime. From end to end it is one man journalism, and each of the papers is run for the benefit of the one man who is its proprietor. The Tribune is owned by Joe Medill, the *Times-Herald* and *Post* are owned by H. H. Kohlsast, the *Record* and *News* are owned by Victor Lawson, the *Journal* is owned by the McRae-Scripps league and the *Chronicle* is owned by John R. Walsh, a banker.

The effects of the newspaper trust upon the public are so well known that they need not be further enumerated. Its effects upon the individual worker in journalism are damnable.

The Chicago journalist belongs to the man who hires him, or he moves away, or he starves. That is all there is to it. If discharged by one, he cannot be hired by another. He is blacklisted until the man who discharges him chooses to reinstate him. If employed by one paper and does exceptional work, he cannot go to another one at an increase of salary. This is one of the strongest rules of the trust. His only chance to get approximately what his work is worth is to resign and risk being hired elsewhere, and he will be hired elsewhere in Chicago only if his former owner does not object. He can, too, go to another paper at the same wages and take his chance of a raise.

The result of this is not only to peon men, but to pay them merely living wages. There has never been a time in the history of America when the pay of a competent newspaper man was so low as it is in Chicago. Reporters run from $10 to $25 a week, copy readers get $25 on morning papers, telegraph editors about the same, editorial writers and paragraphers are paid from $30 to $35. Wages in other parts of the business "up-stairs" are formed on a like model. These wages are from one-third to one-half of what are paid in New York. There is no newspaper trust in New York. As it is, the list of unemployed newspaper men in Chicago numbers more than 200. Any one of them would be glad to take a place at starvation wages if he could get it.

There is one gleam of hope for the Chicago newspaper man. It is rumored that W. R. Hearst of the New York Journal intends to start a morning paper there. I do not believe that he will, but if he does he will force some of the trust members to publish newspapers or get out of the business. Hearst is called a "yellow journalist," and what not, and may be he is, but he is a boon to the workers. There can be no manner of doubt about that.

Chicago, October 15.

* * * * *

THE AUTHOR OF EPISCOPALIANISM.

VERSAILLES, Mo., August 31.—Editor, ICONOCLAST: Will you please inform me who was the father of Anne Boleyn, second wife of Henry the Eighth, giving citations.

JOHN D. BOHLING.

Anne Boleyn was the daughter of Henry VIII. of England, and Lady Boleyn. This is so well known to every student of history that "giving citations" seems superfluous; but of the first that comes to my mind I'll furnish a few: Dr. Bayley ("Life of Bishop Fisher") says that before the wedding of King Henry to Anne occurred, Lady Boleyn addressed to the former these words: "Sir, for the reverence of God, take heed what you do in marrying my daughter, for, if you record your own conscience well, she is your own daughter as well as mine"; to which the king replied: "Whose daughter soever she is, she shall be my wife." Dr. Sander ("Anglican Schism") says that Henry VIII. was the father of his second wife, Anne Boleyn. Dr. D. Lewis, in his introduction to the book, says that both Lady Boleyn and her daughter Mary were King Henry's mistresses, and adds: "Nothing remains but to accept the fearful story told, not by Dr. Sander only, nor by him before all others, and say that, at least by the confession of the King and both Houses of Parliament, Anne Boleyn was Henry's child." Van Ortroy (Vic de B. Martyr Jean Fisher") says that Anne was the daughter of Henry, and that the fact was so generally known that it was the subject of ribald songs in continental capitals. William Cobbett ("History of the Protestant Reformation") says that Anne Boleyn became first the mistress and then the wife of her father. Gasquet, in his notes on that work, endorses the statement. By act of Parliament (28 Henry VIII C. 7) Elizabeth, daughter of Henry and Anne, was declared a bastard; that "certain just and lawful impediments" were unknown to the King when the marriage occurred, but had since been officially "confessed by the said Lady Anne." Archbishop Cranmer, who divorced Henry from Catherine, also divorced him from Anne, declaring in his latter decree "in the name of Christ and for the honor of God, the marriage was and always had been null and void." This sentence was signed by both houses of Convocation. It was approved by Parliament. Yet Cranmer, the Convocation and Parliament recognized Henry's divorce from Catherine as valid. According to English law, both religious and secular, Henry had no other wife when he married Anne, she no other husband. The only "lawful impediments" to the marriage were those stated by Anne's mother. They were positively known before Anne's marriage to Henry, the first official head of the Church of England, and who formulated and enforced its first body of doctrine, and there is every reason to believe that they were known at that time to Cranmer, the first archbishop of the parent of Episcopalianism, the sweet-scented author of the "Book of Common Prayer."

* * * * *

Dr. Rufus C. Burleson is not a perfect man. He has not always treated the ICONOCLAST either with Christian charity or courtesy; but as men go, he's far above the average. While he was president of Baylor University its students did not get drunk. They were not encouraged to arm themselves and commit lawless acts of violence. All the good that is in Baylor University is due to his untiring efforts and self-sacrifice. There would be no Baylor University to-day but for Dr. Burleson; yet after nearly half a century of service, he has been pitched out and humiliated and lied about by creatures who are not worthy to breathe the same atmosphere. The Baptist fight is none of mine; but I am the champion of fair play; and I say here that even in his so-called "dotage," Dr. Burleson has more brains, more good morals, more manhood, than have Carroll, Cranfill, and all their scurvy crew. If the enemies of Burleson triumph at the coming state convention, then the Baptist sect ought to perish from the earth. Shake, Doctor; Baylor has treated you a damned sight worse than it has treated me.

*   *   *   *   *

A GIPSY GENIUS.

BY WILLIAM MARION REEDY.

Men are the only things worth while, in this world, and I purpose to write briefly of a man, who, though living in these, our own, so-called, degenerate days, would have found a perfect setting in "the spacious times of great Elizabeth." He would have been a worthy companion of Raleigh, half-pirate and half-poet. He had in his time but one soul-kinsman, and that man was at once England's shame and glory, embalmed forever in the ominous work, Khartoum.

Sir Richard Burton was the last of the English "gentleman adventurers." He came late into the world, but he had in him the large, strong qualities that have made England master of the world. He was a Gypsy genius, though his utmost research could never find more clew to a Romany ancestry than the fact that there was a Gypsy family of the same name. He looked the Gypsy in ever feature, and he had upon him such an urging restlessness as no man ever had, save, perhaps, the Wandering Jew. His life was an epic of thought, of investigation and of adventure. The track of his wanderings laced the globe. He loved "the antres vast and deserts idle," and he had the *flair*, the houndscent, as it were, to find the hearts of strange peoples. His "Life," by his wife, is the most interesting biography since that of Boswell, and strangely enough, it is, like the famous "Johnson," as interesting for its revelation of the biographer as for its portrayal of the subject. Burton's wife was the loving-est slave that ever wedded with an idol. The story of the courtship is ridiculous almost to the verge of tragic. As a girl, a gypsy woman named Burton, told Isabel Arundell that she would marry one of the palmist's name, would travel much, and receive much honor.

One day, at Boulogne, she was on the ramparts, with companions, when she saw Burton. She describes him raptuously; tall, thin, muscular, very dark hair, black, clearly-defined, sagacious eye-brows, a brown weather-beaten complexion, straight Arab features, a determined looking mouth and chin. And then she quotes a clever friend's description, "That he had the brow of a God, the jaw of a Devil."

His eyes "pierced you through and through." When he smiled, he did so "as though it hurt him." He had a "fierce proud melancholy expression," and he "looked with contempt at things generally." He stared at her, and his eyes looked her through and through. She turned to a friend and said in a whisper, "That man will marry *me*." The next day they walked again. This time this man wrote on the wall, "May I speak to you?" She picked up the chalk and scrawled, "No, mother will be angry." A few days later they met in formal manner, and were introduced. She started at the name, Burton. Her naif rhapsodies on the meeting are refreshing. One night he danced with her. She kept the sash and the gloves she wore that night as sacred mementoes. Six years passed before she saw her Fate again. He had been in the world though, and she had kept track of his actions. In 1856 she met him in the Botanical Gardens "walking with the gorgeous creature of Boulogne—then married." They talked of things, particularly of Disraeli's "Tancred." He asked her if she came to the Gardens often. She said that she and her cousin came there every morning. He was there next morning, composing poetry to send to Monkton-Milnes. They walked and talked and did it again and again. "I trod on air," wrote the lady in her old, old age. Why not? She was one woman who had found a real hero. He asked her if she could dream of giving up civilization, and of going to live there if he could obtain the Consulate of Damascus. He told her to think it over. She said, "I don't *want* to think it over—I've been thinking it over for six years, ever since I first saw you, at Boulogne, on the ramparts. I have prayed for you every day, morning and night. I have followed all your career minutely. I have read every word you ever wrote, and I would rather have a crust and a tent with *you* than to be Queen of all the world. And so I say now, yes, yes, yes." She lived up to this to the day of his death, and long after it.

In 1859 she was thinking of becoming a Sister of Charity. She had not heard from Burton in a long time. He had left her without much ceremony to search for the sources of the Nile with Speke. Speke had returned alone, Burton remained at Zenzibar, and she says, "I was very sore "because Burton, according to report, was not thinking of coming home, to his love, but of going for the source of the Nile once more. She called on a friend. The friend was out. She waited, and while waiting Burton popped in upon her. He had come to see the friend to get her address. Her description of the meeting is a pitifully exact reproduction of her emotions over the reunion. He was weakened by African fevers. Her family, ardent Catholics, opposed the idea of marriage. The lovers used to meet in the Botanical Gardens, whence she often had to escort him fainting, to the house of sympathetic friends, in a cab. He was poor. He was out of favor with the government. Speke had pre-empted the honors of the expedition. But she was happy.

Then one day, in April, 1860, she was walking with some friends when "a tightning of the heart" came over her, that "she had not known before." She went home, and said to his sister, "I am not going to see Richard for some time." Her sister re-assured her. "No, I shall not," she said, "I don't know what is the matter." A tap came at the door, and a note was put in her hand. Burton was off on a journey to Salt Lake City, to investigate Mormonism. He would be gone nine months and then he was to come back, to see if she would marry him. He returned about

Christmas, 1860. In the later part of January they were married, the details of the affair being appropriately unconventional, not to say exciting. The marriage was, practically, an elopement. Lady Burton's description of the event, and of every event in their lives, ever after, discloses an idolatry of the man that was almost an insanity. She reveals herself as a help-mate, with no will but her husband's, no thought that was not for, and of, him. She annihilated herself as an individual, and she has left in her own papers a set of "Rules For a Wife," that will make many wives, who are regarded as models of devotion, smile contemptuously at her. She was utterly happy in complete submission to his will. She described how she served him almost like an Indian squaw. She packed his trunks, was his amanuensis, attended to the details of publishing his books, came, or went, as he bade, suffered long absence in silence, or accompanied him on long journeys of exploration, uncomplainingly, was proud when he hypnotized her for the amusement of his friends. One can but feel deeply sorry for her, for with all her servility, she was a woman of the finer order of mind. The pity of her worship grows, as the reader of his life, and hers, realizes how little return in demonstrative affection she received as the reward for her vast, and continuous lavishment of love. She strikes me, in this, as a strange blend of the comic and the tragic. The world neglected Burton. He almost deserved it; so great a sacrifice as his wife consecrated of her life to him would compensate for the loss of anything. You admire it; but you catch yourself suspecting that this consecration must have been, at times, an awful bore to him. He was unfaithful to her, it is said, with ethnological intent, in all the tribes of the earth. He had no morals to speak of. He had no religion, having studied all. He was a pagan beyond redemption, though his wife maintained that he was a Catholic. Unfortunately, for her, his masterpiece refutes her overwhelmingly. He wrote the most remarkable poem of the last forty years, one that is to be classed only with Tennyson's "In Memoriam" and the "Rubaiyat" of Omar Khayyam. By this poem, and, probably, by the revelation of the love he excited in one woman, he will live. This poem expresses himself, and his conclusion, after years spent in wandering, fighting, studying languages, customs and religions. To understand the man and his poem, we must understand what he did, and since the time of the Old Romance, no man surpassed him in "deeds of derring-do." He was a modern, a very modern, Knight of the Round Table. He was the possessor of innumerable abstruse, and outlandish accomplishments. He was a scientist, a linguist, a poet, a geographer, a roughly clever diplomat, a fighter, a man with a polyhedric personality, that caught and gave, something from and to every one. And he died dissatisfied, at Trieste, in 1890, at the age of sixty-nine, and Swinburne sang a dirge for him that was almost worth dying for.

What he did is hard to condense into an article. I can do no more than skim over his career, and make out a feature here and there. He was an unstudious youth. He was not disciplined. He grew as he might, and he absorbed information at haphazard from any book he found to his liking, but he was a sort of intellectual Ishmael. He studied things not in the curriculum. He plunged into Arabic and Hindustani, and was "rusticated." He cared nothing for the classics, yet he left a redaction of Catullus that is a splendid exposition of that singer's fearful corruption, and with all of his art. He entered the Indian Army, and he became so powerful, though a subordinate, that he was repressed. His superiors feared, that in him, they would find another Clive or Hastings. Then he joined the Catholic church, but he joined many a church thereafter to find its hidden meaning. He was trusted to a limited extent by Sir Charles Napier, and he so insinuated himself with the natives, that he was one of them, and sharer of their mysterious powers. Kipling has pictured him under the name of "Strickland" as an occultly powerful personage in several of his stories. He was close to the Sikh war, and he mingled with the hostile natives in disguise, until he knew their very hearts. His pilgrimage to Mecca was a feat that startled the world. He was the first "infidel" to kiss the Kaabba. To do this he had to become a Mohammedan, and to perform almost hourly minute ceremonials, in which, had he failed of perfection, he would have been torn to pieces. His book on this journey is a narration that displays the deadly cold quality of his courage, and indeed a stupendous consciencelessness in the interest of science. Next we find him in the Crimea in the thick of things, and always in trouble. He said that all his friends got into trouble, and Burton was, usually, "agin the government." It was after the Crimea that he met the lady who became his remarkable wife, in the remarkable manner I have sketched. Then he went off to discover the sources of the Nile, and with Speke navigated Lake Tanganyika. He knew that he had not discovered the source, and he wanted to try again, but he and Speke quarreled, and pamphleteered against each other in the press. Burton, deficient in money, and in sycophancy, was discredited for a time, although now his name is immortal in geography as a pioneer of African travel. We have seen how he left his betrothed to study the Mormons, and he studied them more closely than his wife's book intimates, for she everything extenuated and ignored for her God-like Richard.

After his experiences of marriage in Mormondom, undertaken it now seems, in a desire to ascertain if polygamy were not better for him than monogamy, he returned to London, and was married despite the objections of Isabel Arundell's Catholic family. The lot of the couple was poverty, although now and then, thoughtful friends invited them to visit, and they accepted to save money. After a long wait he was appointed Consul at Fernando Po, on the West African coast. This was a miserable place, but Burton made it lively; he disciplined the negroes, and he made the sea captains fulfill their contracts under threat of guns. He went home, and then went back to Fernando Po, and undertook delicate dealings with the king of Dahomey, and explored the west coast. He went to Ireland, but Ireland was too quiet for him, but he found there were Burtons there, which accounted to himself for much of himself. After that he went to Brazil as Consul at Santos, Sao Pablo, another "Jumping off place." He explored. He found rubies, and he obtained a concession for a lead mine for others. He met there the Tichborne Claimant, and invented a Carbine pistol. He visited Argentina. All this time he was writing upon many things, or having his wife take his dictation. She went into the wilds, down into the mines, everywhere with him. Next he was transferred to Damascus, where his honesty got him into trouble, and his wife's Catholicity aroused great sentiment against him. He went into Syria, and he created consternation among the corrupt office holders in Asia Minor. One can scarcely follow his career without dizziness. By way of obliging a friend, who wanted a report on a mine, he went to Iceland, and came back to take the Consulship at Trieste. He went back to India and into Egypt, and then returned to Trieste to die. He wrote pamphlets, monographs, letters and books about everything he saw, and every place he visited. He had information exact, and from the fountain head about innumerable things; religions, races, ruins, customs, languages, tribal genealogies, plants, geology, archaeology paleontology, botany, politics, morals, almost everything that was of human interest and value, and besides all this, he was familiar with Chaucer's vocabulary, with recondite learning about Latin colloquialisms, and read with avidity everything from the Confessions of Saint Augustine to the newspapers. He wrote a "Book of the Sword," that is the standard book on that implement for the carving of the world. His translations of the "Arabian Nights" is a Titanic work, invaluable for its light upon Oriental folk lore, and literal to a degree that will keep it forever a sealed book to the Young Person. His translations of Camoens is said to be a wonderful rendition of the spirit of the Portuguese Homer. His Catullus is familiar to students, but not edifying. He wrote a curious volume on Falconry in India, and a manual of bayonet exercise. He collated a strange volume of African folk-lore. He translated several Brazilian tales. He translated Apulius' "Golden Ass." And he had notes for a book on the Gypsies, on the Greek Anthology, and Ausonius. The Burton bibliography looks like the catalogue of a small library. All the world knows about his book, "The Scented Garden," which he translated from the Persian, and which, after his death, his wife burned rather than permit the publication of its naked naturalism. It was in the same vein as his "Arabian Nights," and contained much curious comment upon many things that we Anglo Saxons do not talk about, save in medical society meetings, and dog Latin.

When such a man sat down to write a poem, embodying his view of "the Higher Law," what could have been expected but a notable manuscript. With his poem, "the Kasidah," we shall now concern ourselves. It purports to be a translation from the Arabic of Haji Abdu El Yezdi. Its style is like that of the Rubaiyat. It is erude, but subtile. It is brutal in its anti-theism, and yet it has a certain tender grace of melancholy, deeper than Omar's own. It is devoid of Omar's mysticism and epicureanism, and appallingly synthetic. It will not capture the sentimentalists, like the Rubaiyat, but, when it shall be known, it will divide honors with the now universally popular Persian poem. Burton's "Kasidah" is miserably printed in his "Life," but Mr. Thomas Mosher, of Portland, Maine, has issued it in beautiful and chaste form, for the edification of his clientele of searchers for the literature that is always almost, but never quite completely forgotten. The "Kasidah" was written in 1853, and it is, in its opening, much like Fitz Gerald's Rubaiyat, though Burton never saw that gem of philosophy and song, until eight years after. "The Kasidah" was not printed until 1880. It is difficult to interpret, because it so clearly interprets itself. It must be read. It cannot be "explained."

The Kasidah consists of about 300 couplets of remarkable vigor in condensation. It reviews all the explanations of "the sorry scheme of things" that man has contrived, and it holds forth the writer's own view. He maintains that happiness and misery are equally divided, and distributed in this world. Self cultivation is, in his view, the sole sufficient object of human life, with due regard for others. The affections, the sympathies, and "the divine gift of Pity" are man's highest enjoyments. He advocates suspension of judgment, with a proper suspicion of "Facts, the idlest of superstitions." This is pure agnosticism. There runs all through the poem a sad note that heightens the courage with which the writer faces his own bleak conclusion, and, "the tinkling of the camel bell" is heard faint and far in the surge of his investive, or below the deepest deep of his despair. In Arabia, Death rides a camel, instead of a white horse, as our occidental myth has it, and the camel's bell is the music to which all life is attuned. Burton reverts from time to time to this terrifying tintinnabulation, but he blends it with the suggested glamour of evening, until the terror merges into tenderness. The recurrence of this minor chord, in the savage sweep of Burton's protest against the irony of existence, is a fascination that the "Kasidah" has in common with every great poem of the world. The materialism of the book is peculiar in that it is Oriental, and Orientalism is peculiarly mystical. The verse is blunt, and almost coarse in places, but here and there are gentler touches, softer tones, that search out the sorrow at the heart of things. It is worthy, in its power, of the praise of Browning, Swinburne, Theodore Watts, Gerald Massey. It is Edward Fitz Gerald minus the vine and the rose, and ali Persian silkiness. The problem he sets out to solve, and he solves it by a petitio principii, is

> Why must we meet, why must we part, why must we bear this yoke of
>   Must,
> Without our leave or ask or given, by tyrant Fate on victim thrust?

The impermanence of things oppresses him, for he says in an adieu,

> . . . Haply some day we meet again;
> Yet ne'er the self-same man shall meet;
> the years shall make us other men.

He crams into one couplet after another, philosophy after philosophy, creed after creed, Stoic, Epicurean, Hebraic, Persian, Christian, and puts his finger on the flaw in them all. Man comes to life as to "the Feast unbid," and finds "the gorgeous table spread with fair-seeming Sodom-fruit, with stones that bear the shape of bread."

There is an echo of Koleleth in his contempt for the divinity of the body. It is unclean without, impure within. The vanity of vanity is proclaimed with piteous indignation.

> "And still the weaver plies his loom, whose warp and woof is wretched
>   Man,
> Weaving the unpattern'd, dark design, so dark we doubt it owns a plan.
> Dost not, O Maker, blush to hear, amid the storm of tears and blood,
> Man say thy mercy made what is, and saw the made and said 'twas
>   good?"

And then he sings:

Cease Man to mourn, to weep, to wail; enjoy the shining hour of sun;
We dance along Death's icy brink, but is the dance less full of fun?

In sweeping away the old philosophies and religions, he is at his best as a scorner, but he has "the scorn of scorn" and some of "the love of love" which, Tennyson declares, is the poet's dower. His lament for the Greek paganism runs:

And when at length, "Great Pan is dead" uprose the loud and dolorous
    cry,
A glamour wither'd on the ground, a splendor faded in the sky.
Yes, Pan is dead, the Nazarene came and seized his seat beneath the sun,
The votary of the Riddle-god, whose one is three, whose three is one.

* * *

Then the lank Arab, foul with sweat, the drainer of the camel's dug,
Gorged with his leek-green, lizard's meat, clad in his filmy rag and rug,
Bore his fierce Allah o'er his sands
Where, he asks, are all the creeds and crowns and scepters, "the holy
    grail of high Jamshid?"
Gone, gone where I and thou must go, borne by the winnowing wings of
    Death,
The Horror brooding over life, and nearer brought with every breath.
Their fame hath filled the Seven Climes, they rose and reigned, they
    fought and fell,
As swells and swoons across the wold the tinkling of the camel's bell.

For him "there is no good, there is no bad; these be the whims of mortal will." They change with place, they shift with race. "Each Vice has borne a Virtue's crown, all Good was banned as Sin or Crime." He takes up the history of the world, as we reconstruct it for the period before history, from geology, astronomy and other sciences. He accepts the murderousness of all processes of life and change. All the cruelty of things "Builds up a world for better use; to general Good bends special Ill."

And thus the race of Being runs, till haply in the time to be
Earth shifts her pole and Mushtari-men another falling star shall see:
Shall see it fall and fade from sight, whence come, where gone, no
    Thought can tell,—
Drink of yon mirage-stream and chase the tinkling of the camel-bell.
Yet follow not the unwisdom path, cleave not to this and that disclaim;
Believe in all that man believes; here all and naught are both the same.
Enough to think that Truth can be; come sit me where the roses glow,
Indeed he knows not how to know who knows not also how to unknow.

He denies the Soul and wants to know where it was when Man was a savage beast in Primeval forests, what shape it had, what dwelling place, what part in nature's plan it played. "What men are pleased to call the Soul was in the hog and dog begun."

Life is a ladder infinite-stepped that hides its rungs from human eyes:

Planted its foot in chaos-gloom, its head soars high above the skies.

The evolution theory he applies to the development of reason from instinct. He protests against the revulsion from materialism by saying that "the sordider the stuff, the cunninger the workman's hand," and therefore the Maker may have made the world from matter. He maintains that "the hands of Destiny ever deal, in fixed and equal parts their shares of joy and sorrow, woe and weal" to all that breathe our upper air. The problem of predestination he holds in scorn. The un-equality of life exists and "that settles it" for him. He accepts one bowl with scant delight but he says "who drains the score must ne'er expect to rue the headache in the morn." Disputing about creeds is "mumbling rotten bones." His creed is this:

> Do what thy manhood bids thee do, from none but self expect applause:
> He noblest lives and noblest dies who makes and keeps his self-made
>   laws.
> All other Life is living Death, a world where none but Phanton's dwell,
> A breath, a wind, a soul, a voice, a tinkling of the Camel's bell.

He appreciates to the full the hedonism of Omar but he casts it aside as emptiness. He tried the religion of pleasure and beauty. His rules of life are many and first is "eternal war with Ignorance." He says: "Thine ignorance of thine ignorance is thy fiercest foe, thy deadliest bane. The Atom must fight the unequal fray against a myriad giants. The end is to "learn the noblest lore, to know that all we know is naught." Self-approval is enough reward. The whole duty of man is to himself, but he must "hold Humanity one man" and, looking back at what he was, determine not to be again that thing. "Abjure the Why and seek the How." The gods are silent. The indivisible puny Now in the length of infinite time is Man's all to make the best of. The Law may have a Giver but let be, let be!

> Thus I may find a future life, a nobler copy of our own,
> Where every riddle shall be ree'd, where every knowledge shall be
>   known;
> Where 'twill be man's to see the whole of what on earth he sees a part;
> Where change shall ne'er surcharge the thought; nor hope deferred shall
>   hurt the heart.
> But—faded flower and fallen leaf no more shall deck the parent tree;
> A man once dropt by Tree of Life, what hope of other life has he?
> The shattered bowl shall know repair; the riven lute shall sound once
>   more;
> But who shall mend the clay of man, the stolen breath to man restore?
> The shivered clock again shall strike, the broken reed shall pipe again;
> But we, we die and Death is one, the doom of brutes, the doom of men.
> Then, if Nirvana round our life with nothingness, 'tis haply blest;
> Thy toils and troubles, want and woe at length have won their guer-
>   don—Rest.
> Cease, Abou, cease! My song is sung, nor think the gain the singer's prize
> Till men hold Ignorance deadly sin till Man deserves his title, "Wise."
> In days to come, Days slow to dawn, when Wisdom deigns to dwell with
>   men,

> These echoes of a voice long stilled haply shall wake responsive strain:
> Wend now thy way with brow serene, fear not thy humble tale to tell—
> The whispers of the Desert wind: the tinkling of the Camel's bell.

So ends the song. The notes appended thereto by Burton are a demonstration of his learning and his polemic power. The poem is his life of quest, of struggle, of disappointment coined into song more or less savage. It seems to me that he overlooked one thing near to him that would have lighted the darkness of his view, while looking To Reason for balm for the wounds of existence. He ignored his wife's love which, silly and absurd as it seems at times, in the records she has left us, is a sweeter poem than this potent plaint and protest he has left us. He explored all lands but the one in which he lived unconsciously—the Land of Tenderness. This is the pity of his life and it is also its indignity. He was crueler than "the Cruelty of Things." He "threw away a pearl richer than all his tribe"—a woman's heart. But—how we argue in a circle!—that he, with his fine vision could not see this, is perhaps, a justification of his poem's bitterness. Even her service went for naught, seeing it brought no return of love from its object.

Burton was a great man, though a failure. His wife's life was one continuous act of love for him that he ignores and her life was a failure, too, since she never succeeded in making the world worship him as she did. Still "the failures of some the infinities beyond the successes of others" and all success is failure in the end. Still again, it is better to have loved in vain than never to have loved at all, and fine and bold and brave as was Richard Francis Burton, his wife, with her "strong power called weakness," was the greater of the two. She wrote no "Kasidah" of complaint, but suffered and was strong.

St. Louis, August 16th, 1897.

*   *   *   *   *

MARRIAGE AND MISERY.

BY ETHELYN LESLIE HUSTON.

Charles Goodwin, editor Salt Lake Tribune, puts into the mouth of a figurative John Bull, who is lecturing his children, the following sentence:

> "Why, ours is an old family. One of our ancestors was knighted by Henry VII for stealing cattle from the Scotch some time in the fifteenth century. I am tracing up the lineage, and I believe we are all barons. I expect to get the title confirmed, and then each one of you boys must sell himself to a beautiful American girl for from 75,000 to 250,000 pounds. Under the rose, it will help the stock damnably, for your mother was a barmaid. Things are working all right, my lads. Our conquest of the United States still goes on."

Apropos of a snub given the Prince of Wales by an American girl, Lillian Russell—even our much-married Lillian—raises her voice in protest at international marriages, and incidentally American snobbery.

What is marriage? as we see it. The veneered vulgarity of the international marriage goes on merrily notwithstanding public opinion freely expressed. We bury the individuality and personality of our daughters and give them as so much chatel to the physically and financially anaemic nobility across the water, to infuse into its diseased and impoverished veins pure blood and into its depleted exchequer pure gold. And this we call marriage. The weak-minded chattel and fatuous mother should be promptly chloroformed without benefit of clergy. But they are instead solemnly consecrated by their clergy, their church and their Fifth Avenue Christ.

And yet, to go back to first principles, is it not that the time are out of joint, and the America herself is responsible for her daughters' shame? America has blinded her eyes with avarice and glutted her brain with greed. She has starved her intellect and gorged her ambition. She has bartered her birthright of nobility and sold her soul to crawling sycophants. She has prostituted her sceptre of power to trusts for tinsel and cowers under the lash of corporations because they bind her brow with a cap of bells that tinkle an empty song of "Freedom." In the mad rush for gain, America has forgotten its greatness, and in their blind struggle for gold Americans forget what is grand. We have sold our freedom to Britain, we have sold our pride, our individuality, our independence, our self-respect, our power, our dignity and our daughters.

The gods have given us brains to make of our country a brawny one, and we have used our talent to corrupt what was once equality into the unequal factions of power and poverty. The gods have given us genius to soften the crudities of the early century and to brighten our homes and our lives, and instead the inventions and the creations but serve to gild the mansions of the monopolist and to gird the iron more tightly on the wrist of the toiler. We are avaricious, we are vulgar, and we are base. We have lost the dignity of Nature that gave to a fragile lily a royalty before which Solomon's grandeur paled. We have piled stone and brick where the forest oak towered, and voice our strident city cries where the imperious roar of the forest king once startled the echoes. We have turned the oil and filth of our refineries into the streams that once crept purling and laughing through the wild-flowers and grasses, and the black smoke of our factories has silenced the plaintive note of the thrush and strangled the wondrous song of the nightingale. Our grandeur is ostentation and our dignity a dead-letter. The greatness that once longed for new worlds to conquer has degenerated into yellow-fingered grasping for ginger-bread display. The powerful figure of the pioneer could swing its mighty as into the forest root, but in the rythm of labor there was time to pause and rest and listen where "soft music ripples along shore, as the lake breathes." In the stillness Nature's god speaks, and in the patient face of the woman, shading her eyes where she watches him from the cabin door, is sweeter and nobler dreaming than ever finds resting place in the sharpened and querulous features of our modern rushed society woman.

In English homes are the friendships of generations and beneath their spreading trees their lives epitomise the lotus eater's religion—"There is no joy but calm." Our women know neither the one nor the other. Our social creed and dogma know nothing of friendship, and calm to them is as Greek papyri in a kindergarten. Thus have we grown avaricious and vulgar and in their weariness of things as they are, have our women grown base. They know that their lives miss something, they know that their fierce rivalry and feverish straining for precedence bring them no nearer the Mecca that closes its austere gates to their aching eyes. And for the dignity and pride their lives have lacked, they give their fortunes and sell their bodies and exchange, for a title, the name of which they have grown ashamed. They perhaps shrink, in physical repulsion, from the man who they feel despises while he endures them. They perhaps hunger, with all the woman-nature their pitiful lives have left them, for other lips murmuring in slumber beside them. But over their burning eyes they press the metal circle for which they have crushed their hearts and outraged their sex, and around the delicate limbs they draw the ermines that cannot hide their shame, and in all their poor, empty glory they only read in the cold eyes of the patrician women around them the chill contempt that stamps them as among, but not of their order. "I sometimes think it wisest not to think," and this warped and twisted human nature has a pathos in all its chasing after a gilded butterfly that has always a grinning skull peering through the gold of its wings. The hunger that finds but Apples of Sodom, the life-labor that wins but the gold of Midas, the ambition that crushes its toy baloon—"and man plods his way through thorns to ashes."

America freed her blacks but rests her social aegis on barter far more hideous. Optimists prate of the world growing better, with their eyes on the mountain tops, but when one reads of frail Lais fined ten dollars in the court-room for earning her daily bread in the only manner possible to a nature in which sin has been bred in the bone by generations of ancestors, and then pictures Dr. Brown of exclusive St. Thomas', New York, murmuring "Benedicite!" over an international marriage ceremony, his handsome face and melodious voice and aristocratic bearing doing full justice to the grandeur of the occasion—it is a contrast in which there is a bitter humor, a farce in which there is something horrible, a comedy that smells of the charnel house.

Is there plan and purpose in all the meaningless mystery and misery? Is "heaven but the vision of fulfilled desire, hell the shadow of a soul on fire?" And are we both? Are we improving? Look on life within its gates. Are we retrograding? Strip the curtains from the hearts of men and women. And marriage, the great pivot upon which swings life itself, what is it? Is it covenant with deity, or contract with the devil?

Boise, Ida., October 1.

*　　*　　*　　*　　*

SALMAGUNDI.

My attention has been several times called by the citizens of Nevada, Ia., to a series of articles appearing in a little boiler-plate paper published at that place by an old plug named Payne and his idiot son. The articles purport to have been written by one G. W. Bailey, from West Point, Columbus, McComb, Magnolia, and other places in Mississippi, and are the most brutally slanderous of the South and the Southern people of anything yet put in print. As the writer is too gross-ly ignorant and hopelesly imbecile to concoct a falsehood to deceive a diapered pickaninny, I should pay no attention to his screeds, but for the indignant protests of the Iowa people. One gentleman sends me some excerpts from the articles and says: "Do not imagine us big enough fools to be deceived by this lying scoundrel. He would, if necessary to get his name in print, defame his own parents. Bailey is an intellectual bawd with an abnormal itch for notoriety. The paper in which his screeds appear has a very limited circulation. I have never detected anybody in the crime of reading it, hence it can do no harm. I was in the federal army and know something about the South. I learned it at Pittsburg Landing. Some mischief-mak-ing, blatherskites ought to have their d——d tongues cut out." Another gentle-man writes from Iowa: "It seems that this fellow Bailey once got a small Federal appointment to some place in China. He remained their long enough to pick up a few curios, contract the opium habit and the name of 'Tankkee.' He returned and began lecturing on China, but the dope was too much for his little encephalon. He took the Keeley cure for the opium habit, but he's as great a liar as ever. You know what Macaulay says about Bertrand Barere? Well, this fellow can outlie the 'Witling of Terror' and not half try. I think if he should accidentally tell the truth about anything he'd drop dead.

Now for Christ's sake don't judge Iowa people by this peripatetic Ananias. Where he was born I don't know; neither do I care a d—n; but I suspect that he was begotten in some back yard during the dark of the moon, spawned in a dry goods box and raised on bones." So Bailey is "Tank-Kee." If I mistake not there was a Tank-kee trotting around Texas some years ago beating school-children of the small towns out of their pennies by dressing like a Chinese joss with a double-bar-relled jag and exhibiting a lot of old junk. It is my impression that he's a half-breed of some kind, but whether half Chinese or coon I cannot with certainty say. If he is hacking around from town to town in Mississippi he is doubtless working a fake of some kind-swindling the people while defaming them. If the Mississippians can locate G. W. Bailey they had best hold him and wire me for copies of his articles in my possession. One thing is cock-sure—"Tank-kee" had best keep out of Texas.

* * *

The suspicion is growing that Dr. Gutieras, the government expert, has a pint of yellow fever baccilli in his cerebrum. He carries the plague with him, just as a man suffering with *mania a potu* carries his cargo of monkeys. Had he been called to see Simon's wife's mother, he would have declared that she had a case of Yellow Jack and spread a panic through all Judea. Should he find a man suffering with katzenjammer he would pronounce him a "suspect." As Barney Gibbs says, all the yellow fever patients Gutieras discovered during his tour of South Texas were up "hunting either a drink or a job" ere this peripatetic expert was well out of town. I'll gamble four dollars that there is not in the United States to-day a genuine case of Yellow Jack. There's every indication that the cases at Mobile, New Orleans and Biloxi are identical with the disease discovered by Gutieras at Galveston—noth-ing under heaven but the dengue. Who the devil ever heard of the mortality in a yellow fever epidemic averaging only about 6 per cent.? Why la grippe will beat that as an angel-maker and beat it blind. When good old-fashioned yellow fever reaches for people they begin to sing "Heaven is my home," I'd rather have the "plague" now rioting in New Orleans than to contract the buck ague or the itch. These "experts" make my soul aweary. An insanity expert thinks everybody crazy but himself, while a yellow fever expert would isolate a case o' cucumber colic. What the South needs to do is to quarantine against these special doctors.

* * *

A few American newspapers and magazines of the genus mugwump, enemies of Cuban liberty and apologists for the Weylerian butcheries and brutalities, are now busily engaged in belittling those who enabled Senorita Cisneros to escape from her captors, are heaping their feculence upon Mesdames Jefferson Davis, Jno. A. Logan and the other "old women" who had the temerity to appeal to the Spanish Queen Regent in behalf of the young heroine—are even repeating the stale lies of Weyler's understrappers reflecting upon her chastity. What brave American journalists! How proud of such sons Columbia should be! It is quite possible the New York *Journal* undertook the young lady's rescue for advertising purposes only; but just the same, she is on American soil, and she can well afford to ignore the petty malice of emasculated mugwump editors, knowing as she must, that the chivalry of this country is with her to the last man. I do not believe the statement of the Spanish official whom Senorita Cisneros accused of insulting her, and who retorted that she had thrown herself at his head. A gentleman could not make such an assertion even though it were true, for a woman's illicit favors set upon the lips of the recipient the seal of eternal silence. The defamer of Senorita Cisneros is but another Don Matthias de Silvae of Le Sage.

* * *

The coon seems to be forging rapidly to the front in some portions of this country. On October 2, Mrs. W. E. D. Stokes, a wealthy white woman and owner of one of the largest stock farms in Kentucky, gave a ball and banquet near Lexington to 300 colored people and filled 'em full of beer. Whether Mrs. Stokes danced with the bucks the dispatches do not state.

* * *

My attention has been several times called to one W. D. McKinstry of Watertown, N. Y., by people of that place. They plead with me that he is really spoiling for a "roast." McKinstry is publishing a little paper which somewhat resembles an over-ripe dish-rag, or an unlaundered sheet from the bed of a colored baby; but I have no idea why he is so unpopular. It may be because he possesses the physique of a bull elephant and the brains of a doodle-bug. It may be that the appearance of such an animal outside a dime museum, or a pig sty, angers the people. I can see nothing in his editorials at which to take offense. Reading them were like drinking the froth out of a pop-bottle or filling one's belly with the east wind. McKinstry is trying to settle the "negro problem" for the South; but that has so long been a favorite occupation of Smart Alec editors who never saw a cotton patch that no one minds it any more. Waco has the coon and Watertown has McKinstry, hence it is in order for the two towns to mingle their tears instead of animadverting each upon the other's misfortune. If I might advise the mighty McKinstry I would suggest that he change his occupation. As an editor he is a dismal failure, but he would be a dazzling success as ballast for a canal boat.

* * *

A correspondent notes that the New York *World* devotes two illustrated pages to the Vanderbilt-Marlborough brat, and wants to know what I think about it? Why, I think that old Josef Phewlitzer has succeeded in elongating the Vanderbilt leg. No editor ever publishes such tommyrot unless paid therefor, because he knows that no sane person will read it. It was an advertisement, ordered and paid for by somebody, probably Consuelo's rather gay mother, who, albeit divorced from her first husband for cause, has the distinguished honor to be gran'dam to an incipient duke, who will probably grow up to be as utterly worthless as his daddy.

* * *

Jno. H. Holmes, editor of the Boston *Herald*, writing on the "New Journalism." says: "Huge circulation is extremely profitable. It produced revenue from the sale of the paper, and a still greater revenue from the volume of advertising." In other words, the average "great daily" is simply a mercenary advertising graft. It may "produce revenue," but seldom profit from circulation, for the price to agents is frequently below the cost of white paper and expressage. The subscription price is usually placed below the profit line, and extra inducements offered in the way of "premiums." Somehow, a circulation, bona fide or fake, must be worked up as an excuse for elongating the business man's leg. And he is a "dead easy mark." The yap who purchases checks of strangers and bets on monte is no more gullible than the average victim of the advertising grafter. A sucker is said to be born every minute; and strange to say, most of them are produced in the cities. The business man who makes an advertising contract without investigating the circulation claims of the publisher, would invest in confederate bonds or buy gold bricks. If he suffered the loss it would not much matter—would be simply another case of the fool and his money soon parted; but it is shifted to the consumer. The people must pay the merchant's advertising bills, just as they pay his rent and insurance; and the amount of which they are annually fleeced to pay for what has no actual existence, would meet all expenses of government and leave a tremendous surplus in the treasury. This nation wastes annually for worthless fake advertising more than it pays for education.

* * *

A Galveston traveling man writes me as follows:

> "I have been for two years past gathering up scraps of your history, and now have the honor to advise you that according to the testimony of many very pious people, among whom are not a few preachers, you are an avowed anarchist who was suspected of being concerned in the Haymarket massacre; that you served two terms in the penitentiary before you were born; that you are a renegade Jew and an Italian Jesuit, that for 30 years you were a Baptist preacher, but were bounced out of the ministry for drunk-

enness and immorality; that you have been a blasphemous Atheist from your youth up; that you deserted from the federal army in the same year that you were four years old; that you have been discharged from all the Texas dailies for incompetency, and are the author of editorials in the Chicago *Inter-Ocean* slandering the South; that you are a big over-grown bully who abuses weaker people, and a miserable little poltroon who has been kicked by every cripple between New York and Denver. All this is doubtless correct as far as it goes; now will you please inform me whether you have been guilty of anything else?"

This is a fairly correct list of my crimes thus far; but being still a young man, I may reasonably hope to add to it considerably if not shut off by the sheriff. The greatest drawback to my career as a criminal is my inability to lie so consistently as some of my dear brethren in Christ.

* * *

The ICONOCLAST's recent comments on Dean Hart of Denver, provoked the following poetic outburst on the part of a singer of that city:

Do you mind him as he walks the street,
The Dean?
With his highly elevated nose,
The Dean.
And his old imported hat
And his time worn black cravat,
Any one could tell that
He's the Dean.

He is "furnist" this country,
Is the Dean,
"It's nothing like old Hingland,"
Says the Dean.
In language somewhat torrid,
With a countenance quite florid,
He says our schools are "orrid,"
Does the Dean.

To many it's a mystery why
The Dean
Doesn't leave us and for England hie away;
No doubt he can explain it,
In England he's not "in it,"
But in this "blooming" country
He's a Dean.

* * *

All the sycophantic little sassiety sheets are now engaged in the delectable task of belittling Miss Edna Whitney, selected by Chillicothe, Mo., as maid of honor to the Kween of the Kansas City Karnival, but objected to by the snob management on the ground that she was a working girl. The sheets aforesaid have discovered that since that event brought her into public notice Miss Whitney has accepted $500 from a cigarette firm for the use of her photo, and are now industriously arguing that a young woman who will permit her portrait to be so employed is not a proper person to be brought for a moment into contract with the eminently respectable sassietyest. Rats! ditto rodents. The Karnival was not a "social function," but a commercial scheme gotten up by the merchants of Kansas City to draw trade to that enterprising town. It was a blowout for everybody; the world was invited—the gates thrown open to the Canary in his Canaryism as well as to Sir Alymer in his Alymerism. Lady Vere de Vere and the chambermaid in the dollar-a-day hotel were alike invited to make themselves at home, enjoy the show and spend their siller. Unfortunately, the management of the affair was committed to an incorrigible snob, and he decided that a young lady who earned her own living was not a fit theatrical associate for the patrician daughters of successful soap-boilers and pork-packers, thereby offering an unforgettable and unforgivable affront to all the legions of labor. I do not approve of Miss Whitney's sale of her photo to a cigarette firm; but I do say that the act is infinitely more excusable than the practice among high-fly society women of paying for the publication of decollete portraits and sickening "write-ups" of themselves. Miss Whitney is poor and, I am told, supports a widowed mother. To a girl so situated $500 is a great sum. She could scarce be expected to have the fine aesthetic feelings of a highly educated woman reared in the lap of luxury. Her portrait had already been hawked about in the daily papers,—like those of the swell society set—and, like the latter, freely commented upon by bummers and bawds. She has the excuse of necessity for the sale of her picture, while her sisters in society are driven solely by a prurient itch for notoriety to exploit themselves in the public prints. It does not necessarily follow, as the sassiety sheets would have us believe, that every woman is unchaste whose portrait is found in a cigarette package—I have seen Queen Victoria's, Mrs. Cleveland's and the Princess of Wales' in the same place. These pitiful sheets, which are belittling Miss Whitney to ingratiate themselves with the snobocracy of Kansas City, are entirely destitute of shame. Their editors are, in most instances, a cross between Jeames de la Pluche and Caliban. Their presence at "social functions" is tolerated for the same reason that nigger waiters are admitted. They are used by the parvenues and heartily despised by the very people whom they so obsequiously serve.

* * *

Mr. Brann: You state in a recent issue of the Iconoclast that McKinley's popular plurality "represents the votes of niggers and the scavangers of Europe's back alleys." I denounce that statement as a falsehood. The votes of native-born Americans elected Mr. McKinley.

Americus.

Waco, Texas, September 10.

My correspondent is indeed "A Merry Kuss" else he could find no pleasure in calling a man a liar in an anonymous letter. To call that creature a cur who flings an insult which he fears to father, were a damning libel on every decent dog in Christendom. My correspondent is probably a mongrel cross between a male hyena and a gila monster, begotten in a nigger grave-yard, suckled by a sow and educated by an idiot. But, perhaps, being familiar with his own birth and breeding he will consider this a compliment. McKinley coralled more than 90 per cent. of the nigger vote and carried every state in which foreign-born people exceeds 21 per cent. of the entire population. He received his largest majorities in Illinois, Wisconsin, Michigan, North Dakota, Minnesota, California, Massachusetts, New York and New Jersey, one-third of whose people, collectively considered, are of foreign birth; his smallest majorities in Kentucky, Indiana, West Virginia and Maryland, where those of foreign birth amount to about 8 per cent. of the entire population. Virginia, North and South Carolina, Georgia, Florida, Mississippi, Arkansas, Texas, Missouri, Kansas constituted Bryan's strongholds and their people collectively considered, show a foreign birth of less than 5 per cent. Colorado is the only state having a considerable foreign-birth population that stands in the Democratic columns, all the others having gone for McKinley. While it is true that thousands of our foreign-born citizens are intelligent, honest and patriotic—a credit to the land of their adoption—it is likewise true that following in their wake we find Huns, Pollocks, Sicillians, "Souwegian" and other undesirable offscourings of the old world, imported by Mark Hanna and other "industrial cannibals" to degrade our labor and debauch our politics. It is the vote of this latter class, and the scarcely less corrupt and ignorant "coons" which constitute McKinley's popular plurality. McKinley was the candidate of the assisted immigrant and the Ethiopian, Bryan of the native-born Americans; and I submit it to a candid world which of these two parties was likely to have the good of this country most at heart, or know best how to promote it.

* * *

I am obliged to my friends for divers and surdry scraps of information regarding the cur-ristian trustee of Baylor who led the last assault upon me in the name of a long-suffering Savior. It would make interesting reading for Waco Baptists no doubt, but I can put these columns to better use than rehashing ancient history. Those who are anxious to learn what kind of an animal this member of Baylor's board of managers actually is, are referred to the Galveston News of July 26th, 1883. Any one can secure access to the files of that paper for the asking. I cannot afford to "damn to everlasting fame" every backwoods hypocrite who raises a howl. The Iconoclast leaves such cattle to the bill collectors.

* * *

I would like to have a flash-light photo of W. S. Densickr of Lebanon, Ind. Ter., not for publication, but to add to my private gallery of hypocritical rogues. Densickr wants to build a temple of pure gold twelve miles square and 60,000 high for some backwoods congregation, but of what denomination he has evidently not yet discovered. He insists, however, that the Redeemer demands such a temple, and that the general public should be forthcoming with the necessary cash. He is working what he calls a "church chain"—all for Christ. He writes you a letter asking you to contribute 5 cents to the cause and thereby obtain the blessing of God. He requests also that you send an exact copy of his letter to three of your friends whom you deem most likely to invest their small change in heavenly grace. The "chain" of letters runs from 1 to 100, and a Cleburne gentleman who was "touched" figures it out that the 25th No. means more than 282 billion letters and more than 21 millions of money if every sucker bites at the bait. If the "chain" doesn't break before the 100th number is played it will corral all the wealth of this world. Mr. Densickr hath a great head. He's a church financier for your galways. Still I opine that the man who complies with his apparently modest request is one large piebald ass who ought to be saddled, bridled and ridden around the block, then turned loose to do the Nebuchadnezzer act.

*   *   *   *   *

THE GOO-GOOS AND TAMMANY'S TIGER.
BY H. S. CANFIELD.

For the giant spoils of Greater New York three contestants are in the field. They are the regular Republican organization, Tammany and the "Citizens' Union." The regular Republican organization is headed by United States Senator Thomas C. Platt, and its active, or rather its most visible manager, is ex-Representative Lemuel Eli Quigg. Tammany still has John Croker for its boss, although John C. Shenan is its official head. The "Citizens' Union" is composed of the truly good and every man is its chief. It has for its candidate Seth Low, president of Columbia University.

This organization is one of the results of a long continued era of official corruption that has no parallel in modern municipal history. Until times quite recent Tammany has had things all its own way in the Eastern metropolis. The extent of corruption was not suspected until the Lexow investigating committee brought it to light. It is certain that not even the committee itself conceived the vastness of the system of thuggery and blackmail. Having begun its labors, evidence poured in upon it in a constantly increasing stream. It could do no less than go ahead. Its prosecuting attorney, John C. Goff, who not so many years ago was a counter jumper in a big New York store, and is now the city recorder at a salary of $12,000 a year and perquisites, woke to find himself famous. The Lexow committee was indirectly a result of the Parkhurst crusade and the Parkhurst crusade was made necessary by an unheard of state of public immorality. Of Parkhurst and Lexow the "Citizens' Union" is the child and more than the child. It stands for purity in politics and the rights of the honest citizen. It objects to high salaries and little work. It desires economy in public places. It wants each vote counted once and only once. It believes in the civil service. It swears by Teddy Roosevelt. It thinks that the workingman is able to judge for himself. It does not think that the world is governed enough. It is certain that it has in its ranks young men of vigor and intellect who would draw salary and serve the public in a manner hitherto never approached. It boasts that it is "the better element." It does not know the alphabet of politics. It is virtuously theoretical and practically impotent. It cannot be brought to understand that successful politics demands a "machine." Each of its individual members is a boss. They have been derisively termed "goo-goos," which is a contraction of "goody-goods." They are youthful, sanguine, patriotic, impertinent, impractical and self-sufficient. Their idea of conducting a campaign is nebulous. They believe that a number of voluble young men, clad irreproachably in evening dress and touring the city in carts after nightfall, stopping on corners and haranguing the multitude, cannot fail to command success. They have a large campaign fund, which will go to the printing of esoteric literature and the hire of carts. There is good in them and any amount of energy. Recognizing this, the leader of the regular Republican organization asked them for a conference. They bouncingly refused. It was explained to them that the best effort of every honest man in Greater New York was needed to defeat Tammany and that a divided front meant defeat, but they would have none of it. "Come into our camp," they said, and be soldiers under us. Accept our commands. Do as we say, work as we direct, spend as we decide, or go to the devil." This being so, the veterans of the regular Republicans, men who have fought through dozens of campaigns and know the meaning both of victory and defeat, naturally decided to go to the devil.

Mr. Low, the candidate of the "Citizens' Union," is a good man. He is a kind man. He is a gentleman and a scholar. He is an educator. Columbia University loves him. All through the campaign its students will give their college yell for him with vigor and much satisfaction to themselves. He has friends who believe in the massive strength of their own influence. But it is to be feared that he will be butchered to make a tiger's holiday. His personal characteristics are all that they should be. His morals could not be improved, but he will know more in November than he knows now. It is to be doubted that the New York voter will rush to the polls and plump ballots for him with the frenzied enthusiasm of which he has been told. The New York voter is a low animal at best, much lower than the Chicago voter, and he enthuses only when filled with beef and beer. Tammany understands him. Thomas C. Platt understands him. Tammany and Thomas C. Platt are not saying a word. They are sitting still and watching the inception of the meteoric canvass of Low.

Integrally the "Citizens' Union" is all right. The trouble lies in the fact that it believes that no good men can come out of Nazareth. There is but one right way, and it has that way. It is purse-proud, bull-headed and inexperienced. It will hold daily conferences with Mr. Low. It will fill him with vain hopes and longings and it will send out the young men on the carts. Also it will publish essays on the dignity of the American ballot. These essays will be written by its own scribes, who will joy to see themselves in print, and they will be scattered broadcast through the city. They will serve to wrap up butter pats and as tails to small boys kites. They will not be read, of course, for who, in the hurly-burly of a city campaign, has time or inclination to read tracts?

The Citizens' Union will not make a house-to-house canvass; it will not make and keep a record of the name, business and preference of every voter; it will not have trained proselyters at work; it will not organize clubs; it will not descend to the brutish level of the torchlight procession; it will not employ the agonizing brass bands; it will not send out men on election day whose business it is to see that every voter gets to the polls at least once, and more times if necessary.

The regular Republican organization ought to win, but it entered the contest heavily handicapped. If the tiger of Tammany again inserts a paw into the public treasury and converts the humblest office into a reward for rascality, the responsibility will rest directly upon the "Citizens' Union" — whose self constituted mission is to purify politics and elevate the ballot box.

The success of Tammany would be deplorable—calamitous. It would mean the restoration of the old era of trickery, jobbery and blackmail in a richer and wider area. But, owing to the split among those who ought to know better, it has never in its history had a better opportunity, nor has it ever fought for so grand a prize. "Greater New York" is composed of the original city, Brooklyn, which by the census of 1890 contained more than 900,000 people, several Long Island towns, suburban to Brooklyn, and a large part of Westchester county, lying north of the city proper. The total population will approach 4,000,000. The taxable wealth is enormous. The number of salaried place holders is close to 25,000. The salary list that is disbursed monthly runs far into the millions. Once in possession of this enormous power, Tammany would build up a machine to pale the records made by the administration of Boss Tweed. There was never any reason for the formation of "Greater New York" other than the fear that Chicago would oustrip the old town in the race for pre-eminence among American cities. There were grave reasons against it, chief among them being the acquisition of an enormous debt and the affording of an opportunity for plunder at the hands of the organization that now threatens. It is certain that the citizens of older New York have carried their pigs to a bad market. If history teaches anything, they will live to regret that they allowed urban pride to run away with common sense.

The methods of Tammany are well known. It is preeminently the American representative and practitioner of the low and effective in politics. It is the oldest and most powerful political society this country has ever known, and possibly ever will know. It is twofold. There is the Tammany general committee, to which any citizen of the city who is a Democrat, may belong. It numbers some 100,000 members. There is a wheel within a wheel, called the Society of Tammany. This is a secret concern, whose lodge-room is in the hall on Fourteenth street, near Third avenue. All of the leading Tammanyites belong to it. From its ranks the executive committee is chosen. It keeps the rolls and the records, makes the assessments, appoints the captains of the various election precincts, holds them responsible for the discipline of their men, rewards faithful service and punishes treachery. The society makes no special pretensions to purity. Its motto is to the victors belong the spoils. While Democratic in politics and of large influence in the national councils of the Democracy, it has never hesitated to sacrifice a national candidate for local gain. It is of and for New York City first, last and all the time. Occasionally it is loyal to a presidential candidate, but more often it is disloyal. Trades are always possible. For instance, it was true to Mr. Cleveland in 1884 and untrue in 1888. It was true again in 1892, and there is no doubt that at the last general election its members were told to knife Mr. Bryan whenever they wished.

It is the most persistent and thoroughly equipped warrior in our political lists. There is not a square foot of New York City that it does not know. On the day before election it is able always to tell within a fraction the number of votes it will poll. Every member is forced to go to his voting place and deposit his ballot. The political preference of every man in every precinct of every ward is known. Its agents are everywhere and always at work. It spends money like water. It is quick to reward and fierce to punish. It has no sentiment. It battles for so much place, so much power and the handling of so many dollars. If it wins, its spoils are promptly and equitably divided. Against such a machine, so intelligently and mercilessly handled, a divided enemy is almost certain beaten. The Republican party of New York and the respectability of New York are able to defeat Tammany when they go hand in hand, but only when they go hand in hand. It is to be feared that the chasm between them in the present campaign is not to be bridged. Their active and unscrupulous foeman may be trusted to leave no stone unturned and no device untried.

Chicago, Ill., October 1.

*   *   *   *   *

THE HON. BARDWELL SLOTE, OF COHOSH.
BY JUNIUS.

The man whom poor dead Billy Florence used to make the dominant, laughter-breeding memory-haunting figure in "The Almighty Dollar," is with us still. He infests Washington for many months of each year. He saves the country with persistency. I purpose to tell of him as I have known him. A residence of three years in the Capital City and a daily converse with its legislators has convinced me that nearly all congressmen are Bardwell Slotes, more or less. It is a fact that to a dweller in the District of Columbia there are no great men. Washington people are valets to these heroes. They get to know them with their rouge and corsets off. The sight is not pretty, but it is instructive. Sometimes it fills a man with despair of the future of this country. It convinces him that the greatest republic of history cannot hold together for another century. It makes him think that statesmanship is dead, never to resurge, and that its place is taken by narrow foul politics. But generally mirth comes as a relief. There is so much of the ridiculous in the modern American Cicero or Catiline that one's visions of his shortcomings is blurred by the tears that laughter brings.

In nine cases out of ten the man sent to Washington to represent his people is uneducated. In the tenth case he is ill-bred. I once showed to twenty congressmen the following stanza, asking them to translate it.

> "Le bruit est pour le fat,
> La painte est pour le sot,
> L'honnete homme s'eloigne trompe,
> Et ne dit pas mot."

It is the simplest of French doggerel and means, freely translated, that while the fat-headed and the weakly foolish do a great deal of jawing when mistreated by the powerful, the sensible man picks himself up and totes himself far from the neighborhood wherein he is unwelcome and never says a word. Of my twenty congressmen but one offered a translation. That was the dead William H. Crane, of Texas. The men were taken at random, and I may say that I did not expect any translations when I started out. Most frequently a man gets to congress through a practically acquired knowledge of dirty politics backed by the ability to make a stump speech, to tell a smutty story, and to plead for his job with a slavish lickspit-tleism that would disgust a Digger Indian. The ordinary congressional candidate when smitten upon one cheek will turn the other, and when smitten upon the other will hoist his coat-tail and request the honor of a kick.

It is but natural that a job which is obtained by eating filth and drinking filth and sleeping in filth is held to with a tenacity that rises superior to all manliness and all decency. The congressman knows but one God—the people who elected him. He has but one object—to pleasure those people and get a renomination. He does not represent the United States of America. He represents his district. His idea of statesmanship is to get as many federal jobs for the voters of his District and as many and large federal appropriations for his District as he can. That is all of it. Any individual Congressman, if he had his way would fill the government places entirely from his District and erect a Federal post-office and custom house at every cross roads in his Districts. If he could do these things, he thinks he would be certain of reelection, and he is right. Federal patronage is a fanged whip that hangs ever above his shoulders and occasionally it falls. The recipient of the blow cringes, cowers and howls like a beaten hound, but he does not resent. When Grover Cleveland called the Fifty-third congress into extraordinary session, the object being to repeal the Sherman act and utterly demonetize silver, thus completing the vast robbery of 1873, he knew that there was a pro-silver majority against him, but he knew also that he held the handle of the patronage whip in his fat beer-swelled hand and that his slaves would troup to do his will at the first crack of its lash. The result justified his confidence. The Democratic party had a majority of nearly 100 in the house of representatives, but that majority voted directly against its convictions. It was told that it would get no jobs for constitutents until it had surrendered its honesty. American history contains no such pitiful instance of cowardice and grovelling meanness. Instead of one Benedict Arnold selling his soul for temporary gain, we had fifty. It did the soul of me good to read the returns of the next Congressional election and to know that the truckling, craven disgusting majority was wiped out as a boy rubs a wet sponge across a slate.

The Hon. Bardwell Slote is a large man at home and a giant to his wife. In his first term he comes to Washington a month ahead of the date set for the assembling of Congress, because he wants the Capital to get used to him gradually. He hires a couple of rooms in a hotel. His wife puts some flowers on the mantel piece in the sitting-room and wears her best dress all the time while she is waiting for the president's consort and the cabinet ladies to call. They do not call. The Hon. Slote is shocked almost to dumbness to discover that the Capital does not know that he is on earth. Beyond a two-line "personal" in the morning paper, jammed among the "hotel arrivals," no mention is made of his coming. He has bills in his trunk providing for a public building at Bungtown and a deep water harbor at Squashville and a light house on Jim Ned creek and the establishment of a federal court at Eden and a governmental survey of the bad lands around Dogtown, and the Bungtown Bazoo and the Squashville Cresset and the Eden Echoe and the Dogtown Democrat have all stated that he intended to make speeches on every one of them, but the general public does not seem to take much interest in these foreshadowed cataclysmal events. Posing on the sidewalk in front of his hotel, with his legs wide apart, his hands behind him and his breast well out, a couple of small boys passing remark that he is "de new jay f'on Injyanny," and that is all the notice he gets. The attitude was very effective at home, but it does not seem to excite awe in the District of Columbia.

Once in his seat on the floor of the House he discovers that he is merely a unit in the majority or the minority. Nobody asks his advice about anything. The tally clerk calls his name in a careless manner. He cannot catch the speaker's eye. He bobs up half a dozen times in the first hour with intent to make a motion about something and sinks back limply. The voice, face and manner that were wont to still the conventions at home are no good. The newspaper men in the gallery over the speaker's head point at him and whisper to each other and then they laugh. It makes him uncomfortable. The next day the clipping bureau sends him thirty or forty paragraphs like this:

> "The Hon. Bardwell Slote, of the Cohosh district, Indiana, made his first appearance on the floor yesterday. He experienced some difficulty in delivering his half dozen speeches on the various manuscripts in his trunks. The speaker was savagely oblivious. The Hon. Slote will add much to the gaiety of nations. The distinctive articles of his attire were a red cravat, a coat of the vintage of '49, a tobacco-stained shirt-front and a whisp of oakum-colored chin beard. As a bit of bric-a-brac, or a curio from one of the oldest portions of the unhallowed west, he will be of value in the interior decoration of the Capitol, but it is to be feared that his oratorical vent has been choked up for some time to come."

As time goes on the Hon. Slote finds his uses. He visits the departments with persistency. He is followed by a trail of officeseekers from home. He finds that he must wait like a servant in the ante-rooms of the secretaries. He does not wield much influence. His party leaders realize the value of his vote and order him to cast it when they want it. The qualities of the man bring him forward. He has been a heeler in the small politics of his own county and he becomes a wrestler with two or three hundred heelers from other parts of the republic. The professional widow, clad in the sable habiliments of woe, takes him into a quiet corner and leans against him hard. The Hon. Slote becomes wildly excited and promises to leg for her bill. He legs for it until it passes and goes up to the court of claims. Then the widow knows him no more. A young lady, with freshly colored cheeks and golden hair streaming down her back, looks at him tenderly in the House restaurant. He follows her outside the Capitol and boards a car with her and scrapes acquaintance with her, and goes back to his lean but fiery wife some time that night, looking and feeling like a dissipated tom cat stealing homeward over the roofs in the gray of a chilly morning. He is introduced to the poker game at Chamberlin's and finds that he can hold more big hands and get more of them beaten than in any place he ever saw in his life. He discovers that the whisky sold in the Capitol is sudden death at a distance of 150 yards against the wind. He draws his first month's wage of $416 and finds that his resolution to save $316 of it might as well not have been made. His mileage money has been spent long before. The fact is borne in on him that it is necessary only that he answer to his name at 12 o'clock roll call. He will not be allowed to make speeches anyhow and can, if he chooses, fill in his time talking to the professional widow and the young lady of the restaurant.

At the end of the two years' term he returns to his home a wiser man. He encourages the idea that in order to get good results it is necessary to return a congressman for many sessions. He has had a taste of the fleshpots. He is sent back. At the next session he is an "old member." His capacity for chicanery has been increased by experience. Having little morals to start with, he is now as utterly conscienceless as it is possible for a man to be and keep out of jail. He gets his bills through by "fine work." He prefers to be known as a mole that works under ground. He has formed an ability to add materially to his income. He would get rich, but for the fact that his expenses have increased with his earnings. He has from one to four female employes of the government "on his staff." He seeks constantly for youthful typewriters. He has learned to dress in a manner that does not shock the populace. His voice takes on an unctuous greasy timbre. He has become something of an authority on canvas-back and wines. His head is full of "schemes" and the pre-requisite of them all is governmental appropriation. In return for his vote in favor of several more or less iniquitous measures, grabs and steals, he has obtained appropriations for the federal building at Bungtown and the light house at Jim Ned creek. The money for the deep water harbor at Squashville is carried in the general rivers and harbors bill and he has hopes that the federal court will sit at Eden the next year. He is more solid with his constituents. Many of them have been made postmasters and railway postal clerks and inspectors of various kinds. One of them has even been given a consulate at Demerara and writes many letters home bearing strange looking stamps. The Hon. Slote at this period is puffy under the eyes. Three Turkish baths a week keep him going. His wife has learned not to question him too closely, and, possible, has found consolations of her own.

So he goes on from year to year. He does not sink any lower in the scale of morality, because already he is about as low as he can get. When a man reaches a stage where he depends for his living altogether on public office and to obtain that office is compelled to fight politicians with their own weapons, not much more need be said than a simple statement of the case. When the day of his decapitation arrives—and it comes to him soon or late—he is apt to develop into a lobbyist. Having been a congressman gives him the right to the floor of the House or Senate. He will be found later on championing any bill that has money in it, no matter how patent the steal.

This description of the Hon. Bardwell Slote, of Cohosh, is not in any way over-drawn. It is, in fact, conservative, If an exact portraiture of him were given, the

Iconoclast would be unmailable. There are some men in the American House of Representatives who are ornaments to the Republic. They are honest, patriotic and intelligent. But they are woefully few. Slote may stand for the ruck of them. They are immoral and pestiferous demagogues, robbing the public whose pay they draw, and willing to go any length to maintain their seats. Washington is notoriously a rotten city, sexually and politically, and the representatives in Congress, more than any other component of the body civic, help to make it so.

This state of affairs will continue until men are chosen by the people distinctly for merit and past services, and for these things only. There are in the state of Texas to-day, and in every other state of the Union, for that matter, a hundred demagogues who are known to be demagogues. They have fed like buzzards upon the rotting offal of politics and the people continue to vote for them. Every now and then the Iconoclast reaches out and whacks one of them a fell blow upon his sconce, but, having tied up his head, he once again returns to his business of craving alms at the hands of his fellows.

If I wanted to send a daughter of mine to perdition, I would leave her in Washington dependent upon the influence of some congressman on the wrong side of forty. If I wished to insure for my son a liberal and eternal dose of hell-fire, I would set before him any one of two hundred representatives and tell him to follow their example in all things. The girl might land as a leader in low-necked bare-armed and swell-busted society or in a bagnio and the boy might land in Congress or in the penitentiary.

Washington, D. C., November 23, 1897.

*   *   *   *   *

MONDE AND DEMI MONDE.

BY ETHELYN LESLIE HUSTON.

Once upon a time in the city of Detroit there lived a society woman who was very wealthy. Her home was one of the most regal of the Woodward avenue mansions. Her aristocratic limbs were clothed in the softest of silks, her delicate hands were weighed down with costliest jewels, her retinue of servants were worthy the princely hospitalities she extended to those of her august order, and her charities—upon occasion—were as munificent as the gifts of gods.

This woman was very fair to look upon, and her life seemed a path of rose leaves upon which all the graces smiled. But there was a canker at the heart of all this loveliness, the deadly breath of the Upas tree sometimes pierced its incense, the hidden head of a coiled asp now and then stirred the laces nestling at her breast. And the tiny asp that slept on her heart was Rumor, that she could not kill, yet whose sting meant death. And when it moved, her lips whitened with fear, but she soothed it back to the warmth of slumber and strewed lavish gifts on the altar of charity. And then for awhile, the asp slept. And so it was that upon one of these occasions the asp moved restlessly, through the soft music of the cultured voices around her there crept an ominous hiss as the little green head parted the perfumed lace.

And the woman knew that her frailties were many and the hiss was Truth, and that all her loveliness was but a whited sepulcher that hid the ghastly bones of a murdered womanhood.

So with her jeweled hand she soothed the asp and gathered about her the women of her kind and told them that as the man of Nazarath had walked among the fallen so ought they. And these women arranged that they should go to the Magdalens of their city and teach them the error of their way and lead them gently into the treadmill of factory and sweat-shop to earn their daily bread and butter and olives.

So in a holy band of six they sought the gilded haunt of sin and asked Madame R— —if they might talk for a while with her-er-young ladies. The former smiling-ly acquiesced and they were courteously ushered into a stately drawing-room, where a number of the-er-young ladies listened with equally smiling interest to their dissertations on the beauties of a moral life. She of the asp moved to the rear of the drawing-room, where a woman with a delicate, refined face was sitting at a grand piano. Her eyes had a touch of tragedy and a great weariness in their depths, but as they rested gravely on her guest there was the faintest soupcon of amusement under their drooping lids. "My dear," quoth the grande dame, very gently, "forgive me if I intrude on delicate ground, but I want to ask—to know— that is—," very regretfully, "just tell me why do you lead a sinful life?"

The other woman was silent for a moment, then she spoke with equal gentle-ness:

"Madame, I was deserted when a girl-wife with a little child to support. I led this sinful life to support my baby and myself. And now, may I ask in return what is your reason?"

Here the chronicle ended, but the incident is still fresh in the memories of the City of the Straits' most exclusive 150. It is reluctantly admitted by those who labor sincerely among the world's unfortunates that the reformation of a fallen woman is more difficult than the twelve labors of Hercules. They are of two classes—the naturally depraved and the victim of circumstances. The former is utterly hopeless because her nature is too coarse-fibred to even realize, let alone heed, her own infamy. The latter is equally hopeless because she realizes too much. And how reform the half-world when society leads so gaily? "We dance along Death's icy brink, but is the dance less fun?" If morals are lax for sheer amusement, among those of the purple, what wonder if Moses' tablet grew dim to the people! Did the glorious and glittering sin of the French patricians teach the grisette patience with her lowly lot? Or did not her frantic fingers twist in the soft, perfumed tresses of proud heads, with shrieks for the guillotine the more fierce because of the toil-worn hands?

But she of the *monde* draws her costly laces over the little asps and gives with the dainty hand of a pictured Lady Bountiful, while her word smiles approval. And she of the half-world, who realizes too much!—what she is, who gave heart and soul and body to a supreme self-abnegation only to be struck back from the blaze of her heaven with the brazen clamor of its closing gates clashing through her stunted brain—she gathers the rags of her life around her and flies, a haunted and a hunted thing to the blackest depths, that can strangle thought and memory and brain. She laughs, too, over her whited sepulchre, but it is a laugh with painted lips and a merriment whose end is madness. We do not ask her for charity,—when we remember her at all, it is to clutch her wages of sin from her grasp to add to the city's tax. And it is not the green asp of Rumor that sleeps in her breast, covered by jewelled fingers, but under her thin hand burns the flame of Vathek, eating always with its crimson torment till heart and reason are charred and black and dead.

We cannot forgive her, so we fine her. Her name is in the Black List, not the Blue Book. She sins and suffers, while the other sins and smiles, and we lash the woman while we laud the wanton.

Of what avail are our home and refuge and retreat—empty shells of stiff formula and strict red tape? Hospitals to the coarse class, perhaps, but is it there a racked soul would turn while in her tottering brain the armed hosts of heaven and hell wage war?

Of what avail are creed and dogma and ritual, when we ourselves "bow the knee to pomp that loves to varnish guilt"? Of what avail our benevolence that offers, not the Christ-touch of pity and understanding, but the bitter bread of craven servitude and Pharisaical condescension, that says "thou art vile and lost for all time?"

We laud the wanton because she has wealth and power. She buys our favor with her wines and feasts, and blinds our willing eyes with her gifts and charities, and we only murmur with pensive gentleness "who shall judge!"

We are such cultured black-mailers, such refined bribe-seekers, such sensitive sycophants, while she obeys the eleventh commandment and is properly discreet she feeds us epicurean favors as she feeds her English pug bon-bons. And we are careful that the face of the dog shall express the greater intelligence.

And the woman with the flame in her heart? From her we have nothing to gain so—what would you? Her nature was too great to be discreet. She sinned grandly, but the height of her sin made deeper the depths of her soul abasement and her self-torment was too horrible to clothe itself in the tawdry draperies of diplomacy. She bared herself to the whips of the avenging furies, she cowered before the wrath of outraged God, and to her there was no guerdon possible for the shattered chrystal of her girlhood. When her heaven thrust her out, to her there was only left the world's hell of lost souls. And we in our wisdom accept her own sentence and our lips are silent. We feast the wanton who is wise and bracket Marguerite with Messalina. We kiss the one and curse the other, because the one is a hypocrite in the halls of splendor and the other honest in the haunts of shame. We hover around the one with flatteries and soft courtesies, and we hound down the other with pitiless vengeance, human and divine.

And in all this does our world show its shallowness and its immeasurable stupidity. How dare woman say to her sister woman, "I am better than thou!" In how much has she been tried and tempted? How much does she know of life and its hideous tests? How much does she know woman's love that is at once her glory and her shame, her crown and her crucifix, her heaven and her Calvary? How dare she judge? Has she ever faced the uphill battle where her two hands alone fought the ravenous wolves of Want and Hunger? Has she ever slipped her bared arm thro' the iron staples and held it there, while they howled in fury outside, and this iron cut and bruised and tore flesh and nerve,—till her teeth sank through tongue and lips and her eyes grew misty and dim with torture worse than death? Has she ever done all this—while her strength reeled and failed and through it all she cursed God for the white fear in the faces of those who loved and lived upon her? Has she ever felt that sickening *give*, as the hell-hounds swept her back and down, and in her blind despair she would clutch at aid though it were steeped in all the infamies from here to hades? Has she ever known all this?—she who would draw her silken shirts aside? Then if she have not, let her strip her heart of its stainless selfishness and her limbs of their ignorant ease; let her go out into the world where women live and strive and suffer, and let her humbly crawl to the feet of those women whose toil worn hands and weary faces and scarred hearts and souls shame her shallow usefulness, and let her lay her mouth in the dust and cry "Peccavi!"

How dare she judge! Who is she, with her pitiless eyes and useless hands and ignorant heart and narrow life,—who is she to question lives that in all their ruins are as grand, compared to hers, as a ruined temple compared to a child's painted toy. Would she write of Rome with the pearl and gold bauble on her dainty, inlaid desk? Would she measure the Pantheon with the little yardstick of her own intellect? Would she weigh Caesar's life and motives on the jeweled letter-scales of her own experience? Would she gauge Jove by the character of her curate?

If she can do this, then is she competent to voice her judgment on the most profound of all mysteries—human life.

Boise City, Idaho, November 12.

*   *   *   *   *

MACHIAVELLI.
BY WILLIAM MARION REEDY.

One of the best books issued this year is the thin pamphlet, you might call it, which contains Mr. John Morley's lecture on Machiavelli. It will repay any reader from what standpoint soever he may approach the character. "The veering gusts of public judgment have carried incessantly along, from country to country, and from generation to generation, with countless mutations of aspect and of inuendo, the sinister renown of Machiavelli."

Truly this man of all men, since Judas, has attained an immortality of infamy. Long was it thought that the common domestic title of the devil, "Old Nick," was an abbreviation of Machiavelli's Christian name. Hudibras fathered that myth, but now we know, Mr. Morley says, that the familiar appellation of the Evil One is a remnant of Norse mythology, deriving from Nyke, the water-goblin.

For three centuries all the evils of all political systems and policies have been attributed to the evils of Machiavelli's logic. Church and State alike have claimed he was the champion of the other's cause. He was Jesuit and atheist as it suited the turn of any vituperative polemist. He was Reformer and "Romanist" as the advocates of Rome or Reformation happened to interpret him. His is, certainly, an unique greatness. There has been in his work, as in all great works, something for all men; but that something has been always, for three centuries, something bad. It is no wonder, therefore, that there prevailed once, a belief that the Devil himself had written his chief book. I have always had an idea that Goethe in drawing Mephistopheles, glanced from the tail of his mind's eye at Machiavelli for a model. Machiaveli appears to come nearer than any human being to realizing the Goethe conception of Intellectual Evil.

The man, still, may be infamous, but—he is intensely human. The baseness of him has its basal strength in his founding upon man. He is the only realist philosopher. Besides him Bacon is a dreamer. Machiavelli was and is the master misanthrope, and,—God help us!—we must admit that his misanthropy only too well is founded on fact. He seems to have been the most perfect incarnation of that "accomplished and infamous Italy," which gave us the Borgias and the terrible Elizabethan plays of Tourneur, Webster and Ford, with their plots of incest and murder, that Italy which was a veritable Hell out of which rose the Renaissance. He was the philosophy of that Italy. He first said, in effect, that nothing succeeds like success. He first cast aside Plato and his dreaming and Aristotle and his elements. He was the father of the philosophy of "practical politics." Francis Bacon learned of Machiavelli, who "wrote what men do and not what they ought to do." This is the philosophy of fact. He dealt with men as he found them. He was a sublime, almost a diabolical opportunist I have often thought Benjamin Franklin, with his "honesty is the best policy," is another Machiavelli, only touched a little with the pharisaism of the Puritan. With the Italian anything that would win is the best policy, and this is his honest estimate of men. The best policy was the policy adopted, after looking the facts of life and of human nature squarely in the face and finding that the end was to be attained easiest either by honesty or dishonesty. To "get there," as we say, was the faith of Machiavelli.

Idea and ideal meant nothing to the author of "The Prince." What we know as "moral forces" this Italian ignored. He judged humanity by its lowest average of motive or intelligence. There was but one general law, for him, and that was that it was right to deceive, if force were of dubious effect, in affairs of State. It were well to be honest, if one could, as a ruler of the State, but it was his duty to rule and triumph by any means between the extremes of simple lying on the one hand, and poisons or other assassination on the other.

Machiavelli was born in 1469. He was a governmental secretary in Florence and met many of the strangely fine and fiendish characters of that time. He went on four missions to the King of France; was an intimate of Caesar Borgia; was an emissary of the Florentine republic to Pope Julius II, and was with Maximilian to Innsbruck. Those were stormy times, and Machiavelli studied the storms. He belonged to the popular party—and his masterpiece is a manual for tyrants. After 1512, with the return of the Medici, he lost his place, was imprisoned, was put to the torture, was amnestied by Leo X and withdrew to San Casciano, where he lived a life almost idyllic in its manner, to judge by a description from his own pen which Mr. Morley has incorporated in his lecture. It was there he wrote the book "The Prince," at forty-five, dedicating it to Lorenzo the Magnificent. The dedication was a bit of palaver to the tyrant who had destroyed Florentine freedom. It was several years before he was rewarded by a small employment and then he was commissioned to write the history of Florence which he finished and dedicated to Leo X, in 1527. Here, also, it is supposed, he wrote a comedy, much praised and unremembered. He was a shrewd man, as his writings aver, yet he made a failure of his own life, to a large extent. He was cheerful in his ill-fortune, however, and he "clung to public things," and, after his comedy, wrote the dialogues of the "Art of War," to induce his countrymen to substitute for mercenary armies a national militia—to-day one of the organic ideas of the European system. Just as Machiavelli entered public life Savonarola had gone to the stake for an idea. The spirit of Dante touched him not at all. He was a man of his time, but not of the very best of his time. And yet he wrote that he loved his country with his whole soul. Mr. Morley says, "and one view of Machiavelli is that he was always the lion masquerading in the fox's skin, an impassioned patriot, under all his craft and jest and bitter mockery. Even Mazzini, who explained the ruin of Italy by the fact that Machiavelli prevailed over Dante, admits that he had 'a profoundly heart.' " Machiavelli died in 1527.

He was a man of affairs. He had read the ancients who dealt with politics, and he assimilated what he read, Mr. Morley says that it was as true of Florence in the Sixteenth Century as of Athens, Corinth, Corcyra in the Fifth Century before Christ, as set forth in Thucydides, that it was a prey to intestine faction and the ruinous invocation of foreign aid. "These terrible calamities," says Thucydides, "always have been and always will be, while human nature remains the same. Words cease to have the same relations to things, and their meanings are changed to suit the ingenuities of enterprise and the atrocities of revenge. Frantic energy is the quality most valued, and the man of violence is always trusted. That simplicity which is a chief ingredient of a noble nature is laughed to scorn. Inferior intellects succeed best. Revenge becomes dearer than self-preservation, and men even have a sweeter pleasure in the revenge that goes with perfidy than if it were open." If any reader of the ICONOCLAST desires a splendid picture of this Italy, I refer him to Vernon Lee's "Euphorion," which pictures the land as an inferno. Mr. Morley, too, gives a vivid picture of the time, saying that Italy of that date "presents some peculiarities that shed over her civilization a curious and deadly irridescence." How one thinks of Ingalls and his "honesty in politics is an iridescent dream." To resume our Morley. "Passions moved it in strange orbits. Private depravity and political debasement went with one of the most brilliant intellectual awakenings in the history of the western world. Another dark element is the association of merciless selfishness, violence, craft and corruption with the administration of sacred things. If politics were divorced from morals, so was theology." Hired crime, stealthy assassination, especially by poison, prevailed. Contempt of human life, the fury of private revenge and the spirit of atrocious perfidy were characteristic of the luxurious Italian renaissance. Genius, according to John Addington Symonds, it was assumed, "released man from the shackles of ordinary mortality." These

Italian tyrants were touched with the Neronian malady. They were mad with power, with luxury, with ennui. Flowers of Evil bloomed profusely. In Italy, fair as it was, with the poets singing everlastingly of Spring, it seemed God has forgotten the world. The demonaic fascination of the land, then, is something the reader finds difficult to shake off. You move among and hold converse with splendid cultured monsters. The church alone kept alive purity, though it did not escape corruption. I think Dante and Michael Angelo proved that the pure religious spirit was not dead in a time when it was proclaimed that "it is best to sleep and be of stone, not to see and not to feel, while such misery and shame endure." There was a spirit recognizing the "misery and shame," and that spirit was in the church. Mr. Morley admits that Michael Angelo was such a spirit and Dante wrote in "La Vita Nuova" the first, pure, spiritual love-poem of the world.

Environed thus, and with a peculiarly Italian *morbidezza*, or *plasticity* we find Machiavelli. Others before had written of politics, but Machiavelli "had the better talent of writing." He wrote to tell things clearly. Imagination he had none, as an historian, and his comedy is in Limbo. He is all intellectual strength, but the moral influence is missing. He is, says Mr. Morley, simple, unaffected, direct, vivid, rational. He is as literal as a woman. His literal statement is his finest effect of irony. Mr. Morley's analysis of the Machiavellian style is itself a masterpiece of serene expression, rising with a solemn sense of the fearful absence of all principle, as we understand it, in the work, to a richly eloquent, and even tender, tribute to the moral beauty of life. I wish I might transcribe it and I hope that many will read it. It is rarer than anything you may remember of Macaulay's essay upon the everlastingly execrable Florentine.

"Men are a little breed" might have been Machiavelli's motto. Or he might have said "the more I see of men the better I like dogs." He is remorseless in seeing only that men are ungrateful, fickle, deceivers, greedy of gain, run-aways before peril, readier to pay back injury than kindness. "Worst of all they take middle paths." Upon these, his observations, he proceeds to tell a story of a State and he tells it icily. He lays bare the foulness of man. He doesn't lecture, he does not preach, he never laughs, never scolds, is never surprised. He shows, says Mr. Morley about "as good a heart as can be made out of brains." In my opinion, that sentence is the most terrible indictment in the book. It marks him as a monster worse than Frankenstein.

Machiavelli has no opinion to argue about; nothing but men's passions as they were and are. He is alive, always and everywhere, because he shows us men. He maintains, according to Mr. Morley, that the world grows no better and no worse. There is for him no "one far-off, divine event to which the whole creation moves." Nothing for him but Power. Good and evil concern him not. He recited what we call a crime as impassively as he recited a virtue. So-and-so did such and such. This followed. That is all. He is a fatalist with no more sound philosophy than this: "It is better to be adventurous than cautious, for Fortune is a woman, and to be mastered must be boldly handled. He was a republican, but he believed that strength was the secret of government—strength in itself and in mastery of those who make up the State. No half-measures for him. The State is his idol, if he have one. The State must be supreme in will, in vigor, in intelligence; unflinching, unsparing, remorseless. The humility of Christ has no part in his scheme. He knows no mercy and no justice. One almost can admire his inhuman disregard of men. He cared as little for them as Napoleon. He scorns all gentleness. And yet he thought well of the people, of their prudence and stability. He deemed them liable to err as to generalities but apt to be right as to particulars. Our experience, I dare say, is otherwise—no matter how we stand on the financial question. "Better far," he repeats an hundred times, "than any number of fortunes is not to be hated by your people." Not to be hated! That was as near as he could come to love. He is opposed to dictators and he speaks out plainly enough, in his discourses, about the unwisdom of slaying fellow-citizens, betraying friends, being without mercy, without religion. He is conventional enough in all this. When he comes to describe the Prince, who is to save the divided State, he does so in lines that make a picture at once to fascinate and affright mankind.

The Prince must save the State. He must be as good as he can be; at least, he must have no vices that will hurt the State, i. e. endanger his government. There are but two ways to govern, by law or force. The Prince must rule by one or the other, as necessity may dictate. He must mingle the lion and the fox. A Prince cannot keep faith, if keeping faith will hurt the State. Why? Because others will not keep faith with him. "It is frequently necessary—and here is the sentence that has done so much to damn its writer—for the upholding of the State, to go to work against faith, against Charity, against humanity, against religion; and a new Prince cannot observe all the things for which men are reckoned good." Reason of State is the only universal test for an action. Anything that may preserve the State is right. I wonder what Professor Felix Adler would think of this, with his proposal to make the State "take the place of the personal deity that is passing out of men's lives. Machiavelli was a fetich worshipper of the State. Preserve the State, say Machiavelli regardless of justice, or pity, or honor! As Diderot, quoted by Mr. Morley, said of this, it is an argument which should be headed, "The Circumstances under which it is right for a Prince to be a Scoundrel."

Caesar Borgia, the fiend, was Machiavelli's model, a man who rivalled all the atrocities of the worst Roman emperors. But Borgia failed. That matters not to Machiavelli. His failure was "due to the extreme malignity of fortune." Mr. Morley's rapid sketch of Caesar Borgia, ferocious, lustful in insane ways, treacherous, splendidly vile, is a glance into the Hell that was Italy. Machiavelli was in this man's train and frankly admired him and his methods. All the men of the times seemed to be wild beasts, and Borgia was as courageous, supple and sly as those with whom he dealt. Machiavelli, to do him justice, thought that Caesar Borgia and his father, the Pope, had design to pacify and to unify Italy. They worked with the material and with the tools to hand. Men did not shudder at treachery and assassination in those days. We must judge men by their surroundings. And it is difficult, even now, *vide* Turkey and Greece, "to govern the world by paternosters." As Mr. Morley says, "It is well to take care lest in blaming Machiavelli for openly prescribing hypocrisy, men do not slip unperceived into something like hypocrisy of their own. Each age has its own hypocrisy. Mr. Morley traces the influences of

Machiavelli, and finds them strong in William the Silent, Henry of Navarre, and Good Queen Bess. All these rulers dallied with creeds and were diplomats to the Machiavellian limit of duplicity. They burned and hanged and tortured on the plea of the strong State. Frederick, the Great, too, Mr. Morley classes as a pupil of Machiavelli, though, once, the "crank" on tall grenadiers threatened to write a refutation of "The Prince" and thereby drew from Arouet de Voltaire a characteristic mot. Napoleon, with his "reasons of State," was Machiavellian. Machiavelli presided at the shooting of D'Engheim. It was one of the last things which showed "what reason of State may come to, in any age, in the hands of a logician with a knife in his grasp."

From the influence of Machiavelli upon the Absolutists, Mr. Morley comes down to his influence in the Republican camp. Mazzini, he says "could not curse the dagger" and yet Mazzini was "in some respects the loftiest moral genius of the century." Mr. Morley does not believe that Machiavellism has pervaded party politics in Europe or America. I wonder if this be not a sample of Mr. Morley's Machiavellism—a reason of state at this time. If not Machiavellism, what, in God's name, are our platform straddles, our expediency candidates, our deals and dickers in tariff-bills, our endeavors to catch all kinds of votes from all kinds of "interests." I am not a silverite, but the regular Democrats made and out-and-out platform and did not hedge. I am a Democrat and glad that, though it "split us wide open," we fought out the issue just as we fought out the slavery issue. True Democrats, gold or silver, despise only the Machiavellists who talk of compromise. Machiavelli seems to have seen but one side of life—the worse. He knew but one kind of men—Italians of the sixteenth century. They were not normal. It is true that Nature is not moral, but if Machiavelli be right it were just as well that we should return to the conditions of life in Stanley Waterloo's "Story of Ab." Whether Nature be moral or not, at least men are. We must look at the facts. We have civilized our code of warfare. The greatest living diplomat is Leo XIII, and no one deems that he succeeds by deceit. Bismark says there is no success in lying, in diplomacy. Reasons of State are not, in the common consent of mankind, good reasons *per se*. "Talleyrand was false to every one but true to France." He was an avatar of Machiavelli, and he is despised, universally.

The Roman State has passed away. The Venetian and the Florentine States have passed. All the supreme States have vanished and they begun to fade just as soon as the Machiavellian idea began to prevail. The State is not the end of the existence of people. The State must grow broader and broader until, let us hope, we shall see "the parliament of man, the federation of the world." Our sympathy with Cuba, with the Armenians, with Ireland, with Poland, rises up to refute Machiavelli and his right of the State to crush for mere pleasure of power. "If Machiavelli had been at Jerusalem two thousand years ago, he would have found nobody of importance save Pontius Pilate and the Roman legionaries," says Mr. Morley. He forgot the moral force of the world. Machiavelli's fault is the Renaissance fault. The Renaissance turned to the past to reconstruct everything, and it copied, save in its architecture, only Antiquity's faults. It became diseased, trying to adjust itself to dead things. Life itself became corrupted; the Renaissance was to a large extent a birth out of degeneration.

Machiavelli was a scientist—a vivisectionist I should say. He preached, with a vengeance, the survival of the fittest. He is vital in his books today because he stands for the vitality of men's passions. He saw them and studied them and knew them. But upon passions nothing ever was builded. They shift and change. They cannot give a foundation of permanency to a State. They were the essence of that chaos out of which he thought to bring order in anarchic Italy, working on them and on them alone. Cunning, jealousy, perfidy, ingratitude, dupery were the instruments with which he would fashion out a State. And he knew that the State so wrought could not last, for he said the world grew no better; what made his State destroyed it, inevitably. Machiavelli ignored charity, which is in itself, justice, fidelity, gratitude, honesty and all the virtues. He was a man without hope and a man without love. What a great sad mad man he was, indeed.

St. Louis, November 15.

*   *   *   *   *

THE AMATEUR EDITOR.

The country appears to be overrun at present with amateur editors. When a man learns by sad experience that he hasn't sufficient sense to successfully steer a blind mule through a cotton patch, where the rows are a rod apart, he exchanges his double-shovel plot for the editorial tripod and begins "moulding public opinion" and industriously exchanging advertising acreage for something to eat. When Will Carleton's old farmer discovered that his son Jim was good for nothing else on God's earth he concluded to "be makin' an editor outen o' him." That practice prevails throughout the country to a very considerable extent to-day—the sanctum divides with the pulpit and the stage those incompetents who aspire to mount above the plow, yet lack the necessary brains to succeed in business, in medicine or at the bar. When a man fails at everything else he is apt to be seized with a yearning ambition to become an editor. He gets trusted for a shirt-tail full o' pied type, a pre-Raphaelite press, lays in a job-lot of editorial "we's" and a sawdust cuspidore, girds up his loins and begins to commence. His first task is to reform the currency system and instruct the universe in the esoteric science of economics. He may not be able to successfully float a butcher's bill, but he writes of finance with all the assurance of Alexander Hamilton. He may not know whether Adam Smith or Tommy Watson wrote the "Wealth of Nations"; but he doesn't hesitate to take issue with every economist from Quesnay to Walter—to utilize his paste-pot for arc light and play at Liberty Enlightening the World. These amateur editors are the curse of the country. They Guldensuppe John Stuart Mill and play Leutgert to Lindley Murray. It is some consolation, however, to reflect that they seldom last long. They unfold their wing-like ears and make a frantic flutter at the sun, only to come down beam first on some rocky islet in the Icarian sea. Their creditors do not have even the mournful satisfaction of contemplating the hole—the amateur editor invariably pulls it in after him. But until his first notes fall due he is an iridescent glory. He adores himself with a long-tailed hand-me-down Albert Edward and carries the universe in his arms. He pokes his meddlesome proboscis into everything and gives oodles of advice, unasked. He may not have as much principle as a tomcat in rutting time, but he poses before all men as a "guardian of public morals." When he places the awful seal of his disapproval upon a fellow mortal he expects to see him shrivel ups like a fat angle-worm on a sea-coal fire. He's a modern Balaam, peddling God's blessings and curses—for the long green. He imagines that an eager multitude sit up every night to catch the first dank copy of his little matutinal mistake—to see what he's got to *say*. He's garrulous as a toothless gran dam at a sewing circle, as busy as a canine eunuch when his kind do congregate. He discourses of everything, from the creation of the universe to Farmer Brown's visit to Bugleville. He fairly riots in editorial "leaders." He gives his "moral support"—and nothing else—to those local enterprises whose promoters jack him up with gobs of taffy on the mistaken hypotheses that his "flooence" may be useful. He has an idea that his miserable little journalistic misfit is "making the town" and is entitled to great wads of gratitude—that should his towline break the whole community would go awhooping to hades, the bottom would fall out of realty values and the streets be overgrown with Johnson grass. So he toils and sweats and stinks—imagines that he is roosting on the top rung of the journalistic ladder when he hasn't even learned his trade. Finally he falls through the bosom of his pantalettes. The sheriff levies on his stock of editorial "we's" the paste sours, the office cat starves, spiders festoon the sawdust cuspidore and the dust settles like a pall on his collection of worn type and wood-base railway cuts. The second-hand engine ceases to snort, the rat printers disperse and the wheezy old cylinder press no longer alarms the neighborhood. But in a little while another yap scraps up $40 in cash, catches a sucker to endorse his note and there's a renascence of the old plant. It is from shyster lawyers without clients, quack doctors without patients and peanut politicians without pulls that the ranks of amateur journalism are constantly recruited. Such people always imagine it dead easy to "run" a paper—that it is only necessary to grab the editorial stylus and pour forth their inexhaustible fund of misinformation to set the woods on fire. Such papers usually manage to wiggle through the fall and winter, for they can then sell advertising space at a dollar an acre, take pay in soft-soap and second-hand sad-irons and still make a reasonable profit—the time of their manipulators being worth nothing a week; but when the long dull summer dawns they go "up agin it" with a dull hollow groan. Every town between Sunrise and Last Chance has had experience galore with the amateur editor. He is one of those unhung idiots who rush in where angels fear to tread. He is an incorrigible but an unabateable nuisance. He never succeeds in making money for himself; he always manages to lose it for somebody else. You may mark this; The quack cannot achieve permanent success in any profession, in journalism least of all, for there his shortcomings cannot be concealed. To become a successful newspaper man one must begin at the bottom and climb by pure strength through long days of labor and nights of agony. It is the most exacting profession in the world today. It is true that some so-called yellow journals succeed in making money; but while they employ perverts they have no use for Smart Alecs and amateurs. Amateur journalists, like dog-fennel and jimson weeds, usually blossom in Jayville. Most Southern towns have suffered from their reckless depredations and will hail their excoriation with delight; still it

so much that he will pay handsomely for it and the charlatan finds a market for his wares. He does not like the plain truth bluntly stated. No one does. We do not admire those who wrestle and strive with us. Nevertheless, they alone strengthen our muscles and, hence—

* * *

Verily I say: "Ye who listen with credulity to the whispers of fancy, and pursue with eagerness the phantom of hope—who expect that age will perform the promises of youth, and that the deficiencies of the present day will be supplied by the morrow," need not attend to the history of Rasselas, Prince of Abyssinia, except for the passing pleasure of the reading, because the story can be told in fewer words, to wit: Happiness is a personal equation—"what is one man's meat is another man's poison." Rasselas found the Happy Valley irksome and intolerable. There never has been a Happy Valley since that could furnish continuous content to any one. The nearest approach to happiness comes with juxtaposition to one's tastes and aspirations. The simpler the tastes and the less discursive the aspirations, the nearer happiness comes and the longer it remains. Happiness does not come from conditions or surroundings, nor are these conditions or surroundings always understood. Actual conditions do not reveal themselves to perspicacity much less to casual observation. The multi-millionaire in his mansion or the king on his throne, surrounded by all the comforts and conveniences, all the marvelous treasures, all that is pleasing to the eye and to the senses, may not be happy—may be unhappy. The rustic who follows the plow through furrowed fields, unkempt, clownish, toil-stained, weary and overworked, may brawl raucous roundelay at even-tide and enjoy the fullness of earthly bliss. His neighbor similarly situated may suffer agonies because his tastes and ambitions are higher. Those who imagine "plow hands" have no ambitions to gratify know little of life. Sometimes they aspire to be presidents, and sometimes they gratify those aspirations, but they never know happiness. They may be as wise as a dozen Solons, but they can not provide happiness by legislation. They may reach the summit of earthly glory and strive to seize the fulgurant prize that lured them on, only to find a penumbra—the shadow of a shade. And if conditions are actually known they prove nothing, generally. Each case must be specialized. Children and grown people, for that matter, are subjected to involuntary fasts and oftimes go hungry, in fact are always hungry, but they suffer less and are healthier than those who are stuffed and pampered and sated. The joy of eating when food comes compensates for the previous scantiness of the fare. There are deaths from insufficient alimentation; ten to one are the deaths traceable to over-feeding. There is suffering for lack of food. There is ten to one more suffering by gouty and dyspeptic gourmands. The beggar shivers in the cold for lack of clothing; there is ten to one more suffering from over-swathing. For pain, actual, excrutiating; for pain invincible, somber and unutterable, one proud woman reduced to a last season's frock suffers more than twenty arrayed in customary rags and tatters. God tempers the wind to the shorn lamb, but not to the dowdy woman. The occupant of the cottage or cabin as he hurries home on Saturday night with his hard-earned store perhaps envies the occupant of the mansion where lights burn brightly and music fills the air, but the master of the mansion may be driven to the verge of insanity in an unequal contest to keep up appearances and a style of living that is grinding his heart into dust. Gladly, he thinks, he would court the modest shelter of the cottage or cabin but, alas! sorrow and suffering, want and wickedness might follow him there. From natal bed to mortuary box happiness escapes us—the faster, the more we pursue it.

We mistake appearances for realities and misbestow our sympathy. Had some of the more tender-hearted met Audubon when he returned from one of his trips in the forests, his clothing in shreds, his shoes gone, travel-stained and unkempt, alms would have been unhesitatingly bestowed. And how amused would the great man have been! He was too great to have been irritated. If, as it is claimed, human happiness is the aim and object of philanthropists, they seek the unattainable and destroy that which they would save. A sudden wrenching from the one condition to another is misery. The eagle would rather starve in his native forests than feast in a cage. The Indian maiden who graduates at Carlisle and who captures all the medals, returns to her blanket and the dirt, dogs and squalor of her tribe as soon as she reaches the reservation. There is a strain of the Huckleberry Finn in all natures that resents a too sudden metamorphosis and which will return to its rags, its back alley and empty cask. Charlatans of the law and of literature inculcate the idea that a change in conditions means the acquisition of unqualified bliss, and they assume that the poor are necessarily unhappy and endeavor to convince them—not a difficult task, that it is the fault of someone else that they are not rich! Folly! The hod-carrier and helot who works from dawn to dusk, who goes in rags, who fares on coarsest food, whose wife and children live in squalor, may be considered unhappy, but they never experience real suffering, acute, unasuageable, poignant grief, until they become possessed of money and mansions and modern grandeur, only to find themselves coldly isolated. Sudden wealth has made them too grand for their former friends, it cannot secure them entrance into the society which they would affect, or, if it does, they find themselves ill at ease, out of place, miserable. Those who imagine that all bliss comes from lucre or legislation know little and are "ignorant of their own ignorance." They do not know that "our own felicity we make is final, and that through the cultivation of individual inherency and personal sufficiency. They listen to the charlatans who, on the plea of bringing balm, inflict incurable wounds; who would bring happiness by sowing the dragon's teeth of discontent. "Coal-Oil Johnny," who threw away hundreds of thousands of suddenly acquired dollars, was a philosopher. The money put him out of harmony with himself. It was to him a curse. And he wisely rid himself of it. There is peace and pleasure in the jangling discord and in the pains of effort, a peace which, otherwise, the world can not give, a pleasure found nowhere else; and this peace and pleasure are not to be sought by effort; are not to be attained by effort; but are found in the effort itself. There is pleasure in dressing a field or in painting a house, but not in the dressed field or in the painted house. In other words, there is pleasure in individual assertiveness and not in inertia. No doubt either Calypso or Circe was more attractive than Penelope, but Ulysses was not content. He had to continue his wanderings even to his own home, and when he had killed of all the suitors and was restored to his diplomatic spouse, there were doubtless days when he wished himself back with the enchantress on the lovely isle—days when he would have changed places with his father, Sisyphus, and rolled the ever re-turning stone with will and energy. Ease and passivity were a torture to him.

A picture of life is painted by that wonderful artist, Gabrielle d'Annunzio, in "The Triumph of Death." Yes, I hear the hurtling of such missles as "decadent," "obscene," "vulgar," "impious." Nevertheless d'Annunzio is one of the great masters. His pigments may be mud or muck. His brush is the brush of an Angelo. His finished product is life itself, breathing, pulsing life, through which the blood rushes loud enough to be heard. Life in all its phases, from the loftiest to the lowliest. Demetrius, wealthy, scholarly, meditative, one would suppose needed no legislation or literature to make him happy. He possessed all the world had to give. "A mild, meditative man, with a face full of virile melancholy, and a single white curl in the center of his forehead among the black hair, giving him an old appearance." He sought earnestly and sedulously for the secret meaning of life. He tried to reach and unravel its symbols and allegories; he tried to interpret the furtive gestures which he beheld in the shadows, and he passed into deeper shadows and more oppressive silences through the ghastly gates of suicide, while his idiotic sister remained to chatter and grimace. Jaconda remained gibbering and pleased with the world and with herself. George saw this and he saw many other things which he could not understand. He saw "Oreste of Chapelles" firing the simple minds of the people to fanaticism as he went up and down like a fury. He saw the pilgrims at the sanctuary and the beggars and cripples on his return from the sanctuary to Cassalbordino—horrible monsters, not fashioned, or scarce fashioned in God's image, and he saw that they had their families and their belongings with them, that they piteously plead for alms and that they danced and sung, cursed and caroused, made merry over the deformities of each other, and presented a phase of life wholly incomprehensible. Laws or literature could not increase their happiness. Their apparent miseries were not real. He saw Colas, ignorant, stupid, superstitious, but content. He saw Candia, proud of her fecundity, slaving, singing. He saw Favetta, the young singer with the falcon-like eyes, the idol of her friends, simple, modest, happy. He saw the peasants in their mysterious rites "consecrating the nativity of bread" in the harvest field. They needed neither laws nor literature to improve their condition. They were the happiest of mortals. And he saw the dark tragedies of this remote world. Liberata carrying her dead child on her head to the burial place. No laws or literature for her, poor woman: her baby was dead and her reason was gone. He saw Riccangela, the widow, on the beach, with her large rough hands, pouring forth her heart in a wild monody over the remains of her puny boy, who was drowned, while the homicidal sea chanted a lugubrious accompaniment or mocked the agony of the song. George sought the meaning and the key to life's mysteries and found them not. Subjective study and spiritual contemplation drove him mad. They had driven his uncle Demetrious mad. He recoiled from them and plunged into life as he found it, endeavoring to extract from it the honey of happiness, or at least, immunity from misery. If carnalism could furnish content, one would think George would have found it. Rich to opulence, young, idle, he met Hippolyte, "a compound of pale amber and dull gold in which were mingled perhaps a few tints of faded roses." He won her and subjected her, "the bloodless, wounded creature who used to submit with profound astonishment, the ignorant and frightened creature who had given him that fierce and divine spectacle—the agony of modesty felled by vicious passion." He idolized her and idealized her in the struggle for perfect bliss. He took her to the deserted abbey and placed on "the summit of the high marble candelabra which had not heard the voice of the light for centuries," where she burned before his eye in the inextinguishable and silent flame of her love, and, as he believed, illuminating the meditations of his soul. Folly! His apotheosis was a farce. She developed, but not spiritually. What he supposed was a pure flame of love proved to be a base erotic fever. The bloom of pudicity was brushed off. She acquired a strange power over him; she, the once innocent and frightened creature. "She possessed the infallible science and knew her lover's most secret and subtle sensibilities and knew how to move them with a marvelous intuition of the physical conditions that depend on them and their corresponding sensations and their association and their alternatives." And from the thing of beauty and light, seen with enraptured eyes as she stood "on the summit of the marble candelabra which had not heard the voice of the light for centuries, she became a loved and hated thing, "the flower of concupiscence," "an instrument of low lasciviousness." The union of these two, perfect in all outward appearances, blessed with love and leisure, beauty and youth, and all that wealth could buy, was a mocking and a delusion because lacking in spirituality, because unsanctified and unholy. It was a monstrous tragedy, this union, presented on a stage of ashes over a volcano. (Unions in polite society, where forms are observed, laws obeyed and customs followed, but where the moving impulse is sordid, where the marriage is for money or for social position, do they, too, not drift toward mutual hate and abhorrence, to divorce or death? I only ask the question. There may be more Georges and Hippolytes in the world than we care to admit). When at last he discovered his true condition, when he realized that he was in her power that he could not live with her or without her, that she obstructed his way of life and his way to death, he caught her in his arms and hurled both over the precipice upon the rocks below, making a ghastly ending for a ghastly tragedy. No law or literature could have brought happiness to him. He sought it in the various ways, in every way but the one, simple and only right way—the effort to confer happiness on others. Frantic intoxications, the culminations of carnal pleasures, which amount to unspeakable ecstasies, are mere temporations which are followed by lassitude, exhaustion and disgust, and these soon turn to a fiercely implacable hate. The search for happiness, when carried to the extreme, becomes a torture. The desire for happiness is selfish, and selfishness is never happy. Happiness dispensed is like bread cast upon the water, and will return after many days. Those who seek it stray from it. All laws and all literature that arouse the spirit of discontent, of selfishness and of desire for happiness, are vicious because they defeat the very object which they seek to accomplish, and make people more miserable than they were by increasing their capacity for suffering without a coexistent power to gratify the desires aroused. What is this George Eliot puts into the mouth of the radical, Felix Holt? "This world is not a very fine place for a good many of the people in it. But I've made up my mind it shan't be the worse for me if I can help it. They tell me I can't alter the world—that there must be a certain number of sneaks and robbers in it, and if I don't lie and filch somebody else will. Well, then, somebody else shall, for I won't—I will never be one of the sleeks dogs—I would never choose to withdraw myself from the labor and common burden of the world; but I do choose to withdraw myself from the rush and scramble for money and position. Any man is at liberty to call me a fool, and say that mankind are benefitted by the push and scramble in the long run, but I care for the people who are alive now and will not be living when the long run comes. I prefer to go shares with the unlucky."

Irrefragible philosophy! The true and the wise proceed not to stir up the lees of passion and greed and avarice and ambition. They remain with the world, go with it in its devious ways and through its torturous windings, removing the thorns and briars from before naked feet, shielding the weak, sheltering the naked, encouraging and dispensing light and hope and love. The true and wise who love their fellows avoid strife and carnage, and conflict with the ineluctable, but they meet the inevitable calmly and courageously. They are superior to laws and literature. They are supremely blest.

Memphis. Tenn., November 10.

    *   *   *   *   *

TOMMIE WATSON'S TOMMYROT.

Somebody whom I have never harmed sends me an A. P. A. tract entitled "A Good Catholic," and issued by Tommy Watson, who once tried to run for vice-president on the Middle-of-the-Muck ticket—for the purpose of turning back the reform tide and electing the humble peon of the gold-buggers, high-tariffites and trusts. Tommie's Ape tract is simply an "ad." for a weekly paper which he seems to be getting out all by his little self somewhere in Gooberdom. On the front elevation of this bombshell with which he expects to blow the Vatican across the yellow Tiber, the statement is made in display type that, for the trifling sum of one dollar in hand paid, "You can read the brilliant, patriotic editorials of Hon. Thos. E. Watson" for an entire year—granting, of course, that their Promethean brilliancy fail to set your shirt-tail afire in the meantime. There is no provision for the return of your money in case Tommie's exhuberant patriotism should overpower you. We are then assured that "no Roman Pope or American Cardinal can coerce" the architect of the "brilliant and patriotic editorials" aforesaid. Now that's the kind of a man I admire! Hang a Georgia editor, say I, who sells himself to the Pope of Rome for six bits, or rushed around to an American Cardinal every morning before breakfast with the proof-sheets of his labored lucubrations, humbly asking permission to print. The brilliant and patriotic editor of a Georgia paper having a paid circulation of 710 copies can not be too independent. It is his solemn duty to keep watch and ward over this country and promptly put a kibosh on every conspiracy of the Pope. Like most brilliant patriots, Tommie has sacrificed a very great deal for conscience sake. When he tried to save the country by playing second tail to the Bryan kite for the purpose of dividing the reform forces and electing a Republican president, the Pope and all his "priest-led citizens" straddled his collar, rode him into an open grave and piled a cathedral on top of him to hold him down—at least I suppose they did from the way in which this raucous little Buzfuz is chewing the rag. Had he been "A Good Catholic" he would have been elected with votes to burn; for did not Dick Bland have to hide out in the Ozark hills to escape the presidential nomination the moment it was rumored that his wife was a "Romanist"? Did not Generals Sherman and Sheridan have to insulate themselves to avoid the presidential lightnings which played around them continuously because they were Catholics? Sure! Tommie is doubtless correct in his assertion that the Pope controls American politics and dictates every act of congress. That is amply proven by the fact that after all these years the Catholics have a representative in the president's cabinet. That all Catholics are sworn enemies of this republic and peons of the Pope is demonstrated by the fact that the "Romish" attorney-general refused to permit his people to erect at their own expense a chapel on government ground at West Point—the general public being taxed meanwhile to maintain an Episcopal clergyman at that place. Tommy protests that he is both a Baptist and devoid of bigotry. If he can make this claim good I will undertake to secure for him an engagement at $1,000 a day in a dime museum as the greatest curio ever seen in this country. Doubtless there are many good people who are Baptists but God's sunlight never fell upon one who was not a bigot. The man who concedes that it is possible for one to reach heaven except he be soused bodily into some sacred slop-tub is not a Baptist. If he thinks he is, he has made a faulty diagnosis of his disease. The Baptist church breeds bigotry just as a dead mule does magots. It dominates politics wherever it is strong enough to do so. It boycotts every publisher who dares suggest that it doesn't hold the one only key to heaven. It is the sworn foe of Catholicism, yet not one of its members in a million has the remotest idea what Catholicism means. It assumes that the great body of Catholics are ignorant clowns, while itself absorbing 60 per cent. of the illiterates of this land. The more ignorant an animal is the more bigoted Baptist it is likely to be. I cannot at present think of a single American of distinction who was a member of that denomination. I have passed in mental review the great American statesmen, soldiers, authors and inventors, and find only one among them who was web-footed. Garfield was a Campbellite—and had he not been murdered no one would have suspected that he was a great man. If any of the immortelles was of the Baptist persuasion he was probably ashamed of that fact, as he kept it concealed. It is possible that in soaking the original sin out of a fellow any latent germs of genius he possesses may be extracted also. Tommie solemnly assures us that Catholics dare not read a book or paper that has not been formally approved by the Pope. What a foolish falsehood! I'll wager a pint of peanuts that Watson cannot name half a dozen American books, papers or magazines that bear the Papal imprimatur, and another pint of the same luscious circus fruit that even his own rabid A.P.A. rot has never been placed in the index prohibitorius. If it is not there every Catholic in this country is privileged to read it without consulting Rome. Of the most bigoted sect of pseudo-religious fanatics that ever cursed this country the Hon. Tommie Watson is perhaps the most intolerant and narrow-brained little blatherskite. And the worst of it all is that while in religion he's a fool, in politics he's a knave. While pretending that the cause of the common people was the apple of his eye, he lent himself to a scheme to defeat their tribune and elect a ligneous-headed hiccius-doctius owned soul and body by Mark Hanna, the "industrial cannibal." Bryan would be president to-day but for this busy little blabster whom accident placed in a position where he could betray the people. Avaunt! thou contumacious little coyote, thou pestiferous pole-cat. Benedict Arnold was a gentleman when compared to you, for his treason was open and avowed, while you stabbed the cause of the people in a friendly embrace, struck in the back. You have had no parallel since Judas Iscariot conspired with the plutocracy to betray the idol of the people—and even Judas had decency enough to hang himself as expiation for his infamy. Shut up, thou hatchet-faced, splenetic-hearted, narrow-headed little hypocrite, for verily the world is aweary of Tommie Watson. His "brilliant and patriotic editorials" are used only to underlay carpets, paper pantry shelvest and for purposes less polite. I cheerfully risk my reputation as a prophet on the prediction that in less than two years his windy little "reform" paper will go to the bone-pile. Tommie, you are the pin-worm of American politics—a more aggravating little parasite than even Miltonius Park. Take a gentleman's advice and apply the soft pedal to your wheezy calliope—get off the political stage in time to avoid the coming cataclysm of sphacelated cabbage and has-been cats. The day of your destiny's over and the star of your fate is in the mullagatawny. You are simply a fragment of worthless political seaweed cast with flabby jelly fish and dead sting rays upon an inhospitable shore, there to rot and befoul the atmosphere. You have "a very ancient and fishlike smell, a smell not of the newest." You may howl a lung out, but will only evoke laughter or disgust. Occasionally some lonely Middle-of-the-Roader, dragging his No. 12's painfully through the dust may turn to look at you, perhaps toss you a dime; but you are politically dead. You may play the Baptist racket for all it is worth; but the brethren while long on zeal are shy on boodle. Even Jehovah Boanerges Cranfill, the champion leg elongator of the universe, finds it hard work to keep fat in the Baptist field—must add professional beggary to his schemes of predacity. You may tie your abortive little paper to the tail of the "Ape," but that animal is too weak in the hinder legs to pull it out of a financial hole. Go plug yourself. Shuck your long-tailed hand-me-down Albert Edward, trade your paper for a double-shovel plow, gird up your yarn galluses and make a reasonable effort to earn an honest living. Had you expended half the nervo-muscular energy in the cotton patch that you have wasted in working your jaw-bone you would have money to burn. Mene mene tekel upharsim—which means that you are entirely too light at both ends.

*   *   *   *   *

PILLS AND POLITICS.

My attention has been called by several disgusted doctors to one Jay Jay Lawrence who tacks A.M., M.D. to his patronymic, evidently as an anchor to hold it to the earth. Jay Jay and his vestibule-train title are conducting a sickly concern at St. Louis, sporting the euphonious cognomen of *The Medical Brief*, a monthly devoted to patent medicine and politics, blue ointment and economics, vermifuge and philosophy. Although Jay Jay finds it necessary to mix display ads with his reading matter to make the latter palatable, he declares that his painful monthly emission has "the largest circulation of any medical magazine in the world"—thereby indicating that while his mentality may be atrophied, his imagination is intumescent.

I have long noticed that journals having large bonafide circulations do little toot-ing of their own horns on the house-tops—they don't have to. It is a species of journalistic quackery which every thorough-bred publisher regards with con-temptuous pity. Brains win, in the journalistic world as elsewhere, and "blowing" a circulation were equivalent to employing a brass band to call attention to the abnormal size of the editorial encephalon. Still I wouldn't be without Jay Jay's truly remarkable magazine for ten times the money. I haven't a very high opinion of it as a medical authority, as it has "Cagliostro" written on it from cover to cover; but as a humorous journal it is 'way ahead of anything since the "Wax Wurx" of Artemus Ward. When I weary of the professional fun-makers, when I tire of laugh-ing at Brer. Rockefeller's heroic attempt to suppress the Iconoclast by excluding it from his little gate-system railroad; when the senatorial candidacy of Chollie-Boy Culberson becomes a weariness to the spirit, and the Texas Baptist convention, with its stage accessories of snuffles and snot develops into nux vomica, I can turn to Jay Jay's flamboyant cyclopedia of misinformation and observe with ever in-creasing interest the attempts of ye able editor to diagnose the disease of the body politic and steer it clear of the funeral director. Jay Jay is evidently not a progres-sive practitioner, for he is trying to save the country exactly as Gulliver's Lagado Galen tried to cure a dog of wind-colic. I note with unalloyed pleasure that the Brief has contributors to its medical department, at Purdon, Cove and Dilworth, Texas, Jones, Switch and Burnsville, Ala., Nassawadox, Va., Salt Springs, Mo., Claypool, Ky. and other great centers of therapeutical information indicating that it spares no pains to give its patrons the worth of their money without adding any tea-store chromos or electric belly-bands by way of rebate. But it is not the startling discoveries of these doctors, not the sophomoric essays of new-fledged Hippocra-ti now struggling manfully with buck-ague, snake bite and new babies at Nassaw-adox, Jones' Switch and elsewhere that constitute the chief charm of Jay Jay's ver-satile journal. The feature of most interest to the lay reader is the political homilies of the editor himself. Not only are they deeply interesting to the *hoi polloi*, but in-valuable from a therapeutical standpoint, being successfully employed in cases of itch, smallpox, etc. as a counter irritant. I opine that one of these read in a loud voice to an Egyptian mummy would result in its immediate resurrection. If it had the faintest conception of humor it would wake up long enough to laugh, and if it hadn't it would come to life for the express purpose of hitting Jay Jay Lawrence, A.M., M.D., across the sterno cleidomastoidens with a well-seasoned obelisk. It is impossible to reproduce the flavor of this intellectual hippocampus' politico-eco-nomic emulsions, they being evidently compounded with thaumaturgis incanta-tions while he is surrounded with jars of jalap, pile remedies, aphrodisiacs and patent liver pills. They should be labelled allopathic purgatives and kept tightly corked. In the copy before me Jay Jay assured his readers—who are supposed to be numerous as the sands of the sea, but are probably confined to himself and his country contributors—that there is a Russo-Franco-Germanic alliance against En-gland and that it is the sacred duty of America to come to the rescue of her much-ly-beloved "mother country," lest the 'orrid bawbawians make 'way with the old woman, overturn the civilization of all the centuries and rip human liberty up by the roots. What my contemporary seems to need is a mild cathartic that will move his brain—say about a tablespoonful of Theodorus' Anticyrian hellebore. The continental powers will not harm England so long as the old harlot behaves herself, but there's no denying that they are becoming dead-tired of her predacity and impudence. If the senescent old British lion attempts any funny business with the Russian bear it is liable to lose its umbilicus, and the surgical operation will be performed without the use of anaesthetics. If John Bull gets his proboscis ingloriously bumped it will be none of Uncle Sam's business—unless the gentleman in the Star-spangled cut-a-way happens to be the party of the first part in the bumping business. Just why we should expend blood and treasure fighting the battles of the old buccaneer only an Anglomaniacal doctor enervated by his own dope could possibly imagine. Russia has ever been our friend, England our foe. The sympathies of Russia are with Republican France, with Republican America—the hand of England has ever been against the world. She has ruthlessly despoiled wherever and whenever she possessed the power, while slavishly obsequious when confronted by equal force. "Human liberty," your gran-dam! How long has it been since England repealed the Test Act?—since she granted political equality to Jews?—to Catholics? In this respect she even legged behind the Ottoman Empire. She is the only "Christian" nation on earth to-day that sanctions human slavery. There are still fools extant who imagine that all the liberties enjoyed by Americans were inherited from "dear old England"; while the fact remains that in the matter of liberty England has been following 50 to 75 years behind the United States ever since the Flag o' Freedom first adorned the atmosphere. But it is when Jay Jay ribs himself up with a powerful nervine and tackles government by injunction that he really rises into the realm of pure humor—becomes serious, so to speak. He inadvertently leaks the information that labor organizations "are animated by anarchistic impulses, their chief desire is to force property owners to divide with them or lose their property"; and naively adds: "the injunction is really a guarantee of individual liberty." Sure! It guarantees to employers the right to combine to lower wages below the starvation point, while preventing those who are thus despoiled seeking the cooperation of their fellows in an attempt to right the wrong by the simple expedient of taking leave of their tools. It guarantees to workmen the liberty to be shot down like dogs for peaceably assembling and walking unarmed on the public highway—for asking other men to cease work until there is a better adjustment of wages. Of course a man who isn't willing to work in a coal mine for 90 cents a day, who lays down his pick and asks better pay, is an anarchist who is trying to drive other people to divide with him their property. Jay Jay is so much wiser than all the labor organizations in the land, than the framers of our fundamental law, than a majority of the American judiciary, a—veritable Daniel come to judgment. Give him a crown as large as that of King Midas, which was designed to hide the ears of an ass. It is, however, when he assails W. J. Bryan that he becomes intensely interesting. According to this learned Theban, Bryan is a Populist and Populists are people who do not pay their doctor bills. They call the M.D. out of his comfortable bed at 2 g.m., and after he has frozen his nose and toes to puke or purge 'em they refuse to even haul him a cord o' slippery-elm firewood or a load o' pumpkins in payment, but, accuse him of incompetence! 'Ow 'orrible! Jay Jay must have obtained his information from those forks of the creek medicos who constitute the chief contributors to his columns—and who would probably encounter fewer charges of incompetence if they expended less time in scribbling "rot" and more in careful reading. Still I can scarce refrain from weeping over such a tale o' woe. In the terse vernacular of the "mother country," hit touches me 'eart—so much so that I hereby authorize anybody to whom W. J. Bryan owes a doctor bill to draw on me for the amount. If he doesn't owe anybody a doctor bill it follows, according to Jay Jay's diagnosis, that he is not a Populist—may be a dyed-in-the-wool Democrat. Classing Bryan and his followers as Populists, then denouncing all Populists as chronic dead-beats, must be very soothing to a majority of the medical men of the West and South, but it is about what might be expected of a man so infamously ignorant that he calls England our mother country, so idiotic that he would have us take up arms for the international pirate in the name of human liberty. The best thing Jay Jay Lawrence, A.M., M.D., can do is to apply a ten-horse power poultice to his head and see if he cannot draw a few brains into that resounding hollow. In the meantime he should eschew politics and confine himself to the publication of essays by village doctors and the exploitation of patent medicines. When he next feels an impulse creeping on to invade the realm of economics he should chloroform it, or hit it with a club.

*   *   *   *   *

BEHIND THE SCENES IN ST. LOUIS.
BY ISEULT KUYK.

Col. Robert Ingersoll once said of the city of St. Louis that, as to Missouri, it was "a diamond pin in a dirty shirt." I will not maintain the immaculateness of the shirt; but the diamond has flaws, and is, in some respects, as a gem not far removed from the "phony."

They call St. Louis "the solid city." It is solid. Also stolid. It's a little Chinese. It regards the stranger as the enemy. In St. Louis they don't gather in the stranger and skin him, as they do in Chicago; but if he happens to have four dollars to invest he is regarded as having designs upon the coagulated capital of a select assortment of "stiffs," known as leading citizens. If he have brains, they dicker with him and let him in on their deals for a share in his. St. Louis is a close corporation. Less than twenty men run it. Jim Campbell, Dave Francis, Geo. A. Madill, Sam Kennard, Ed. Butler, Charlie Maffit, John Sculin, Edwards Wittaker, Thomas H. West, Julius S. Walsh, George E. Leighton and a few more own the town. They dare do anything. They control the banks, the trust companies, the street railroads, the gas works, the telephone franchises and the newspapers. Almost all the ability in the town is engaged in their service. They gather it in as it develops, and the multitude is made vassal to them. They own everything in St. Louis worth owning. They are the local nobility. They can crush anyone who ventures to oppose their desires. When they war among themselves they manage that no interloper shall come in for a share of the spoils. They unite against the newcomer and crucify him. They control municipal legislation. They buy aldermen like cattle. The city is at their mercy. They are all religious and moral men; their crookedness is purely commercial and political. Their different monopolies oppress the town, and the press is their tool. Most newspaper warfares upon them are mere "blinds" to draw off public attention to one quarter, while they gobble up something valuable in another.

St. Louis has had a reputation for a long time, for public spirit. It's there all right, but it is public spirit for private gain. Take the exposition. A job. Public money built the structure. The city gave the ground, right in the heart of the business-district-to-be. All the subscribers are frozen out but a few shrewd ones own the whole business. They have a piece of property worth at least eight million dollars. It is untaxed. They rake in the coin accruing from the exposition. They work the public up into supporting the venture, and three or four men in large retail stores get all the benefit. They advertise their private business by their public spirit, in capturing an enterprise that in its inception was somewhat communal in character.

St. Louis boasts of her fine Planters Hotel. Well, eight or ten men have confidenced the public out of that property, and its stupendous increment. Once there was subscribed $600,000 for what are known as the Fall Festivities. There were illuminations for a few years, and the Veiled Prophet pageant still survives; but there has been no accounting for the $600,000 that anyone has been able to understand. It is a legend in St. Louis that a large wad of the $600,000 was invested in the Planters Hotel, in the names of the individuals who made up the Fall Festivities Association. They are drawing from the splendid institution the earning upon money raised by miscellaneous public subscription. No paper dare take up these matters and discuss them. If one were to do so, it would not have five advertisements of the leading retail dealers in anything in the whole city. Col. Charles H. Jones, when editor of the Post-Dispatch, once criticized Mr. Sam Kennard for something, and forthwith Barr, Nugent, Crawford, Scruggs, Vandervoort and Barney, and the other big dealers withdrew their patronage in order to prevent his making the sum of money each year prescribed in his contract with Joseph Pulitzer as the sine qua non to his retention of his place. They drove him out of journalism finally. You've got to stand in with all this gang, or go to the wall. The only person who gets anything from them is the person who will do their work.

You go to the city hall in St. Louis, the old one, which looks like a rickety tobacco warehouse, or the new one, which is a realization in material of a bad dream consequent upon too much rarebit, and you might as well be in Berlin. You are lost without an interpreter. You must talk German or a Joe Emmet dialect, to make yourself understood. Money only doesn't have to talk German at the city hall. That is transferred without being translated. The mayor of the town talks, in his public addresses, a lingo that would make the fortune of a vaudeville comedian of the Dutch Daly stripe; and his son, who is his secretary, has the physiognomical symptoms of intellectuality that you might expect in a dude who eats with his knife, or any Brummel of "the bad lands." The lower branch of the municipal legislature is a bedlam. Its sessions are eruptions of obscenity. Talk is indulged in that would cause the ejectment of the talker from a bawdy-house parlor. The august body never rouses into activity save over some measure with "stuff" in it. The combine will take as low as twenty-five dollars to beat or pass a bill. They introduce bills to induce the franchise holding syndicates to put up money to kill them, and business is at its best when two or three street railroad bosses can be led into bidding against each other for the passage or defeat of some measure. The St. Louis house of delegates is as fine a gang of rapacious ruffians as ever invited mob law in an American city.

Politics in St. Louis is practiced by the pimps and pothouse habitues, just as in other cities. Two of the best known office holders in the city have been accused publicly of stealing $1,200 that was given them to support a measure for capitol removal at the last general election. They got the money to divide among the members of the city committee, and no member of that body ever saw a copper of it. The check was cashed, however. The governor appointed to their present offices the men who got the money.

It costs more to conduct the city government of St. Louis than it costs proportionately to govern New York. The town is overrun with an army of men drawing salaries, and few sober breaths, but doing nothing else. The present head of government when he left the office of city collector, lost or destroyed his books, that they might tell no tale of the monstrous malfeasance of his administration. Corporations were held up for sums that never appeared on the books. Instead of paying licenses and taxes, merchants, manufacturers, saloon keepers, brewers and others paid tribute to the then subordinates of the present mayor. Corruption is rampant all through the city government. Every one knows it; but no one feels like expressing it for the reason that such exposures are "chestnuts" to the St. Louisan. There have been reform waves in every large city in the Union, now and then. In St. Louis, never. The syndicate of snappers that holds the franchises won't have it. Reform doesn't go. They want the old gang they have been dealing with, in power. No matter which gang dominates, Democrat or Republican, the syndicate owns them. It doesn't like the prospect of dealing with strangers. It likes to buy over and over again the same old crowd to enact or defeat certain bills. When the gang in power is Democratic, Ed Butler does the buying. When the gang is Republican, Chauncey I. Filley takes the money and dictates what his creatures shall do. Butler disgorges something; Filley nothing. Butler deals with Filley when Filley has fooled the people into electing his men, and vice versa. It is Croker and Platt over again on a smaller scale. These two men have all the corporations by their throats. They are both men of genius in their line, commanding an insane devotion among the slums and a certain amount of admiration and awe, from among the wealthy, if not the respectable, of that city.

The St. Louis police force is demoralized by politics. Robberies and burglaries multiply. Purse-snatching from women by white and black ruffians is sunk to a mere commonplace in the daily newspaper reports. Thieves flourish, and are protected by petty politicians. Real estate dealers work the police department about once a year to chase the prostitutes out of one section of town into another. It's all a job. The prostitutes pay big rents, $60 per month for a house that would rent to decent people for $25. One crowd of agents gets the upper hand and starts an agitation to get the "girls" out of the district they occupy into another, in which the agents interested have a great many empty houses. After a time another real estate combination is made, and the poor bawds have to move again. Result of this? Many of the women open assignation houses in the West End, or go "living decent" under some man's care in that quarter, make the acquaintance of good women, and innocent girls, and collect a "maiden tribute" from among the latter for numerous old rakes who prefer the sexually initiative to the referendum in the case of women in the territory known as "tamale town." Kept women, the mistresses of men driven from downtown, have been known to ingratiate themselves, in the West End, with women moving in the very best society. And all this to enable a few real estate men to rent at exorbitant figures a few ramshackle houses to the women who must stay "on the town."

St. Louis society is not so bad and vulgar as society in some other cities. The city is so much like a village that no opportunity is afforded for intrigue or depravity among the swell set. Every one in St. Louis knows the business of every one else. A woman cannot "go wrong" without being discovered. Most of the details that you hear about the corruption of St. Louis society are imagination wholly. There is a great deal of excessive drinking at functions among women, but it is said that this is notable rather because of the amount the girls can stand without showing it than because of its prompting them to ribald Terpsichorean evolutions. The world outside the swell set hears occasionally of some girl who patronizes the punch bowl until she falls into hysterics, but as a rule the up-to-date St. Louis girl can "carry a load" with much dignity and grace.

St. Louis society is cheap and garish in spots. Some of the newly rich are unbearably snobbish. The Granite Mountain set carries its nose in the air most heinously and its chief female representative is celebrated for her absurd malapropisms. There is but one "fast" set in the town and that "fast" set is looked down upon quite generally and quite sincerely. It is composed of gay young married women who affect the Bohemian by drinking cocktails in public and cutting up at the Jockey Club. One of the members of this last set is the daughter-in-law of a Missouri senator and a very pretty woman. Another of this set is the woman who was voted the best dressed woman at the horse show in a newspaper scheme. Her father is a millionaire doctor and her husband is a thoroughbred. It cannot be said even of this set, however, that it is fast in the immoral sense in which that word usually is employed. It is gay and the women are only unfortunate in having nothing to do and in dispelling weariness by silly and flashy pranks in a social way.

There are some awfully funny society people in St. Louis. For instance, I am told that one of the women who has recently blossomed into the society columns is the wife of a millionaire lumber man who lives in a swell place and whose stinginess is peculiar in that it applies to everything but the feeing of the reporters who write up his wife and daughter. There is another woman whose burst into society has occasioned a great deal of comment of late. She is the wife of a cattleman and certainly not well trained in the graces, but she has her name in the papers continually by virtue of presents of such things as bolts of silk to society editresses. The wife of one of the police commissioners, who used to be the widow of a former mayor, is a fearful and wonderful matron in her methods of attaining distinction. She dresses gorgeously at all public occasions and has more color than a spectacular show at the theater. St. Louis society is dull and unintellectual. As a rule, however, it does not mask any corruption. There are not enough men in society to give opportunity for corruption. Nowhere in the country are there so many pretty girls without admirers. They have to go to the theaters with their own fathers and brothers. The few men in society are a lot of "cheap skates" who can not repay their social obligations in the fashion supposed to prevail among them. The St. Louis society belle has no good time of it. She doesn't get rushed to any great extent at any time, and this is the more remarkable because the wealthy girls are as much neglected as the poor but pretty ones. St. Louis is the finest field in the world for a man with nothing who wants to marry money. St. Louis society doesn't patronize the theaters extensively. It is not appreciative of music. It doesn't care for art. It is hopelessly unaesthetical as a whole. The picture dealers, music dealers and book sellers declare that their patrons come mostly from the people who are not in the swell set. A peculiarity of St. Louis society is that its members are as a rule procreative. There is no suppression of increase and multiplication such as prevail in the swell mob in other cities. A woman in St. Louis is not disgraced by having three or four babies. As a rule also St. Louis society women are not disposed to set up a rigid standard of exclusiveness. They have taken up recently the wife of a young man who was a singer with the Bostonians and it is the fad at present to rave over her. The whole world knows, of course, that a St. Louis girl insulted the Prince of Wales by refusing to meet him, when he never had asked to have her presented. That, however, was the most glaring effort ever made by a St. Louis girl to get a lot of newspaper notoriety and at a cheap rate. To the credit of the local high society it must be said that it does not cultivate the newspaper habit of exploitation. It tolerates the journalistic abuses of papers and write-ups. To be perfectly just to society in St. Louis, about all that can be said of it is that it is dull, principally, because it is decent. A man who is an authority upon such matters tells me that there is not in real society in St. Louis one woman of whom there has ever been any scandal. The very highest society in St. Louis—the old families are all Catholics, and very strict Catholics at that, and so there is not the taint of animalism about it that you find else where in the realm of the high flyers.

St. Louis cannot be said to be a moral city. It is as immoral as any in the country. I am told that the professional Social Evil in St. Louis is an unprofitable occupation "because of amateur competition." I am quoting a gentleman who is interested in sociological questions very largely. From what he said I deduce the conclusion that the daughters of the poor are preyed upon by the men so successfully as to account for the prevalence of virtue in the wealthier circles. Fearful stories are current of the immorality of the working girls, but these, I suppose, may be discounted to a certain extent. I hesitate to tell you some things I have heard about the tribute exacted of the girls in some of the big dry goods emporiums. Suffice it to say that these stories are told of three of the great merchant princes. One of them is said to make it a rule that no girl shall be employed who fails to understand that she is liable to his advances. Another merchant prince, portly and domineering, who gained unenviable notoriety because of his attempt at political coercion of his employes, had a bad reputation in this same line. Still another merchant prince who runs a strictly cash store, had one of his girls arrested for stealing goods and refused to prosecute her when she threatened to tell all she knew about how girls held their places in his establishment. As I say, these stories should be discounted, in all probability, but where there is smoke there is fire and most of the stories come from the girls in the big stores.

The city of St. Louis is hopelessly monotonous. It is a big place. A great business is carried on there, but it seems to be done by people somnambulistically. The soporific atmosphere that the readers feel when perusing the *"Globe-Democrat"* or *"Republic"* is characteristic of the town. The great majority of the people seem unable to arouse themselves to any action, even of viciousness. The crowd just lives as if it were soaked and sodden in the city's vast beer output. It is content to let a few men and a few big concerns monopolize all the business. It scarcely has energy enough to try to amuse itself. It goes to bed at half past nine, and never thoroughly wakes up. The town is sleepy, notwithstanding its size and its boasted progress. It grows because it can't help itself. The people appear to be good because they've not energy enough to be otherwise.

St. Louis, Mo., November 10.

*   *   *   *   *

THE STAGE AND STAGE DEGENERATES.
BY ROBERT LEE WYCHE.

Here and there in the big and little towns of America cranks are busily working for the elevation of the stage. Every 2 x 4 newspaper man who thinks he has a mission, every preacher who desires to make a sensation in the pulpit, every maiden novelist whose feminine mind battens in pruriency, every old maid who has missed her opportunity to be manhandled and wishes to reform a race she has done nothing to increase, every two-for-a-quarter evangelist between Bangor and Los Angeles is talking a lung out for the public on the subject of making the stage higher and better. When Col. Hercules, not of Herculaneum, viewed the Augean stables he may have thought that he had a considerable job on hand, but he tackled it with a man's strength and brain. By the help of his good right arm and a river or two he got rid of some thousands of tons of filth which went to enrich the levels lower down. Col. Hercules died in time to save his reputation. If required to cleanse the modern stage, he would pull his beaver over his brows and sneak out of town. Col. Hercules was a man who knew when he was over-weighted. He entered the ring only with such opponents as he stood a chance to best.

Once upon a time I boarded in a little German hotel in this city. Near it was the great Madison Square Garden. In consequence, the little hotel, which was very German—that is to say, clean and cheap,—was patronized by many actors and actresses. They had little rooms upstairs, got their morning coffee in the little restaurant and after the evening's performance sat in the little apartment off the bar, where the floor was sanded and drank beer until the small hours. These men were representatives of their profession so far as America is concerned. There were no stars among them and none of the lowest stratum. They were of the middle class of the people of the footlights. Nearly all of them were married and a few of them had children. They had the small ambitions and the small amusements of their class.

At that time I worked upon one of New York's yellow journals. I reached the hotel each morning between 12 and 1 o'clock, and always found the theatrical symposium in full blast. I was with these people for three months for an hour or two each night and think that I formed a fair idea of what the American stage is like. In those months I heard just two general subjects discussed—grease-paint and copulation. That was all of it. No science, no literature, no art in its higher sense, no news of the day, no politics, no sports, no history, no travel, not anything that goes to make up the intellectual life of the ordinary man. From first to last it was the business of acting, the demerits of some actor not present, the merits of those present, the pursuit of woman and the unholy pleasures of indiscriminate sexual lust. The dominating passion of these people was a petty jealousy. I never heard from them a good word for a successful brother artist. I never heard them breathe one generous hope that other men or women would grow happy and prosperous. I never heard them speak a kindly sentence for one of their ranks who had fallen upon evil days. They were selfish, they were brutally abusive, they were ridiculously conceited, they were all geniuses held down by a conspiracy of managers, they were card and dice sharpers, they were willing at any time to act the part of procurer or procuress for a consideration of drinks and suppers. I was rejoiced at the opportunity to study a type that was new to me, and when I got enough of it I moved out.

I have met these people and their kind many times since then. I have seen them in Philadelphia, Boston, Washington, Chicago, New Orleans and San Francisco. They are everywhere the same. They do not differ in any degree. On the road they are slightly more restrained, for fear of corporal punishment or jail, but the impulse of gluttony and lechery is always there. Any keeper of a second or third-class hotel in a town that is on one of the big circuits is apt to grow eloquent upon the subject of theatrical folk if given the chance. They are noted for a brazen effrontery in demanding everything that is in sight and the laxity with which they regard a debt incurred. I have no doubt that the first man to let his valise down from the second-story window of a hotel, slide down the rope himself and thus square his bill was the leading comedian of that sterling bit of humor, "Hot Times in the Tenderloin." Meantime his soubrette, who was another man's wife, was waiting for him outside, and they went away together.

I do not know that the baleful fire of unchaste amour runs more fiercely in the veins of stage people. I only know that they give it more of a free field. You sometimes hear some bar-room comedian and booze recitationist, who draws a hamfatter's salary in a continuous vaudeville, declare to half drunken listeners that there are good women on the stage. So there are—some. But they are so rare that when they are found they shine like the jewel in the Ethiop's ear. It would be within the bounds of truth to say that for every virtuous woman behind the foot-lights there are ten prostitutes. Even those who try to keep their feet from the mire and succeed are given no credit for chastity by their fellow professionals. One night, in my never to be forgotten German hotel, I was assured in a thing in loud-patterned trousers and a snow-white overcoat with deep black collar and cuffs, that he knew Emma Abbott, then dead, was unfaithful to her husband, Eugene Wetherell, also dead. This was spoken of "honest little Emma." A purer woman never lived. I knew that he was lying and told him so, but he was ready with a tale of time, place and circumstance and brazened it out. In like manner I have been told tales of Mary Anderson and Modjeska and Viola Allen—all of them lies. They were the tributes which my gentle friends, male and female, paid to success in their beautiful but risky profession.

It is not to be wondered that women who go on the stage lose their virtue. The wonder is that some of them preserve it, in spite of the life they lead and the company they are forced to keep. The very talents they possess render them susceptible to adulation and applause. They keep late hours. They are thrown constantly with conscienceless males. They breathe an atmosphere of excitement. If they display unusual capabilities, they are intoxicated nightly with the deep, rich, moving roar of high acclaim. Their nerves need bracing and they take to late suppers and champagne with absinthe in the mornings. From the woman who drinks to the woman who falls is not a far cry. I once asked Lizzie Annandale, the contralto, to tell me why so many stage girls surrendered their most precious possession within a year after their first night behind the scenes. She was a frank old party, willing to talk to a friend:

> "Aw," she said, "that's easy. Women are only human. The girls are cut off from association with decent people. They have to live with stage folks. Society is barred to them. Stage men marry only when they can't help it. The girl must have somebody to look after her, some man to see that her trunks are checked, that she gets a decent seat in a crowded train, that she doesn't get the worst of it all around. A man expects pay of some kind and she hasn't anything to give except herself. That is what he wants. Take our own company, for instance. We are carrying twenty chorus girls. We are bound for the southern circuit. After we play New Orleans we play Texas. After we leave Texas we make a jump straight across the continent to 'Frisco. The girls don't get wages enough to enable them to take berths in the sleepers. They will be forced to herd day and night in the other coaches with the men. You will see the chorus people, male and female, asleep two and two on the seats. The exhausted woman's head rests on the shoulder of her companion, the man's arm around her to hold her steady. What do you suppose happens when a thing like that is kept up for awhile? Aw! W'at t'ell."

Despite the constant efforts of the classes mentioned in the opening paragraph of this story, the American stage is not being elevated to any extent. It is steadily sinking lower. Year after year its plays grow worse, its players more reckless and debased. This, it has been said, is the fault of the public and, to a great extent, this is so. The managers are in the business for money. They give the people that which the people will pay to see. Nobody cares anything for tragedy any longer. Stage classics have become stage stalenesses. Shakespeare is out of date. "The Gaiety Girls," "In Gay New York," "The Merry World," Hoyt's buffooneries, "Problem

Plays," social eraticisms have become the rage. Translations from the French, with all of the French immorality reduced to English grossness, pack the theaters. In New York a manager named Doris put on a pantomime which represented the scene in a bridal chamber. The police closed it up after half the bald-headed men and nearly all the boys in town had seen it. That pantomime, I understand, is now drawing crowded houses in Chicago, having been introduced to the citizens of the western metropolis by Sam Jack of "Adamless Eden" game. Continuous performances are proving mines of gold for their conductors and in the continuous performance the vulgar song and ribald jest meet with readiest applause. Your wife or your daughter, who goes down town for her morning shopping, gets lunch with a glass of absinthe, drops into the continuous show for an hour and comes home with memories in her little head of a song which should be interdicted by law, or of a dialogue that ought to land the speakers in jail, or of Hope Booth, posing in imitation nudity as Venus Aphrodite, or some beefy actor, also an imitation nude, as Ajax defying the lightning, or Antinous, facing the audience full front without a stitch of clothing on him. This is pleasant for the wife and daughter, but how about you? You do not look anything like Ajax and your daughter's brothers bear no resemblance to Antinous.

Thousands of men and women are actors and actresses, but they do not differ in type. They are to be recognized anywhere in any crowd. Hundreds of thousands of dollars are invested in the business, and it is the business of the owners to make them pay. The public wants filth and it gets it. The plays given to patrons have only the purpose to make money. They are not written to educate, to uplift, to ennoble. The men who make them look only to the collection of their royalties. The best play of the year is Gillette's "Secret Service." It is trifling. It does not teach anything. It inculcates no moral. It does not deviate in any way from the well known "war play." In these days there is always some snipe of a federal lieutenant, who gets shot in the heel, or under his coat tail, or somewhere behind, and is quartered on the family of a southern planter, and the daughter falls in love with him, and her brother is in the Confederate army, and there is a whole lot of trouble and everything comes out all right in the end. Gillette's hero is a Federal spy instead of a lieutenant, but that is about the only difference. I imagine that he must have been many times to see Bronson Howard's "Shenandoah," whose favorite novelist in turn, I think, must have been E. P. Roe, of "Barriers Burned Away." The next success, it is supposed, will be something in the line of Mr. Howard's "Aristocracy." This play, its author assures us, was written to demonstrate the danger that lies in an American girl marrying an European nobleman. Instead, it administers a solar plexus blow to American womanhood. The heroine marries a German prince, merely because he is a Prince, discarding her honest and true lover in a scoundrelly fashion, while her beautiful stepmother comes within an ace of surrendering her person to her son-in-law, and is prevented only by the inopportune arrival of her idiotic husband. It is all very "elevating," and a good thing to take your wife and daughter to see.

We arrive at this formula: The American stage is debasing; American stage people are dead beats and women of scarlet. There are exceptions, but they prove the rule. The business is Jew-ridden. They do not act, but they handle the dollars. Everybody knows that your Jew drummer and your Jew theatrical manager are incapable of anything sexually wrong. The big syndicate which has its home in this city and is endeavoring to control the theatrical business of more than half the country is composed of Jews. One of them is an undersized Silenus named Erlanger, who used to be a pensioner upon the personal and mental abilities of the ill-fated Louise Balfe and repaid her for her bread and favors by brutally assaulting her in Arkansas.

Yes, Brother Iconoclast, the 2 x 4 newspaper men and the sensational preachers and the prurient prudes who write novels and the unfructified old maids and the narrow-beamed self-elected evangelists are talking, but they do not elevate the American stage to any great extent. It bids fair to remain the same excellent school of preparation for the penitentiary and the bagnio.

New York, November 20, 1897.

*   *   *   *   *

"THE CHRISTIAN."
BY JULIA TRUITT BISHOP.

If one may judge by the effect it has produced in arousing a storm of criticism, the book of the year is undoubtedly "The Christian," by Hall Caine. Not only the book of the year, perhaps, but of more years than one cares to count, for of books worth reading or remembering, there has been the fewest number within these latter days. And it must be conceded, in the beginning, that Hall Caine has written a book—a live book—and that no one will dissect it without finding blood on his rapier's point.

As for the critics themselves, they have had much to say, after their fashions, and have wasted vast quantities of good ink in giving the author of "The Christian" meanings which he never meant. One of them has found that John Storm was intended to represent Christ himself, come back to earth in this most unbelieving Nineteenth century; a construction which seems to have been as far as possible from anything that was in the novelist's thought. Another finds the plot weak and the *motif*—it is the custom to use French in this connection—strained; and can endure nothing in the book but Glory, who is "altogether delightful." Still another is furious because of the "nurses' ball," and thinks it is reflection upon the whole sisterhood of trained nurses; and there are others who cannot recover from that still further insult to the sisterhood conveyed in the fact that Polly was a nurse.

I have read the criticisms—all I could find—with weariness of spirit, and have felt that the real meaning of the author lay deeper than any of these shallow comments could reach. What difference does it make whether Polly was or was not a trained nurse? The real thing at issue was this—that she was a woman, ruined and played with and tossed aside. For this book is, above all, an earnest book, with bitter protest and lofty purpose running through it, and in such a light as this the paltry errors sink into nothingness. Hall Caine has had something to say to the world, and has said it. The world has waited long enough for a writer with a message. When it comes, let the space-writers and all the horde of small spirits retire for a little while, or go on sounding the praises of this or that "society novel" by Mrs. Van Kortland Van Kordtland, or other of that ilk.

And while there may be lay-figures in the book, as has been charged, the people around whom the interest centers are so terribly real that they cannot stay in the book. They come out of it, and become part of our lives. Glory is a vivid creature, with her moods and fancies, her dual nature, with the one side of her in love with John Storm and his work, and the other side—and so much the stronger side, alas! in love with the world, and filled with merry, buoyant life. One follows her through every step of her course, and feels the moral deterioration coming upon her so gradually and yet so surely. Splendid, wholesome, Glory, pure-eyed and frank-hearted, going through the wild rout of music-halls and theatrical successes, suggestive songs, Derby days and midnight suppers; one follows her with dread as though she were the child of a loved friend, and finds the smell of fire gathering upon her garments. Nothing could so show Hall Caine's art as this. If he had written nothing else worth reading, Glory should make him immortal, for this sweet, wild nature is more a living being to us than many whom we meet every day.

But the real character of the book is John Storm, one of the finest portrayals that the English language has yet given to fiction; a Christian, but not Christ. Nothing could be more human than this man, full of faults, and yet so earnest, so brave, so intense. His love for Glory is the dominant feeling that leads him into many strange paths, for he loves as intensely as he works; but above even this he is a Christian, and trying to do the work of Christ. How natural it is that a man like this, filled with enthusiasm and eager to begin work among the poor and the suffering, should find the shallow hypocrisies and shams of a fashionable church abhorrent to his soul. And the asceticism of the Brotherhood was as far from the possibilities of this man as long-faced and comfortable hypocrisy would have been. It was the fall of poor, ignorant Polly that gave him his life-work; and the discharge of the girl from her position in the hospital, while the man who had accomplished her ruin remained a member of the Board which presided over the destinies of that same hospital.

And Hall Caine could have given no more conclusive proof of his courage and his earnestness of purpose than in selecting as the motif of this book that outrage upon justice, that travesty on morality; the condemnation of woman for a crime that is readily ignored or as readily forgiven in man. It is really such an outworn theme that the very mention of it is greeted with smiles or supercilious shrugs, and even lovers of their kind have grown apologetic about it. If any man like John Storm, fired with the best and truest principles of Christianity, steady of eye and bold of heart and fearless of speech, dared to utter such principles as his in any social circle of any one of our cities, what a consternation he would create; and here as in London he would be called a madman and avoided as an outcast. Yet what was his creed? "Let him that is without sin amongst you cast the first stone at her." We have heard it before, have we not?—but in leaving it out of our Revised Version we have taken care to leave it out of our practice as well, and are very busy casting stones, though in truth not one of us is without sin.

The author of "The Christian" has loosed many a shaft that will surely pierce between the joints of the armor; and not the least of these is the story of a young girl's marriage to the abandoned young lord, the man who had dragged Polly to ruin which ended in suicide. We see such things every day, and it is not polite to call them by their names. For that is the bitterness of it; that ruin and disgrace and the swift downward road to hell are set by society before the feet of the woman who errs, while for the man who was at least her equal partner in crime, there are cordial greetings, and a thousand doors, opened by women, alas!—and he may have some pure girl for a wife, if he likes, and go serenely every evening to a happy home, untroubled by remorse. Is it any wonder, with the scales so unevenly balanced as this, with a premium put on corruption among men, that new and ever new recruits from womanhood are marching down into the infected quarter of our cities, and that the wretched army grows and will grow?

True, there are good women, here and there, making earnest effort to "rescue" some of this miserable horde; and here and there one is gathered into some house of refuge, and is helped to give up her evil life. But even there, are the hopes held out before them such brilliant hopes? One goes back to her old home and her mother, and is thenceforward a marked creature among all the people who have known her, doomed to cold avoidance or impudent familiarity. One succeeds in getting work, of some menial kind, and must live a life of utter subjection of self and utter abnegation of pleasure, or will be suspected that she has a secret longing for the old life. Many hide themselves in convent walls, knowing what kind of welcome the world would have for them if they went forth. If they could look over those walls, and could be gifted with some far-seeing vision, they could see the men who helped them to become criminals, abroad and at ease, riding or driving in the free sunlight, bending over jeweled fingers or whispering pretty nothings into dainty ears, as much approved by all the world as though their records were as pure as snow. Servitude or convent walls for one, even after she has repented; the world and its gaieties for the other, to whom remorse is unknown. No doubt the woman should be punished, and her punishment should be as great as her sin has been; but one would like to see the man who was guilty, equally with her, at least avoided a little; at least made to know that there were circles of society sufficiently refined to shut him out.

"The first stone." Many of these women have fallen through their adoring love for men, for whom they would willingly have given life itself, and would have counted it well lost. Wretched, sinful women, no doubt, but is that any less a prostitution which leads a woman to marry a man she does not love, whose very presence is repulsive to her? Yet that is done every day, to the music of the wedding march, with all the world there to see. If there be any justice in heaven, the unfortunate who falls through love is less a criminal than is the silk-robed bride who became a prostitute under the holy cloak of marriage.

The first stone! The workers of all our large cities have among them hundreds of girls who are doing their faithful best to earn an honest living; who work long hours and endure fatigue, and wear poor clothes, and surrender all girlish pleasures for the simple right to exist. Once in a while comes a lull in business, and scores of these girls are turned off. The employer makes no effort to learn how they will live, meanwhile. "Am I my brother's keeper?" — the old cry, many times repeated in these latter days. How subtle, how alluring are the temptations that come in the weeks and months of idleness; how inexorable seems the choice held out to these helpless working girls — starvation or infamy. It takes so long to starve, and life, after all, is sweet; so they make their choice, shirking from death while age is still so far away, and hope is bounding in the pulses; and having so chosen are shut out from hope forever more. Yet there are items in the society columns of the morning papers only too often, which, if the truth could stand out through the flattering lines, would tell how this or that fashionable girl has sold herself for money, her mother standing by well-pleased, and all her five hundred friends sending presents to commemorate the occasion. There was no bitter hunger urging her to the sacrifice — there was not the slightest excuse or necessity for it in any way. Which was the greater prostitution?

And yet, women who have sinned these gilded sins of society, or who have at least condoned the offense in their friends and intimates, unite in shutting the fallen unfortunate away from light and hope; and women of blameless life and pure name stretch welcoming hands to men who have helped to recruit the army of the fallen and make them outcasts and pariahs in the earth.

An outworn theme, doubtless; but there is enough in it still to thrill the heart and bring tears to the eyes. It is well for the world that a Christian, even in a book, has stood up among men and told them of their crimes, and has told it face to face, in the old Apostolic way; for we have come upon a Christianity, in these latter days, which is silent when the Magdalene is brought out for stoning if it casts no stones itself.

New Orleans, La., November 14.

*   *   *   *   *

SALMAGUNDI.

Bishop Wilyum Doane hath an abiding place at Albany, N. Y., a village on the Hudson where the peons of the political bosses most do congregate to leg for bribes. In his recent annual address to the clergy the Bish. lamented bitterly that the American "jingo" was provoking dear patient Christian England to put on her war-paint. "The English press," quoth he, "has been most patient." Yea, it hath — in the optic of ye animal yclept the hog. For two years past nearly every English paper, large and small, has systematically insulted Uncle Sam — has belched upon him all the feculent bile it could rake from its putrid bowels, all the moldy mucus it could snort from its beefy brain. Even the press of Canada — that Christ-forsaken land of bow-legged half-breeds which continues to lick the No. 7 goloshes of old Gilly Brown's leavings because it lacks sufficient sand to set up for itself — barks across the border like a mangy fleabitten fice yawping at a St. Bernard. But Doane would have America swallow it all — just as the Thibetans swallow pastiles made of the excrement of their Dalai Lama. The Bish. evidently has John Bull's trademark branded on the rear elevation of his architecture. So Hingland is growing blawsted tired of our Hawmewikan himpudence. Aw! Vewy likely, don-cherknow. But we shoved it down the old harlot's throat twice with the business end of a bayonet, and we'll fill her pod again with the same provender whenever she passes her plate. Doane ought to amputate his ears and send them to the British monarch to be used as door-mats.

* * *

My old friend, Major-General Whistletrigger Vanderhurst, of the Amazonian Guard, minister plenipotentiary of the Gal-Dal *News*, has just run a superb "scoop" on all his contemporaries. He rustled out one morning all by his lone self and discovered that prosperity had arrived—that every Texan afflicted with chronic hustle hath greenbacks to burn, and blue yarn socks galore stuffed to the bursting point with "yellow boys," while ye farmer simply slings the silver dollar of our sires at marauding blackbirds. Whistletrigger turns up his patrician nose at all "pessimists" and broadly intimates that the man who hasn't a new silk cady, seventeen pair o' tailor-made "pants," a silken nightshirt and sufficient provender in his pantry to run a Methodist camp-meeting for a month, would starve to death in a Paradise whose springs run Pomery Sec, and whose trees grew pumpkin pies, hot weinerwurst and *pate de foie gras*. Texas, according to this Columbus of prosperity, is a veritable Klondyke bowered with roses instead of imbedded in snowbanks—a place where every financial prospect pleases and only the popocrat is vile. But I note with pained surprise that the farmers are still selling middling cotton below six cents, buying bacon and wearing pea-green patches on the bust of their blue jeans two-dollar hand-me-downs; that I can hire all the common labor I want at 75 cents a day despite the advance in flour; that scores of mechanics are idle; that there is no longer a wage rate in any trade; that the streets are full of able-bodied beggers, while merchants offer me 2 per cent a month for the use of a little money. I note that in every Texas city realty is being cast upon the bargain counter, while great newspapers are cutting down the pay of their employees. There's prosperity and prosperity. Perhaps Whistletrigger has been talking to the agent of some mortgage company or to Colonel Hogg—who's making so much money compromising railroad cases with the Chollie Boy Culberson administration and suppressing prize-fights for $2,500 fees that he really cannot afford to serve Texas in the United States Senate.

* * *

Now that Henry George is dead, those papers and politicians that were wont to abuse and misrepresent him most brutally are fairly falling over each other to do him honor. The post-mortem gush is sickening because of its insincerity. If Henry George was not a great man living he is not a great man dead. If his economic views were fatuous while he was among us they are folly forevermore. I am not of those jackasses that delight in kicking dead lions; I insist that simple justice be done a man while he is in the land of the living—that we should not hound him to the grave with gross misrepresentation then try to make restitution by placing him among the stars. Henry George was a good man, but he was not great. He was an advocate, not an originator. He created no new epoch; he added nothing of importance to the world's knowledge; but he did stimulate most wonderfully economic investigation. He was a thought-compeller. He brushed the mold of prejudice and the cobwebs of partisanship from many a brain. By so doing he rendered the world invaluable service and is entitled to its profoundest gratitude. So long as men can be induced to *think* there is hope for the race. Although his Single Tax theorem will perish, it has served a good purpose.

* * *

A Denver party wants to know if I would *kneel* if given an audience by the Pope of Rome. I would be pretty apt to do so if such action on my part was expected. I would ascertain beforehand what conduct was required, then prove myself a gentlemen by either observing the proprieties or declining the audience. What would the Denver man do? Waltz up to the august head of the Catholic church, slap him on the back and offer to shake him for the drinks? Novalis says: "There is but one temple in the world and that is the body of man. Nothing is holier than this form. Bending before men is a reverence done to this revelation in the flesh." We, whose ancestors for so many centuries bowed, not only to the Pope, but to 2 x 4 kings and petty princelings, should not unduly exalt our Ebenezer—should not become so stiff in the joints that we prove ourselves boors by declining when in Rome to do as the Romans do. Were I to seek the presence of Queen Victoria I would observe all the court etiquette.

* * *

It is said that Miss Rebecca Merlindy Johnson, editress of the Houston Post, and winner of the ICONOCLAST's $500 prize as the most beautiful woman in the world, will be a candidate for the office of lieutenant-governor. If this be true she can depend on the unswerving support of the ICONOCLAST. If there be constitutional objections to her holding the office with both lily-white hands we will amend that remarkable instrument. I will take it upon myself to elect Rebecca and ask no other reward than the privilege of dancing with her at the inaugural ball. She was my first, if not my only love; and although she threw me over for Pinkie Hill, by whose effulgent aurora borealis she was hypnotized, and took to wearing pantaloons in public despite my protest, she has since repented and given all her maidenly heart to me; hence it will be my duty and my pleasure to manage her campaign. Rebecca may safely consider herself elected and discount her salary whenever the *Post* gets into a pinch. I am willing to do anything for Rebecca except pay off the mortgage on her paper.

* * *

Because a young man was killed while playing football, the lower house of the Georgia legislature passed a bill prohibiting that game under severe penalties. To be consistent the same body should now prohibit swimming because some boys are drowned, and possum hunting because some nocturnal sportsmen are killed. Georgia appears to take it for granted that nature makes no mistake—when she finds a man who's good for nothing else in the universe she sends him to the legislature to make laws. There's an element of danger in foot-ball as in all other athletic exercises; but that is no reason why we should confine the youngsters to croquet, mumble-peg and finger-billiards, and allow the race to degenerate into a lobeliaceous aggregation of lollipops. That Georgia legislature is full o' goobers and red lemonade.

* * *

I am rejoiced to learn that the two factions of Texas Baptists, after having for months past denounced each other in language that smelled of sulphur and would have disgraced opposing parties of Parisian gamins—after resorting to all the petty meanness of peanut politics to control the flesh-pots—have kissed and hugged, slobbered and boohooed each on the other's brisket. "How sweet it is for brethren to dwell together in unity!" That's whatever. I'm glad the ruction is over, for it was becoming a rank stench in the nostrils of the Protestant religion. It was enough to drive an intelligent man to Atheism, to make him not only suspicious of religion but ashamed of his race. It seems to me that the ICONOCLAST should have had a reserved seat at the love-feast—should have been forguv and slobbered over with the rest of the sinners, for it had not said nearly as hard things about its dear brethren in Christ as they had urged against each other. It might at least have been permitted to collect the tears of the penitents. That flood of brine, if carefully evaporated, would have supplied Scholtz's Garden with beer salt for a century. And it all went to waste! Doc Hayden and myself were the only Baptist parsons who didn't get hugged. Hayden was made a scape-goat for the sins of both factions and sent to wander in the wilderness, and it was decided to no longer recognize the ICONOCLAST as the official organ of the Baptist faith. It looks as though Hayden and I would have to start a little Baptist hell of our own.

* * *

J. Sterling Morton of Nebraska, one of those "village Hampdens" whom G. Cleveland discovered when raking the country with a fine-tooth comb in a frantic search for intellectual insects even smaller than himself, says the Bryan Democracy is composed of fanatics, bigots and idiots. He must have seen that brilliant *bon mot* in the Chicago *Inter-Ocean*. Poor J. Sterling Morton. Not being born great, nor having the ability to achieve greatness, it was his misfortune to have it driven into him with a maul. And he's never gotten over it. Had Cleveland done naught else evil he would have damned himself everlastingly by pulling this intumescent jay out of a Nebraska turnip-patch to make him a cabinet clerk. I say cabinet-clerk, for the so-called secretaries of the Cleveland regime were merely stool-pigeons for the Stuffed-Prophet. And now this erstwhile seneschal of the Buffalo Beast, this pitiful stool-hopper for the d—est fool that ever disgraced the presidency, turns up his beefy proboscis at the intellectuality of the Bryanites. If J. Sterling Morton would only shave his head he could get four dollars a day for playing What-Is-It in a dime museum. As an anthropological curio Oofty-Gofty or the Wild Man of Borneo wouldn't be "in it."

* * *

The committee sent to Europe by McKinley to talk a little twaddle about international bi-metallism has completed its alleged labors, and the net product is nothing—just as the people knew it would be when saddled with the expense of this high-fly junketing trip to enable the administration to make a pretense of redeeming the kangaroo promise of the Republican platform. The silver problem is not at present the burthen of my song—I simply rise to remark that the American people have been buncoed by this commission business. It was sent abroad at great outlay of boodle to ascertain what is perfectly well-known to every man outside the insane asylum, viz.: that England, being a creditor nation, would not consent to the remonetization of silver. Now let us send a commission to Europe to see if the water over there is wet. O Lord! how long will Uncle Sam consent to enact the role of a long-eared, pie-bald ass?

* * *

I wonder, O I wonder who that "prominent lawyer and sound money Democrat" was who got drunk at Charlie Cortizio's in Austin the other day and toasted Chollie Boy Culberson as "Texas' most distinguished son, the man who has done most to distinguish his state abroad"—just a bummy little boost for Chollie Boy's anaemic senatorial boom? I cannot imagine who he may be, but I was pleased to see his toast followed in my pet daily by an "ad" for a tansy compound warranted to "give relief from painful and irregular periods regardless of cause." I hope that the "sound money Democrat" aforesaid did not overlook the "ad," as he was evidently having a painful period and much in need of relief. I sincerely hope that he doesn't get that way often. It is a trifle difficult to determine whether he was pregnant with a great idea or full o' prunes—whether he needed a tansy compound or a cathartic. Poor Chollie Boy! His senatorial boom must indeed be in a bad way when he must fill old boozers with beer to induce them to boost it. But it is quite true he has been heard of outside the state—the Iconoclast has mentioned him several times.

* * *

I noticed in one of the local papers that "Dallas wants Baylor," $50,000 to $75,000 worth. Doubtless I'm a hopeless heretic, but I don't believe a d—n word of it. If anybody thinks that Dallas will put up $25,000 cash to secure the removal thither of Baylor, he can find a man about these premises who will make him a 2 to 1 game that his believer is 'way of his base. Dallas doesn't want Baylor even a little bit. There isn't a town in this world that wants it except Waco. It is simply another Frankenstein monster that has destroyed its architect. Baylor spends no money here worth mentioning. Its students are chiefly forks-of-the-creek yaps who curry horses or run errands for their board and wear the same undershirt the year round. They take but two baths during their lifetime—one when they are born, the other when they are baptized. The institution is worth less than nothing to any town. It is what Ingersoll would call a storm-center of misinformation. It is the Alma Mater of mob violence. It is a chronic breeder of bigotry and bile. As a small Waco property owner, I will give it $1,000 any time to move to Dallas, and double that amount if it will go to Honolulu or hell. There is no bitterness in this, no desire to offend; it is simply a business proposition by a business man who realizes that Baylor is a disgrace to the community, is playing Old Man of the Sea to Waco's Sinbad. The town could well afford to give it $100,000 to "pull its freight."

*   *   *   *   *

SOME ECONOMIC IDIOCY.

A correspondent calls my attention to the recommendation of a commission appointed by the governor of Massachusetts, to the effect that "all taxes on intangible property be abolished." He adds that, "as much of the wealth of Massachusetts is in stocks, bonds and mortgages this would relieve the rich at the expense of the poor." I could recommend that my correspondent be placed in a well-padded cell in a lunatic asylum and fed on *Ladies Home Journal* literature. The idea that what he calls "intangible property" should be taxed is quite prevalent among the ignorant and a perfect hobby with the half-educated. No writer distinguished for economic erudition recommends laying a tax on notes, stocks, bonds and other such evidence of wealth. Such a tax should never be laid by a government guaranteeing equal right. It is class legislation—it is *double taxation*. This statement may not be at all palatable to the West and South, but the proposition is impregnable. It taxes both the lender and the borrower on the same property and the latter has to pay for both. It must be remembered that such securities are not wealth *per se*, any more than a cook-book is a square meal—they are merely evidences of ownership. Let us say that I hold $10,000 worth of stock in the Illinois Central railroad: The road is my property to the extent of my stock—I am a small partner in the enterprise. It pays taxes to the State of Illinois and to every county and municipality through which it passes. Having paid taxes upon my property in Illinois, where it is located, must I pay taxes upon it again in Texas, where it has no existence? If I must pay taxes upon my railway property, then pay it again upon the certificate that I own it and am entitled to its usufruct, why not compel me to pay taxes on my business block, then pay it again on the deed thereto in my possession. My certificate of railway ownership and my certificate of realty ownership are on an exact parity from an economic standpoint. Each is evidence that I possess tangible property upon which I am paying taxes, and I emphatically object to a double dose. Exactly the same principle applies to promissory notes and bonds. A bond is nothing more nor less than a note. Suppose that I hold Illinois Central bonds to the extent of $10,000 instead of stock: The corporation has borrowed the money of me and invested it. It is paying taxes as well as interest on my property in consideration of use. As the corporation is using the property it must earn all the taxes, by whosoever directly paid, for I can earn nothing with property not in my possession. If I am taxed on my bonds, I must "put it in the bill," just as the merchant puts rent, interest and insurance. If Massachusetts owns ten million dollars of Texas securities she has simply transferred that much tangible wealth to this state for us to tax. If the paper evidence that this property is located here be taxed in Massachusetts, Texas must pay the piper. Let it never be forgotten that a tax is but a toll and can only be taken of something tangible. You cannot get blood out of a ghost or wealth out of a paper evidence of property. The blood must come from real veins and the tax must be drawn from something tangible. It is a contravention of justice and a violation of economic law to tax this man's property once and that man's twice. That the one is rich and the other poor does not mitigate the infamy—it is a fundamental principle of this republic that all men shall be equal before the law. Some years ago a howl was raised that reached high heaven that Jay Gould was worth 50 millions and paid taxes on but 75 thousand. Economic idiots gnawed a file because the ex-house-trap maker objected to paying his taxes twice, and charging his patrons on both the amount and the cost of collection. There are many abnormal fortunes in this country, but confiscation through taxation is not the proper remedy. If the government toll be an ounce in the pound let it *be* an ounce in the pound, whether the citizen possess ten pounds or ten million. Let every citizen contribute to the support of government in exact proportion to his means. To exempt the man who makes $500 a year and place the entire burden upon the man who earns $1,000 a year and upwards is to make of the first a political pauper. The graduated income tax, so-called is wrong to one class of citizens and an insult to the other. Let us tax all property once and only once; but let us see to it that unctuous old hypocrites like Rockefeller are not permitted to rob the public—that they do not build collegiate monuments to their own memory with other people's money.

*   *   *   *   *

AN EPISCOPALIAN MISTAKE.

Sometime ago a correspondent sent the Iconoclast a newspaper report of the "jubilee sermon" of a Rev. Mr. Reed, rector of a Protestant Episcopal church, and inquired if the statements contained therein were true. The clipping has been mislaid, and I do not now remember where Rector Reed is located; but I do know that his statements, so far as I have investigated them, are arrant falsehoods. He affirms that the American Republic is the handiwork of Episcopalian patriots; that more than two-thirds of the signers of the Declaration of Independence and an equal proportion of our generals, statesmen and presidents have been members of that denomination. As the sources of information regarding the religious views of most prominent Americans are shamefully meagre, I was inclined to regard Rector Reed's sermon as a historical document of inestimable value. Being prone, however, to act upon the advice of St. Paul and "prove all things," I began a cursory investigation. Rector Reed neglected to give the source of his information, and to save me I could find but seven presidents, including Washington, who were Episcopalians, and now Col. Patrick Ford, of the *Irish World* calls my attention to Jared Spark's statement that the Father of his country "withdrew himself from the communion service." Jefferson, whom Rector Reed claims as an Episcopalian, was, as every school-boy knows, an avowed free-thinker. The Adamses were Unitarians, Garfield was a Campbellite, Jackson, Buchanan, Cleveland and Ben Harrison were Presbyterians, Lincoln was non-sectrian, Grant and Hayes were Methodists, as is McKinley, while the religion of several others is unknown. Rector Reed's other statements stand examination as poorly as that relating to the presidents. It is pretty safe to judge a church by its clergy, and the clergy of the Anglo-American or Episcopal church were tory almost to a man. As I have made this statement before, and it has been flatly denied in the Chicago press by an Episcopalian bishop, it may be well to quote a few paragraphs from an article by Rev. Chas. Inglis, entitled "State of the Anglo-American Church in 1776." Inglish was at the time Rector of Trinity Church, New York, and afterwards bishop of Nova Scotia. His article may be found in Vol. 3, O'Callaghan's "Documentary History of the State of New York." Inglis says under date of October 31st, 1776:

Reverend Sir: The confusions which have prevailed in North America for some time past must have necessarily interrupted the correspondence of the missionaries with the society. A short authentic account of them, and of the Church of England in general, in this and the adjacent colonies, may be acceptable to the society at this most critical period. The success of his majesty's arms in reducing the city, and driving out the rebels, the 15th of last month, affords me an opportunity of doing this, as packets are now again established between this port and England. I have the pleasure to assure you that all the society's missionaries, without excepting one, in New Jersey, New York, Connecticut, and, so far as I can learn, in the other New England colonies, have proved themselves faithful, loyal subjects in these trying times; and have to the uttermost of their power opposed the spirit of disaffection and rebellion which has involved this continent in the greatest calamities. I must add that all the other clergy of our church in the above colonies, though not in the society's service, have observed the same line of conduct; and although their joint endeavors could not wholly prevent the rebellion, yet they checked it considerably for some time, and prevented many thousands from plunging into it who otherwise would certainly have done so. . . . The present rebellion is certainly one of the most causeless, unprovoked and unnatural that ever disgraced any country; a rebellion marked with peculiarly aggravated circumstances of guilt and ingratitude. . . . About the middle of April, Mr. Washington—commander-in-chief of the rebel forces, came to town with a large reinforcement. Animated by his presences, and I suppose, encouraged by him, the rebel committees very much harassed the loyal inhabitants here on Long Island. Soon after Washington's arrival he attended our church; but on the Sunday morning, before divine services began, one of the rebel generals called at the rector's house (supposing the latter was in town) and, not finding him, left word that he came to inform the rector that "General Washington would be at church, and would be glad if the violent prayers for the king and royal family were omitted." This message was brought to me, and, as you may suppose, I paid no regard to it. Things being thus situated, I shut up the churches. Even this was attended with great hazard; for it was declaring, in the strongest manner, our disapprobation of independency, and that under the eye of Washington and his army. I have not a doubt but, with the blessing of Providence, his majesty's arms will be successful and finally crush this unnatural rebellion."

The ICONOCLAST is indebted to Col. Patrick Ford for a transcript of Rev. Inglis' ebulition. It fully substantiates the statement made by this journal some time ago that the Episcopal churches were, during the revolution, "nests of tories and traitors."

*   *   *   *   *

GLORY OF THE NEW GARTER.

BY JOHN A. MORRIS.

A few seasons ago when Audrey Beardsleyism was the rage and Oscar Wilde a lion in "sassiety" gay plaid stockings in Persian or Audrey Beardsley designs sold as high as $7.50 a pair, enough I should say to enable a poor devil like me to live a week. But this is not all. For spring or June brides of the "swell London sassiety set," fine white silk stockings cost $22.50 a pair must go with a wedding gown and trousseau equally as extravagant, the climax of fashion's freakish ways being the rose-made garter worn over said stockings. Parisian society which smells to heaven in fashionable odors has now originated garters made of primroses, harebells, narcissus, violets and lillies, the same being worn by the ladies at balls and receptions in Paris. Knots of blossoms are caught among the thick flouncings and ruches of the petticoats; and even the embroidered corset has its little bouquet attachment. The inside flounce of the most delicate evening gowns is made entirely of flowers, and the newest garter is simply made to conform to the general harmony of fragrance and color.

The appropriateness of a flower for garter-wearing purposes is considered according to the degree and strength of its perfume, the most highly perfumed being the most highly appropriate. Violets are in great favor, and are used for garters worn with lilac, lavander, delicate green or white costumes. Again, as American women love to ape the fashionable society of gay Paris it may not be very long before in the great cities of the country we may not only have the American morphine fiend and cologne-drinker, but also the perfume faddist. Not long ago a Paris druggist communicated to a few French "sassiety" women the plan of perfuming the skin by means of hypodermic injections. The favorite distilled odors are violet and lavender. I know not how true it is, but I heard that this fashion is already being taken up by some of New York city's fashionable freaks of "sassiety" women.

I have recently been engaged in reading two very interesting histories, the one of the rose, the other of perfume, in reading which I was deeply impressed with the fact that all the civilizations of the past, previous to their downfall, had their rose fetes, their festivals of flowers where luxury and license ruled, where effeminacy ruled supreme, their perfumed halls and extravagant balls and soirees. Before the fall of the Roman Empire, the wealthy abandoned themselves to pleasure, luxury and licentiousness and such expressions as "living in the midst of roses," and "sleeping on roses" had a deep and tragic meaning. Seneca speaks of Smyndiride who could not sleep if one of the rose petals with which his bed was spread happened to be curled. Cicero alludes to the then prevailing custom among the Romans of reclining at the table on couches covered with roses. Ah, my jeweled buddies, there were Adonises in those days!

When Cleopatra, the perfumed serpent of the Nile, went into Cilicia to meet Mark Antony, she gave him for several days a festival such as the gods themselves would not blush to participate in. She had placed in the banqueting hall twelve couches large enough to hold three guests. Purple tapestry interwoven with gold covered the walls, golden vases admirably executed and enriched with precious stones stood on a magnificent gold floor. On the fourth day the queen carried her sumptuousness so far as to pay a talent ($600.00 in our money) for a quantity of roses, with which she caused the floor of the hall to be covered to a depth of eighteen inches. These flowers were retained in a very fine net, to allow the guests to walk over them. According to Suetonius, Nero (the fiddler of burning Rome and the tyrant par excellence of the ancient day) gave a fete at one time on the Gulf of

Baiae when inns were established on the banks, and ladies of noble blood played hostesses to the occasion, the roses alone costing more than four million of sesterces, or $100,000. As the hag Tofana was the inventor of a new and deadly poison, so Lucius Aurelius Verus was the inventor of a new species of luxury. He had a most magnificent couch made, on which four raised cushions closed in on all sides by a very thin net, and made of leaves of roses. Heliogabalus, celebrated for every kind of vice and luxury, caused roses to be crushed with the kernels of the pine (pinus maritima) in order to increase the perfume. Roses were, by the order of this same emperor, scattered over the couches, halls and even the portierres of the palaces were decorated with the same. A profusion of flowers of every kind, lilies, violets, hyacinths, narcissus, etc., filled great quantities of space. Gallien, another cruel and luxurious princeling, lay under arbors of roses sometimes varying the performance by reclining on beds of roses. Before her downfall Rome could spend millions on her royal tables, support the dignity of a single senator at $80,000 a year, employ courts of sycophants and flatterers, impose taxes at the pleasure of her ruler, declare any complaint treason, marry her daughters for money and title, employ notaries to attest the fatness of her banquet fowls, punish a servant for disobedience and trivial offenses with death, while letting the monied thief and murderer go free with a mild reprimand, and making slaves and menials of the profoundest philosophers. The dancer and the buffoon received the homage and the adoration which in the golden age of Greece under the reign of Pericles only scholars, philosophers and artists received. Poverty in those days was crime, so in ours! Augustine of Rome was utterly ignored. "In exact proportion to the sum of money a man keeps in his chest," says Juvenal, "is the credit given to his oath." Verily, reader, these days at the end of the nineteenth century are greatly similar to those last days of Rome. Yvette Gilbert, the songstress of the vile, the recitationist of the vulgar, and Le Loie Fuller, the dancer of the serpentine, live off the fat of the land every day. The songstress and the kickeress get their thousands of dollars per week, while "the poor devil of a workingman" must be satisfied with a dollar a day cash and barrels of unlimited confidence. Caligula's horse wore a collar of pearls and drank from an ivory trough. Nero fiddled while Rome was burning. Cleveland when president drank his morning coffee from a cup worth $100 at least, and went fishing at Buzzard's Bay while the ship of state was plunging among the rocks and breakers of bonded indebtedness. Conde spent three thousand crowns to deck his palace at Chantilly. The Duke of Albuquerque had forty silver ladders. The expression then, as now, was often heard, "the rich are getting richer and the poor are getting poorer.

" San Pedro, Cal., November 11.

*	*	*	*	*

TWO OF A KIND.

BY H. S. C.

The McKinley administration has been in power long enough to show that the only material distinction between it and the Cleveland administration lies in the fact that it is slightly more extravagant. That is the characteristic of the Republican party and no one is surprised. In addition to being the party of violence, bigotry and fraud, it is also the party of gay liberality with other people's money. In the matter of directing the destinies of this country towards a higher and better national existence, there is really nothing to choose between Republicanism and Democracy. Both are equally unwilling and incompetent, both, despite the prating of civil service snobs and snivellers are dominated by spoils, and the managers of both regard a campaign not as a battle for the betterment of America but as a battle for boodle. The McKinley administration has appointed some Negro postmasters in the South. This the Democratic administration would not have done. The McKinley administration has played openly into the hands of the trust. This the Democratic administration would have done secretly. The McKinley administration enacted a tariff law which robs the people openly for the benefit of a few. This the Democratic administration would have done in sly paragraphs here and there, in the meanwhile declaiming loudly against the unrighteousness of tariff barons. The McKinley administration has based its contracted currency solely upon the gold product. This the Democratic administration would have based, with almost equal fatuity, upon the silver product. McKinleyism and the Democracy with which the country has been cursed on two occasions since the war, are six of one and half a dozen of the other. Practically considered, the main difference between Republicanism and Democracy, is the difference between the highwayman and the sneak thief. This being so, the question naturally arises: What are we going to do about it? Nothing. That is, not yet. The time may come when the people will choose public servants for fitness, and will demand that they keep the pledges made as a condition precedent to election, but it is far from us. In many of the years to come we will continue to build up an office-holding class that is now so utterly idle, incompetent, impudent and corrupt that the history of the world can show nothing like it. This will be always so with universal suffrage. A government which permits the ballot of a man who has not a dollar's interest in the good conduct of the government, who can neither read nor write, who cannot speak the English language, who is permitted to vote merely upon the declaration that he intends at some time to become a citizen, will continue to be a rotten government. The wonder is not that the United States has had war internecine and otherwise, but that it has existed at all. It carries within itself the elements of its own damnation. It has within itself the seeds of decay. Unless they are dug out, that which is now one of the worst governments under the sun will be no government at all.

*   *   *   *   *

THE SAW-MILL CHECK SYSTEM.

The ICONOCLAST receives frequent complaints from laboring people in the lumber districts of Texas and Louisiana, that their employers are robbing them by compelling them to accept orders on mill stores, where they are charged exorbitant prices for all they purchase. I have been unable to visit the lumber districts and make personal investigation of these complaints, while letters of inquiry have elicited conflicted evidence. The following statement by a disinterested party, a gentleman of unusual intelligence who has traveled extensively in the lumber districts of the two states, is doubtless a fairly correct account:

The system of issuing checks to saw-mill employees, as practiced in some places, is, in my opinion, an advantage to the laborer. Each mill has a pay-day, monthly, and the checks issued at intervals between pay-days, redeemable in merchandise, pass current among merchants at par. You can buy a big glass of beer for a 5-cent check as you can for a nickel, and buy it anywhere it is sold. You can, in fact, buy anything at any place in these towns for mill checks. The merchants either use them in trading at the mill stores, which are large and complete, or sell them, at a discount of 5 per cent. to parties who engage in building and who use them in paying for lumber, which is sold at the same price for checks as for cash. No one is required to take these checks, which are merely in the nature of an advance payment on wages. Each employee can wait until pay-day and get all that is due him in cash. Many of the mills are large concerns with A1 credit, and being able to buy as cheaply as anybody, can, and I believe do, sell as cheaply. Such is the case with the Beaumont mills and the mills on the Sabine and East Texas road owned by Beaumont parties; but as much cannot be said for saw-mills at some other points. There are some saw-mills in Texas that never have a pay-day; they issue checks on the commissary and charge enormous profits, so that the people who work at these mills are virtually peons. A party told me some time ago that on the H. E. & W. T. railway mill checks of reputable institutions can be bought for 20 cents, 30 cents and 40 cents on the dollar. I do not know that this is so, but I believe it. As for the mills at Orange and Lake Charles, they have no commissaries attached, but I have been told that certain merchants in those towns pay the mill owners 10 per cent. on all orders sent them, and the mills go so far as to turn in each evening to the merchant the time made by each employee to govern them in giving credit. This looks like a fraud on the employee and it is wrong for the employer to pocket money which should rightfully go to his employee. But he reasons that he has an established pay-day, and if his employees will insist on demanding money or its equivalent every evening, and thus force him to retain an extra man to attend to the check-issuing business it is right that the employees should bear that expense. I believe the mills at Westlake have commissaries, but I know the mill-owners and do not believe they practice any extortion. They pay off in checks. They have a monthly pay-day, and if, like railway employees, these should wait until the first Saturday after the 5th or 10th of each month they could draw their wages in cash. No mill at either place mentioned pays off in checks. You might roast such mills as those on the H. E. & W. T. referred to, as they rob not only their employees, but, by thus being able to manufacture lumber cheaper than those who pay wages, force down the price in the open market and compel the honest manufacturer to meet it."

*   *   *   *   *

LOVE AS AN INTOXICANT?

Seymour, Texas, Nov. 4, 1897.

MR. BRANN: Will you please answer the following question and thereby settle a dispute in Seymour: Is love intoxicating?

CHAS. E. RUPE.

My correspondent neglects to state whether Seymour is a Prohibition town. Of course if it is and love is listed as an intoxicant, the blind god will be expatriated for the benefit of the makers of Peruna, Hostetter's Bitters and and other palate ticklers, popular only at blind tigers. Why the deuce didn't the Seymourites set to work and settle this vexatious problem for themselves? Must I undertake a system of scientific experiments in order to obtain this information for the citizens of Seymour? Suppose that I do so, find that love makes drunk come, and am run in by the patrol wagon while supercharged with the tender passion: don't you see that this would militate against my usefulness as a Baptist minister? How the hell could I explain to my congregation that I was full of love instead of licker? Clearly I cannot afford to offer myself as a sacrifice upon the altar of science. Should I proceed to fall in love just to see if it would go to my head, and should it do so, my Dulcina del Toboso might marry me before I recovered my mental equipoise, and I would awaken to find my liberty a has-been and my night-key non est. Of course I should mind it ever so little, but it would be awfully hard on the lady. I have been baptized just to see if it would soak out any original sin; I've gone up in a balloon and down in a coal mine in the interest of science; I've ridden on the pilot of a locomotive for the sake of the sensation; I've permitted myself to be inoculated with the virus of Christian charity just to see if it would "take"; I've tampered with almost every known intoxicant, from the insidious mescal of the erstwhile Montezumas to the mountain nectar of Eastern Tennessee, but I draw the line at love. Will it intoxicate? Prithee, good sirs, I positively decline to experiment. However, if hearsay evidence be admissible I'm willing to take the stand. To the best of my knowledge and belief love will pick a man up quicker and throw him down harder than even the double-distilled brand of prohibition busthead. Like champagne at 2 a.m., it is good to look upon and pleasant to the palate; but at last it biteth like a serpent and stingeth like an able-bodied bumble-bee in a pair of blue-jean pants. Like alcoholism, love lies in wait for the young and unwary—approaches the victim so insidiously that ere he is aware of danger he's a gone sucker. The young man goeth forth in the early evening and his patent leathers. His coat-tail pockets bulge with caramels and his one silk handkerchief, perfumed with attar of roses, reposeth with studied negligence in his bosom. He saith unto himself, "I will sip the nectar of the blind deity but I will not become drunken, for verily I know when to ring myself down." He calleth upon the innocent damosel with soft eyes and lips like unto a cleft cherry when purple with its own sweetness, and she singeth unto him with a voice that hath the low sweet melody of an aeolian harp, and squozeth his hand in the gloaming, sigheth just a wee sigh that endeth in a blush.

And behold it cometh to pass that when the gay young man doth stagger down the door-steps of her dear father's domicile he knoweth not whether he is hoofing it to Klondyke or riding an erratic mustang into Mexico. He is drunken with the sweetness of it all and glad of it. And she? Oh she lets him down easy—sends him an engraved invitation to her marriage with some guy with oodles of the long green whom her parent on her mother's side has corraled at the matrimonial bargain counter. Then the young man has a case of what we Chermans call Katzenjammer, and swears an almighty swore never to do so any more. But he does. When a man once contracts the habit of being in love there's no help for him. It is a strange stimulant which acts upon the blood like the oenanthic of old wine, upon the soul like the perfume of jasmine buds. He has felt its mighty spell, more potent than the poppy's juice or the distillation of yellow corn that has waved its golden bannerets on Kentucky's sun-kissed hills—more strangely sweet than music heard at minight across a moonlit lake or the soul-sensuous dream of the lotus eaters' land. For the spell of the poppy's dreamy drug and the charm of the yellow corn whose spirit breeds dangerous lightnings in the blood, the skill of man has provided a panacea; but "love is strong as death," says David's wisest son. Will love intoxicate? Rather! I should say that Solomon was drunk with love when he wrote the Canticles:

> "Let him kiss me with the kisses of his mouth, for thy love is better than wine."

When a man is drunken he sees strange varieties of serpents. That's what ailed Adam and Eve. They kept intoxicated with their own primordial sweetness until they got the jimmies and saw a talking snake prancing around the evergreen aisles of Eden with legs like unto a prima donna. At least I suppose the Edenic serpent was built that way, for the Lord cursed it and compelled it to go on its belly all the days of its life. Hence the Lord must have pulled its leg. So to speak, or words to that effect. As an intoxicant love affects one differently from liquor. A man drunk on bourbon wants to trail his coat-tails down the middle of the plank turnpike and advise the natives that he is in town. The man drunk on love yearns to hide away from the busy haunts of men and write poetry for the magazines. The one is sentenced to ten days in the bat-cave and the other to pay some woman's board. Verily the way of the transgressor is hard. Some people manage to worry through life without ever becoming drunken on either liquor or love. They marry for money, or to secure housekeepers, and drink pink lemonade and iced buttermilk until there's clabber in their blood. They "like" their mates, but do not love them, and their watery babes grow up and become Baptists. Their affections are to the real article what dengue is to yellow fever. Temperance is a good thing in its way; but the man who is temperate in love is not to be trusted. The true man or woman can no more love moderately than a powder magazine can explode on the installment plan. When the cup once touches their lips it is drained to the very dregs. The chalice is not passed by human hands—the gods give and the gods withhold. Hence it is that we ever find Love's bacchanals beating against the social bars. We laugh at the man who flushed with wine disregards the peace and dignity of the state; but we frown upon the woman who drunk with love sins against our social laws.

Man's brewed enchantments may be set aside by acts of human will; but the wine of love creeps like a subtle perfume through all the senses whether we will or no, filling the brain with madness, the heart with fire.

*   *   *   *   *

THE SWORD AND THE CROSS.

A correspondent asks "whether the great nations owe most to the sword or the cross." That were much like asking whether the usefulness of a watch be due most to the case or the works. Religion has ever been the heart of the body social, the dynamics of civilization. A great nation of Atheists is a practical impossibility, because the basic principle of such a society must needs be selfishness, and from such a foundation no mighty superstructure can ever rise. "Ye cannot gather grapes of thorns nor figs of thistles." War is but an incident in the history of a nation, while religion is its very life. In the latter it moves and breathes and has its being. From the standpoint of a statesman it makes little difference what the religion of a people may be so long as most of them believe it. History abundantly demonstrates that when a nation begins to doubt its gods, it begins to lose its glory. Without religion the contract social is simply a rope of sand. "No union of church and state" is simply a protest against the union of body and soul. The greatest rulers of ancient and modern times regarded religion as the palladium of national power. True it is that religion has time and again strengthened the hands of the tyrant and stoned the prophets of progress; but every good gift bequeathed to man has been at times abused. The sword has been wielded by the assassin; it has been employed to enslave and despoil the people; yet we dare not break the blade. Men of narrow minds, seeing many warring cults, imagine them to be disturbing factors in the human brotherhood—that if they could be eliminated, the body politic would have peace. They cannot understand that the discords of the finite make the harmony of the infinite. They fail to see that these warring creeds are but the necessary differentiations of a common faith. Lay the winds, still the tides, and old ocean, that perennial fount of health, becomes a stagnant pool of putrefaction—a malodorous "mother of dead dogs." Force presupposes friction. Let the sectaries fight, each doing valiant battle for his own dogma, for when they all agree religion will be dead and progress at an end. It is not necessary that you and I should stand close enough to be stifled with the dust of conflict, to taste all the bitterness of sectarian controversy—we may mount above it all and watch it beat like the convolutions of a mighty brain. We may take refuge in the philosophy of religion and say that all are right in conception and wrong in expression; we may call it blind superstition if we will; but if we mount high enough to obtain a clear vision we must confess that religion has ever been the dominant factor in the forging of mighty peoples. Were I required to give a reason for this fact I would say it is because man is not altogether a machine—because he is not content to eat and sleep and propagate his kind like the lower animals. Despite his thick veneer of selfishness, man is at heart a creature of sentiment, and religion is the poetry of the common people. Crude it may be, but its tendency is toward the stars, while all else in man is animalistic and of the earth. Strike the religion, the poetry, out of a people, and you reduce them to the level of educated animals. Annul the power that draws them upward and they must sink back to primordial savagery. The individual may accept logic as a substitute for sentiment, but a nation cannot do so. The masses are not swayed through the head, but through the heart. Sentiment is the divine perfume of the soul. Of sentiment was born the dream of immortality. It is the efficient cause of every sacrifice which man makes for his fellow man. It is the parent duty, and duty pre-supposes the Divine. Could the materialists inaugurate their belauded age of reason, sentiment would perish utterly in that pitiless atmosphere, and the world be reduced to a basis of brute selfishness. The word duty would disappear, for why should man die for man in a world whose one sole god was the dollar. Why should a Damien sacrifice himself if selfish ease be the only divinity? If there be no Fatherhood of God there can be no Brotherhood of Man—we are but accidents, spawn of the sun and slime, each an Ishmel considering only himself. Atheism means universal anarchy. It means a kingdom without a king, laws without a legislator, a machine without a master. An Atheist is a public enemy. He would not only destroy the state but wreck society. He would render life not worth the living. He would rob us of our garden roses and fill our hands with artificial flowers. And why? Because, forsooth, he finds that some articles of religious faith are impossible fables. He sits down with a microscope to examine the tables of the law for tracks of the finger of him whose sentences are astral fire. He finds a foolish contradiction in some so-called sacred book and imagines that he has proven either that man's a fool or God's a fraud. "By geometric scale he takes the measure of pots of ale." He calls himself a "liberal," while fanatically intolerant of the honest opinions of others. He is forever mistaking shadow for substance, the accidental for the essential. He "disproves" religion without in the least comprehending it. He hammers away at the Immaculate Conception and the miracles with a vigor that amuses those who realize that cults and creeds are but ephemeral, while faith in the Almighty endures forever. And of all the Atheists and Agnostics Bob Ingersoll is the most insupportable. He is but a mouthful of sweetened wind, a painted echo, an oratorical hurdy-gurdy that plays the music of others. He's as innocent of original ideas as a Mexican fice of feathers. He gets down on the muddy pave and wrangles with the "locus" preachers. He's a theological shyster lawyer who takes advantage of technicalities. He is not a philosopher—he's emphatically "a critic fly." He examines the Christian cult inch by inch, just as Gulliver did the cuticle of the Brobdingnagian maid who sat him astride her nipple. He never contemplates the tout ensemble. He learns absolutely nothing from the cumulative wisdom of the world. He doesn't even appreciate the fact that the dominant religions of the world to-day are couched in the language of oriental poetry. He wastes his nervo-muscular energy demolishing the miracles. When he gets through with the Bible I presume that he'll take a fall out of aesop's Fables. He doesn't understand that the soul of man has never learned a language—that all sacred books are but an outward evidence of an inward grace. He doesn't know that religion, like love, cannot be analyzed. Because the orient pearls are imbedded in ocean slime he denies their existence. Ingersoll and the "plenary inspiration" people are welcome to fight it out—it's none of my funeral. You may prove Zoroaster a myth, Moses a mountebank, Gautama a priestly grafter and Christ the prototype of Francis Schlatter and other half-witted frauds; but adoration of a superior power will remain a living, pulsing thing in the hearts of the people. It is this poetry, this sentiment, this sense of duty, which transcends the dollar that constitutes the adhesive principle of society and makes civilization possible.

*   *   *   *   *

A COUPLE OF UNCLEAN COYOTES.

There are times when language seems made, as Talleyrand would say, to conceal thought; times when in no known tongue can one body forth his indignation or express a tithe of his contempt—he gropes in vain for invectives that bear upon their sulphurous wings an adumbration of his anger. One must sometimes stand speechless before a subject, else burn his lips with blasphemy or befoul them with billingsgate. Two months ago my attention was called to a precious pair of attorneys at San Antonio, Texas, who seem to have not only touched the profoundest depths of subter-brutish degradation, but to have wallowed there like swine in an open sewer, proud of their own dishonor, infatuated with their rank disgrace. Time and again I have been requested to hold them up to the scorn of human-kind, and time and again I have essayed the subject only to find the product of my pen unprintable—it would have melted the type and burned a hole in an asbestos mailbag. But indignation cools as the days run, philosophy asserts itself, and perchance I can speak of these offenders in language sufficiently polite to escape the attention of the police. The facts may be summarized as follows: A modest, well-behaved German girl named Wulff was brutally assaulted and raped on a lonely road by a negro named Robinson, who decoyed her to the place of her undoing by telling her mother that he had been commissioned by a reputable white woman to secure a serving-maid. His victim dragged herself back to her mother's door, and, half dead with grief and fright, related the awful story of her despoilment. The lying coon was apprehended and tried for his hellish crime. There could not be the slightest doubt regarding his guilt. He was fully identified. His general bad character was amply proven. The doctors declared that the child had been forcibly despoiled. The neighbors testified that she had returned to her home with torn and muddy clothing, half strangled and crying. The good character of plaintiff was demonstrated beyond peradventure of a doubt. Yet in San Antonio, that Mecca of Southern chivalry, there stood forth two white-skinned lawyers to defend the lecher. These were McAnderson and E. D. Henry. Do not forget these names—they represent the sum and crown of infamy. They are names with which to conjure evil spirits. By one shameful act they have been "damned to everlasting fame." Henceforth when babes are naughty their mothers will affright them with these foul bogey-men. In almighty Milton's catalogue of unclean demons there is naught so damnable. These two champions of a rape-fiend first attempted to establish an alibi, to prove that the girl was lying about their sweet-scented protege—that she was laying claim to a sexual distinction which she did not deserve. That having failed miserably, the attorneys changed their tactics. They knew that their client was guilty, yet were anxious to turn the black son of Perdition loose upon society. They admitted that he had debauched the girl, but insisted that it was with her consent—that this modest little German maid was the black brute's mistress. They scared up a brace of worthless brutes who testified to having seen plaintiff bathing naked in a creek with the prisoner at the bar. It was quickly demonstrated that these fellows were guilty of deliberate falsehood. The perjured witnesses were impeached. To say that defendant's attorneys did not know when they placed these witnesses on the stand that they would exploit a foul calumny cooked up for the occasion, were to brand them as hopeless fools. If they did know it they were knaves—and they are welcome to impale themselves on either horn of the dilemma they like. They next attempted to badger and browbeat the poor girl into an admission that she had made an assignation with the Senegambian. The local papers in reporting the case said the language used by these chivalrous (?) Southern gentlemen to the plaintiff was unprintable. They secured no admission of guilt—not one word that could be distorted to her discredit; but they did succeed in driving the child into hysterics with their brutal insults and damnable innuendos. Remember that this was not Muckle-Mouth Meg who was thus publicly accused of criminal intimacy with a coon, but a 16-year old maid of respectable family who was seeking a situation as housemaid to assist her mother. But the foul-mouthed and foul-minded creatures who had undertaken to save the neck of the ravisher cared naught for a young girl's reputation. The villain Robinson was given a life-term in the penitentiary—and his attorneys expressed themselves as "satisfied with the verdict." Why were they satisfied? Because they knew that their client deserved to hang like a sheep-stealing hound. It was a brutal confession that in questioning the good name of Miss Wulff, in branding her as the mistress of a black, they were guilty of a more heinous crime than the beast who defiled her body. And this actually happened in San Antonio, a city whose very name thrills every fibre of American manhood—a city from whose turrets the flags of five nations have proudly fluttered—a city whose every foot of soil has been time and again baptised with the blood of the brave—a city that twice within the century has put Thermopylae to shame! Yet I am told that these unclean birds, who befoul so fair a nest are allowed to live in San Antonio, to walk her streets, to elbow her proud sons and look her proud daughters in the face! How have the mighty fallen! There was a time when to have breathed a word against the good name of an honest girl, howsoever humble, would have meant the bowie-knife's fearful plunge and a dead face staring at the stars. It were curious to reflect what would have happened had the victim of Ethiopian lust been Lady Vere de Vere instead of a scullery maid! What would have happened? Why, the brute would have been torn limb from limb and his carcass fed to the buzzards, while any man who dared hint that she was his paramour would have been hanged higher than Haman. "The trail of the serpent is over us all," the golden calf has become our supreme god, and even in the South it now matters much whether a woman seeking justice be clothed in gowns of Worth or linsey-wolsey.

I once discovered in Massachusetts what I considered to be the world's meanest man. It was Rev. Spenser B. Meeser, engineer of a Worcester gospel-mill. He was a beggar's brat who had been clothed, fed and educated by old Stephen Girard's bounty, but when he grew to manhood—or doghood—he puked on the grave of his benefactor because the latter elected to be an Atheist instead of a bigoted Baptist. I could not at the time conceive of anything meaner wearing the name of man, of a crime blacker than base ingratitude, of aught more damnable than calumniation of the honored dead; but Massachusetts will have to surrender the pennant of infamy to the South. Texas has succeeded in producing two men, either of whom is infinitely meaner than Meeser. The latter did no more than insult the memory of the man whose bread he had broken, and he did this as an excuse for not contributing a little money towards building him a monument. The meanness of Meeser was solely mercenary—he found it easier to slander the dead than to give up a dollar. The San Antonio lawyers sought to turn a black rape-fiend loose to defile the women of the South, to endanger their own daughters; and to perpetrate this crime strove with tooth and nail to commit one even more damnable.

Fifty years ago Macaulay wrote of Bertrand Barere: "When we put everything together, poltroonery, baseness, effrontery, mendacity, barbarity, the result is something which in a novel we should condemn as caricature, and to which, we venture to say, no parallel can be found in history." It is indeed a pity the great essayist did not live to contemplate this pair of Texas attorneys. He would have learned, doubtless to his surprise, that "the Anacreon of the guillotine" was a pretty decent fellow—by comparison. Barere was a monster born of a reign of blood. He gave the friends of his youth to the guillotine. So terrible was his savagery that he became known as "the Witling of Terror." He was an able-bodied and enterprising liar who never told the truth unless by accident; but in his most demoniac moods it did not occur to him to prove recreant to his race, to torture children that he might enjoy their agony, to brand innocent girls, who could scarce look upon their own budding bosoms without a blush, as the depraved paramours of syphilitic Senegambians. Ah Macaulay! from thy Seventh Heaven, reserved for the lords of intellect—the children of genius, who needs must be the favorites of Omniscience—shake down a drop of cold water upon the blistered lips of Bertrand Barere, for they did not frame the supreme falsehood—nor did he strive to unchain a black lecher that he might imperil the honor of the ladies of his native land. Despite all his sin and shame, he would have looked upon that dishonored daughter of the Caucasian race and cried for vengeance.

Carlyle, greatest of critics, the supreme lord of literature—that Scottish Arcturus before whom even Shakespeare's glorious star pals its ineffectual fires—awards the palm of correlated cussedness to Cagliostro; yet the "count" was merely a successful swindler and professional pander. He plucked rich dupes, but I find not in his long catalogue of crime that he slandered youthful serving maids—for a consideration. He was advocate for many an unclean thing, but it is not recorded that he ever took a fee from a negro rape-fiend—that he ever defended a lecherous son of Ham who had dared raise his wolfish eyes to the fair face of Japhet's humblest daughter. Even when put on trial for his own worthless life he did not seek to save himself by the perjured testimony of the sons of slaves.

Cagliostro, Barere and Meeser—the positive, comparative and superlative of infamy hitherto! but we must turn to "Grand old Texas" to find unblushing effrontry and irremediable rascality. Some months ago a creature named Otis, who conducts somewhere in Southern California a putrid abortion miscalled a newspaper, declared in his columns that Southern women are often paramours of black bucks, and that the frequent lynching of so-called rape-fiends are due to discovery of these unnatural liaisons. But as Otis commanded a company of coons during the war—a job which no gentleman would have accepted to save his immortal soul—and as he has a head shaped like a gourd and a face strongly suggestive of a degenerate simian, his foolish lies only produced a general laugh; yet here are two alleged Southern gentlemen, certifying in open court that Otis' cowardly falsehoods have a broad foundation of fact! In the whole world's history there is but one other instance of such shameless infamy, and that too belongs to Texas. When the 14-year old "ward of the Baptist church" was debauched at its chief storm center of bigotry and bile, Baylor University, the sweet scented son-in-law of President Burleson tried to make it appear that she was enciente by a Senegambian—that young and innocent girls committed to its care were so poorly guarded that it was possible for them to have nigger babies!—Yet this defamer of Baptist womanhood has not yet been introduced to a rope by the male students, attacked from the rear by Baylor trustees, or told to leave town! Fortunately the young lady was able to refute this slander of the University and its inmates by putting a white baby in evidence—the pickaninny specialty having been reserved by Providence for the manager of the Baptist missionary board.

One cannot help asking if Miss Wulff has no male relatives, or if gunpowder is no longer sold in the Alamo City. As I understand it, her people are late from the Fatherland—have yet to learn that in some cases society expects a man to overlook the law, to kill as unclean curs those who thus defame a female member of their family. It is possible that there are other shyster lawyers as mean, other bipedal coyotes as contemptible as those under consideration; but if so they have not yet been called to the attention of the ICONOCLAST. True it is, however, that the average attorney cares more for victory than for virtue. Howsoever honest and upright he may be in private life, the moment he enters the court-room he becomes an unnatural monster, willing to accept the devil as client and win his case at any cost. It is likewise true that the courts allow too large a liberty to lawyers in the examination of witnesses for the opposition, permitting them to call in question the honor of men of well-known probity and cast suspicion on the character of women full as good as their wives in order to make an impression on the jury that will redound to the interest of cut-throat clients. It has come to such a pass in this so-called chivalrous country that sensitive women will submit to almost any wrong rather than seek redress in our courts of law, where they are liable to be subjected to studied insult by unconscionable shysters. It were well for the people to take this matter in hand and make it plain to all concerned that courts do not exist for the express purpose of enabling blackguard lawyers to pocket fat fees for aiding professional criminals to escape the legitimate consequence of their crimes, but to secure even and exact justice—to insist that henceforth these legal parasites be compelled to treat them with common courtesy. It might be well for the South to vary the program by lynching fewer rape-fiends and more shysters lawyers.

*   *   *   *   *

COINING BLOOD INTO BOODLE.

Some months ago the ICONOCLAST paid its respects to the old line insurance companies. It demonstrated beyond the peradventure of a doubt that they are but so many cut-throat gambling concerns. It proved that they are consuming the substance of the people by returning in satisfaction of matured policies about one-third what they collect in premiums. Of course, the expose aroused the ban-dogs of Dives, and they made the welkin ring from Tadmor in the wilderness to Yuba Dam. The Iconoclast became a target for oodles of cheap wit and barrels of black-guardism by the journalistic organ-grinders for the insurance buccaneers; but as yet none of the megalophanous-mouthed micrococci have attempted to answer its arguments or to demonstrate that the indictment was too drastic. A gentleman who has made an exhaustive study of the insurance problem sends me some valuable data which I propose to draw upon from time to time, not with the expectation of making high-toned thieves ashamed of themselves and thereby effecting their reformation, but to keep their newspaper panders and potwallopers snarling and snapping until general attention is attracted to the consummate meanness of their masters and thereby curtail somewhat their powers of despoilation. The old line life insurance fake is the most colossal scheme of predacity known to human history. Enough money is annually filched from the people to clothe every pauper like unto Solomon in all his glory and feed him upon the fat of the land. Millions of Americans are today denying themselves creature comforts to pay premiums on policies that will never yield their dependents one penny. The old line fraud flourishes simply because, in the language of the erstwhile P. T. Barnum, the American people love to be hood-dooed and humbugged. I do not by this mean to reflect upon the commercial integrity of all men soliciting old line insurance. Many of them are elegant gentlemen who have engaged, quite unconsciously, in very bad business. The Deity should forgive them for they know not what they do. They really believe that they are engaged in a work of philanthropy, while devoting their best energies to the promotion of a fraud. The average policy-holder knows little or nothing about life-insurance. He desires to provide for his dependants; but being unable to accumulate much property, he scrapes and saves and pays to some remorseless robber all his surplus money. He wants to be doubly sure that the company is solvent and will remain so, hence he selects one boasting enormous "assets." It does not once occur to him that the aforesaid assets have been accumulated in a very few years by bumping the heads of other suckers. He pays the rate prescribed without considering whether it be high enough to keep the company solvent or low enough to stamp his investment as commercial sanity. He is little concerned about "dividends," but wants to be assured that at the time of his death his heirs will be paid a certain number of dollars. So he goes up against a mammoth slot-machine which absorbs dollars while it rolls out dimes. He knows that the widow so-and-so was paid so much insurance, and takes it for granted that it is a good thing. He sees the little pile of coin poured into her lap, but he does not see the greedy hands of the corporation despoiling a hundred pockets to make up treble the amount. He hears much about what the Flim-Flam Life Insurance Co. has paid on policies, but nothing about what it has collected in premiums. So he makes his old threadbare coat do for another decade, lets his wife go without a new gown, feeds his children on slapjacks and sop and surrenders for life insurance the surplus thus saved. No "cheap insurance" for him!—he wants to get into a "time-tried" financial Gibralter. He is told by the agent of an old liner of its enormous "legal reserve," and innocently supposes this to be a portion of its available assets—the one thing which makes it "solid." He contemplates a long array of figures and assumes that Old Mortality might sweep the land with War or pestilence without affecting the solvency of his patron saint. The agent neglects to inform him that the "legal reserve," which looms up like a seventy four in a fog, cannot be utilized in the discharge of death-claims, that insofar as the average policy holder is concerned it is simply a beautiful legend on an advertising blotter. When I was editor of the San Antonio Express the philanthropic proprietor gave me a block of land in the city of Laredo in lieu of a raise of salary, but neglected to supply me with a deed to same. The land is mine, all right enough, but is no part of my available assets—it's my "legal reserve." Like its insurance namesake, it's a liability to the exact extent that it's an asset. It is an awfully nice thing to have, but adds never a cent to my solvency. My correspondent points out that it costs policy holders in old line companies more to maintain the legal reserve than it does to provide for losses by death, and adds that this is proven by the fact that all such companies doing business in the State of New York must have on hand in cash, or in invested assets approved by the insurance department, the reserve belonging to all the policies which they have in force. This means that they must retain or keep invested a sum equal to about two-thirds of all the premiums paid on all existing policies. The moment they part with any portion of this reserve for any purpose whatsoever, they are declared insolvent and wound up by a receiver. In other words, the corporation is d——d if it does and the policy holder is d——d if it doesn't. That the latter gets the sulphur bath goes without saying. The four largest old system companies doing business in New York had, on Jan. 1, 1893, $48,265,798 more in legal reserve than the total amount which they have paid in death losses and endowments during their entire existence! With this fact before him, how in the name of heaven any sane man can be induced by an old system company to enact the role of sucker surpasses my comprehension. Five years ago the net assets of the largest old line life insurance company in the world amounted to $165,000,000, of which more than $158,000,000 was legal reserve. Had a shrinkage of 10 per cent occurred in the value of its investments its reserve would have been impaired and the corporation declared insolvent. So long ago as 1878 the Union Mutual Life Insurance Co. acknowledged over the signatures of its general officers that it had collected from its policy holders more than $45,000,000 "beyond the necessities of our business." It felt so badly about this that it proceeded to raise the cost of management from $5 to $11.57 on the $1,000 and shove up the premium something more than 20 per cent! It is believed that the gutta percha conscience of the general officers is now reasonably easy—that "the necessities of our business" are not on a parity with the ability of the corporation to yank the legs of the guileless yap. In 1873 this company paid in dividends $29 on each $1,000 insurance in force; in 1895 it paid—despite the increased cost of premiums—but $2.16. All the old line companies, so far as I know, have been increasing premiums and cost of management while decreasing dividends. "Loading" is another scheme by which all old line or legal reserve companies rob the people. "Loading" means simply the placing of a sufficient burden on the patron to freeze him out before maturity of his policy and enable the company to pocket all he has paid in premiums. The idea of the old liners is to squeeze a victim dry and get rid of him—to "load" him until his financial back is broken. That the system is proven by the fact that only one policy in seven is ever paid. Six out of every seven people who insure in the old line companies pay heavy premiums for a longer or shorter period and never receive back a cent. They lie down under their "load." By such methods these systematic blood-suckers acquire those vast assets that make them so "solvent." By such practices they are enabled to pay $75,000 salaries to their presidents while the chief magistrate of the Republic must worry along on less money. By the pernicious system of "loading" a patron is charged four times as much for operating expenses at 60 years of age as he is charged at 25, although it costs the same to collect his premiums and furnish a receipt therefor. The idea is that the older he grows the more likely he is to prove a loss to the company, hence his burden is made too grievous to be borne. Life insurance should be a public blessing instead of a bane. Properly applied it would well-nigh eliminate pauperism. As matters now stand it is too often a promoter of poverty instead of a preventative. To shelter one family the old line companies turn two or more into the street. To feed the few they starve the many. They coldly speculate in the holiest affections of the human heart. They remorselessly coin blood into boodle. They wring the last farthing from the thin purse of labor for their own enrichment. They obtain patronage of the ignorant by false pretenses. They permit the people to regard their legal reserve as available for all purposes. They parade eight and nine-figure assets as things to be proud of, when they are in reality the fruits of shameless despoiliation of the poor. They pose as benevolent institutions while the land is filled with those whom they have robbed and wrecked. The government should suppress these eminently respectable gambling games. They have caused more sorrow, destitution and crime than all the cards and dice this side of the dark dominion of the devil. The horse-leech's daughters should be pulled off the body politic. Not only should the government suppress these shameless skin games which collect gold and distribute copper, but it should supply life insurance to heads of families at cost and make it compulsory. It should be an offense against the law, punishable by imprisonment for a man to bring a child into the world without first providing for its support in case of his death or disability, and in no other way can the poor so easily make such provision as by a system of life insurance conducted for the benefit of the many instead of the enrichment of the few.

*   *   *   *   *

A BIGOTED ARCHBISHOP.

All the fools are not confined to any one political party or religious cult. As a rule the Catholic clergy, while ultra-dogmatic, are thoroughly decent. While standing up stiffly for all the claims of their creed, they treat their Protestant neighbors with courteous toleration. There are exceptions to most rules, hence it does not infallibly follow that a man is a gentleman because he is a priest of the Church of Rome. The unworthy are usually discovered and weeded out, but their dismissal does not entirely repair the damage done by criminal or foolish utterance. It is seldom indeed that the Mother-Church permits a small-bore bigot or brainless blatherskite to rise to the dignity of an archbishop, but one such has evidently escaped her watchful eye. Archbishop Cleary, of Kingston, Can., recently distinguished himself by an ebullition of unchristian bile that will long be used as an excuse for the existence of the A.P.A. His utterances were a disgrace to his office. They were beneath the dignity of the humblest neophite of the Church of Rome. They remind one of the old Puritanical tongue-borers and witch-burners. They suggest the Star Chamber of England and the Inquisition of Spain. The brutality staggers the brain and chills the blood. They compel those who have ever felt kindly towards Catholicism to pause and consider. Although the voice of the Vatican is strangely at variance with the astounding mandate of the Archbishop, the latter has been pounced upon and exploited by the "Apes" as an official utterance of the Pope. It appears that a Catholic young lady officiated as bridesmaid for a friend who was married in a Protestant church and according to the rites of that religion. Therefore his reverence proceeded to have a cataleptoid convulsion and cut fantastic capers before high heaven. It was entirely within his sacerdotal province to administer a reprimand. He could, without transcending the proprieties have advised the Catholics of his diocese to refrain from officiating at Protestant marriages in future. He did neither the one nor the other, but proceeded to issue a mandate which, reduced to the last analysis, means simply that a marriage not consummated by the Catholic church is no marriage at all, but simply concubinage born of lust and wickedly sanctioned by human law. He forbade Catholics, under pain of his dire displeasure, even witnessing Protestant marriages or attending as mere spectators at Protestant funerals. Archbishop Cleary has flagrantly insulted every non-Catholic wife in the world. He cast the baleful bar-sinister on the escutcheon of every child born of non-Catholic parents. With all due respect to his holy office, Archbishop Cleary is one ass. He is a brute who should be taken out and bastinadoed. Of course due allowance must be made for the fact that he is a Canuck. Canada is but half-civilized. It is still "loil" to old England, the strumpet of nations, the governmental harlot of history. It continues to take its manners and customs from the old country. It is to the Queen's apron strings like an idiot's scalp to the belt of an Apache squaw. Whenever John Bull whistles it comes a running like a half-grown spaniel at the call of a stable-boy. It has never mustered up sufficient sense and sand to set up for itself. It is the red bandana upon which Britannia blows her protrusive bugle. It is the cuspidore into which she voids her royal rheum. We could not expect much even from a Catholic archbishop in such a country. In fact, the Canadian Catholics, like the Canadian Protestants, are so narrow between the eyes that they can look through a key-hole with both eyes at once. Their heads are small and ill-furnished. The winters are so long that the sap cannot rise to the top—it stops at the belly-band and there coagulates. Canadians of any faith are scarce so broad in the religious beam as Texas Baptists, who believe that unless a man be treated to a sanctified plunge-bath by some acephalous shouter he is headed direct for hell. Still it is something of a shock to hear even a Canadian archbishop branding four-fifths of the people of this world as bastards. It makes one ashamed of the genus homo to hear him forbidding Catholics attending the funerals of their Protestant friends. One cannot help asking, What of marriage and motherhood during the long ages before St. Peter became Pope? Was Eve a concubine and Sara a slut? Has

Archbishop Cleary an hundred generations of harlotry behind him? I am seeking no controversy with Catholicism. With its peculiar ideas of marriage and divorce I have nothing at present to do. I am simply tying a few bow-knots in the ears of an ass. I deny, however, that it is within the power of any church to add to the sanctity of a marriage ceremony. Marriage is nothing more or less than formal notification to the world that a man and woman have already become husband and wife. It matters not how this announcement is made, so long as due respect is shown the established customs of the country, so long as it is generally accepted as sufficient. "What God hath put together, let no man put asunder," cried the Archbishop as he contemplates the possible annulment of a non-Catholic marriage contract. What God hath put together no man *can* put asunder. Even the almighty hand of death cannot break that sacred bond. But how does God join people together?—how does he make a man and woman husband and wife? Is it by the mumbled formula of priests or magistrates? If so, then is a *mariage de conveniance as sacred* as the mating of Cupid and Psyche. Then is the union of a snub-nosed American parvenu with an idiotic European "nobleman" whom she has bought with her daddy's dollars as holy in the sight of heaven as that of old Isaac's son with Laban's beauteous daughter. God joins man and woman together only with the golden links of love. When they are joined thus they are bone of one bone and flesh of one flesh. Were they alone in the world no marriage ceremony would be needful; but being a portion of society they must obtain its sanction. When they are joined together by church or state and love is lacking the union is not of heaven, but of hell. The woman is no true wife, but a kept mistress, and every child born unto her is a bastard. She has sold herself, and the priest or preacher who knowingly sets the seal of his approval upon her sin becomes an accomplice in a subterbrutish crime. But neither church nor state can read a woman's heart—all it can do is to announce to the world, "This woman elects to be that man's wife." There's naught more sacrosanct in the act of church or state in so far as the marriage ceremony is concerned than in the newspaper notice of its consummation. A few years ago a young and cultured woman, a woman beautiful as the dawn and with a suggestion of the Madonna in her fair young face, was persuaded by an ambitious mother to marry an old Silenus whom the political ocean in its madness had scooped out of the ooze and thrown among the stars. Three children have been born to her, and if current report may be credited, all are semi-idiots. Her gross husband is so repulsive to her that her babies are conceived as in some devil's dream and brought forth in despair. Thank heaven this ill-mated couple are not Catholics. But had they been: does Archbishop Cleary mean to tell me that all the power of the Church of Rome could have rendered their union holy? It is quite likely that Archbishop Cleary will not have to wait very long for a letter from Rome. When it comes I opine that it will contain a friendly tip from the Pope not to talk too much. His Holiness is a man of great good sense, and it will naturally occur to him that while reasonable church discipline is desirable it may be enforced without flagrantly insulting the millions of very worthy people who decline to accept his dogma.

*　　　*　　　*　　　*　　　*

SALMAGUNDI.

This year's crop of Christmas accidents appears to be up to the average. As an angel-maker Christmas outclasses St. Patrick's day and is almost equal to the Fourth of July. The North celebrates the birth of our dear Lord by stuffing itself to the bursting point with plum budding, while the South manifests its appreciation of God's mercy by blowing itself to pieces with gunpowder. Dozens of people were killed, hundreds lost more or less important portions of their anatomy while a great army of new-made dyspeptics goes marching onward to the grave. I cannot understand what either plumpudding or gunpowder has to do with saving grace. The man must be very gross who can celebrate with gluttony and drunkenness the birth of the Redeemer. Why should anyone desire to transform the world into a murderous pandemonium because of the arrival of the Prince of Peace? Truth to tell, Christmas has become a secular holiday rather than a day for religious rejoicing, and Deists, Atheists and Agnostics take as much interest in its observation as do those who believe in the divinity of the Babe of Bethlehem. More people get drunk on Christmas than on any other day in the year. It is a time of violence and blood, rather than of "peace on earth, good will to men." I move that we switch, and instead of celebrating the nativity of Christ, observe the birth of Bacchus. We will then be privileged to drink until we are drunken. We can then stuff ourselves with the good things of earth and be consistent. We can then explode cannon-crackers, fire anvils and yoop with our mouths open without being guilty of the slightest disrespect to our God. But what must Christ Jesus think as he looks over the jasper walls, of this high revel, supposedly held as a sacrament? Surely he must be sorry he was ever born of woman. But gluttony, and drunkenness and fireworks are not the full extent of a so-called Christian world's offering. We have perverted the communistic doctrine of Christ in our practice of giving Christian presents. So long as custom confines gifts to immediate relatives and dependents it was well enough, for the largesse was usually selected with discretion and prompted by love; but it has now become the practice to send gifts to pretty much the entire circle of one's acquaintances. The result is the expenditure of tens of millions of money annually in the purchase of useless plunder. And the worst of it is that presents are usually given on the reciprocity plan—the custom has well nigh left the realm of sentiment and degenerated into social tyranny or brute selfishness. The homes of this land are littered to-day with trash which the recipients did not want and cannot use. And half the people who incurred this foolish expense are suffering the inconvenience of poverty. On the day after Christmas a lady shoved me her presents. They made a truly imposing pile. "There's not a solitary thing in the entire load," said she, "for which I have the slightest use. I cannot retain much of the stuff as keepsakes because of the bulk, and I am neither privileged to sell it or to give it away. I would have appreciated a rose or a ribbon from one I love more than all this trumpery from the people who are for the most part mere acquaintances. And I? Oh I adhered to the custom—went broke buying a lot of useless truck with which to encumber others. And now that Christmas is over and we contemplate our thin purses and impossible presents, we all wonder why 'that monster custom' doesn't permit us to exercise a little common sense. Christmas is becoming ever more and more a nightmare to me. The dinners are simply dreadful. The housewife begins a month in advance to plot against the stomachs of her people. I never ate but one Christmas dinner for which I did not feel like apologizing to my doctor, and that was not eaten in strictly religious company. It was a regular Bohemian lunch partaken of on a Pullman by myself, a newspaper man and two other sinners. The everlasting roast turkey, the pudding, pies and all the rest of the greasy, indigestible mass was missing. We had tongue sandwiches and Budweiser, deviled ham and more beer. I remarked that we were awfully wicked, but the newspaper man consoled me by saying the Christ was something of a Bohemian himself. We take an infinite deal of pains and spend an awful sight of money just to make ourselves miserable." One great trouble with the American people is that they do not have nearly enough holidays. In fact, Christmas is the only one really worthy of the name, for on New Year's, and July Fourth, we do not cease business until noon, while on Thanksgiving we forget to chase the nimble nickel merely long enough to feed. Next to gain-getting, eating seems to be the important business of the Universe. It is the manner in which a semi-civilized people express pleasure. Ouida has called attention to this fact somewhere. If a general wins an important battle, if a poet writes an immortal epic, if a Columbus discovers a new world, or if a God becomes incarnate we—eat! Yet there be sentimentalists who say that soul and stomach are not synonymous! It appears that the heart cannot feel, that the brain cannot enjoy unless we're shovelling a varied assortment of provender into the belly. That humble but useful organ seems to be the seat of all joy, as it is the source of most sorrow.

* * *

The American custom of "treating" is receiving some severe criticism from the European press. It deserves it. It is one of the most ridiculous and hurtful that ever cursed mankind. It is responsible for the bulk of the crime and pauperism usually accredited to John Barleycorn. Where there is no treating there's usually little intemperance. When a man steps into a "resort" for a glass of beer he's pretty apt to find a party lined up at the bar. He wants to pay for his beer, drink it and take his departure. But this is not permitted. He may have no more than a passing acquaintance with any of those present, but he must drink with the crowd, and having done so feels obligated to ask the crowd to drink with him. It does so, and he's "out" from one to three dollars. Having drunk with Tom he must drink with Dick and with Harry, and when he departs he's more than half drunk. The chances are that he could ill afford the expense incurred—that if left to himself he would have taken one drink instead of a dozen. "Treating" is a foolish custom that should be abolished in the interest of sobriety. It is good neither for the saloon nor for society. It is not good for the saloon because it occasions drunkenness and disorder and causes it to be avoided by thousands of otherwise good paying patrons. It is not good for society because weak men waste their substance, and a drunken man is an unsafe citizen. But the treating habit has too strong a grip on the American people to be eliminated by magazine essays—it must be made a misdemeanor. I am told that in Germany it matters *not* how friendly the members of a symposiac may be, everybody is expected to order and pay for his own booze. The result is that the German drinking place is respectable as the average restaurant and is patronized by almost the entire people. Temperance is the rule—stimulants are freely used but seldom abused. The treating habit is born of the American desire to "splurge." It means an enormous waste of money. It likewise means a sinful waste of good wine, for when a crowd of men belly a bar and pour stimulants into themselves as swine absorb swill it really matters little whether they drink Pomeroy See or barrel-house booze. They do not enjoy their potations—their only desire is to make drunk come. The treating habit is making of us a swinish people and strengthening the hands of the Prohibitionists.

* * *

The "Rev." Sam Jones of Jawgy has broken loose again. This time he sets his cornstalk spear in rest and charges full tilt at the public school system and pretty much everything else in sight. His pathway is strewn with a gruesome wreck of the English grammar. Sam discussing the merits of education suggest a brindle mule criticising the Venus de Milo or a scavenger expatiating on the odors of Araby. His reverence (?) has become imbued with the idea that it spoils a boy to educate him, which goes to prove that the less a man knows the more he despises knowledge. But we can scarce blame Sam for railing at education. He is but obeying the law of self-preservation. When the people learn to distinguish between a hawk and a heron-saw they will drive this putrid-mouth little blatherskite from the pulpit.

* * *

The New York Press wants all niggers holding federal offices in the South "armed to the teeth" for their own protection. It has an idea that the South is peopled only by "white savages" whose favorite sport is the shooting of nigger officer-holders from ambush. Like the erstwhile Artemus Ward's monkey, the editor of the Press is "a most amusin kuss." The South never gets angry at that kind of an animal. Occasionally a corrupt Republican administration appoints some ignorant Ethiopian to office who becomes insufferably insolent to his white neighbors and is called down with a six-shooter; but for every negro office-holder "assassinated by Southern savages" at least five white women are dragged from their homes by Northern white-caps and brutally abused. Who says so? I do; and I stand ready to prove it by the files of the leading Republican paper of this nation for ten years past. I refer, of course, to the St. Louis Globe-Democrat, the best all-around newspaper in the world. The South has very little affection for nigger office-holders, but they are full as safe as any other class of citizens so long as they behave themselves. The black man is not to blame for accepting an office, it is the Republican administration that deserves censure in thus making him the political superior of his white brethern. It is not the nigger who deserves killing, but the meddlesome Yankee editors who encourage him to be insolent.

* * *

According to press report a fashionable New York society female has dismissed her maid and engaged a valet. Well, if the dear creature enjoys having a man dress and undress her, comb her hair and lace her corsets why should an envious world stand on its hinder legs and carp? New York fashionables must have some antidote for ennui. If it be proper for ladies to have valets I presume that it is permissible for men to have maids. What is sauce for the goose should be sauce for the gander. Verily "the world do move."

* * *

In the morning Mr. Logan wore a doeskin box coat with pearl buttons nearly as large as alarm clocks in two rows on it. His spats were old-gold color to match. In the afternoon he wore a dark plaid coat and trousers and a saffron-colored vest. The vest was garnished with maroon-colored inch-and-a-quarter checks. He wore an Ascot scarf, dark blue, with lavender polka dots. His scarfpin was a gold whip four inches long and set with a half-inch turqoise in the middle. He wore ox-blood shoes in the morning and ox-blood gloves and in the afternoon his shoes and gloves were buff colored. In the evening he wore full dress.—*Chicago Times-Herald.*

And still we wonder at the increase of crime! Could any self-respecting Texan with a six-shooter concealed about his person be expected to meet such a gorgeous bird o' paradise and suffer it to escape? I wonder if Mr. Logan scrapes his tongue, manicures his toes and puts his moustache on curl papers? And I wonder what the devil old "Black Jack" would say could he wake up long enough to take survey of his clothes-horn of a son? And I wonder what the deuce the woman who married it will do with it? And I wonder why the hades his ma doesn't lead the little man out into the woodshed, remove his panties, lay him across the maternal knee and hit him 'steen times across the rear elevation with a green cypress shingle? Think of a featherless he animal playing peacock—no mission in God's world but to dress and undress itself three times a day.

* * *

The New York *Medical Record* says that "a custom prevails in this country that ministers should be considered as free from pecuniary obligation to the doctor for service rendered." The *Record* then proceeds to file a very vigorous kick because of the aforesaid custom, broadly intimating that sky-pilots in general are long on gall and short on gratitude. There is certainly no reason why the preacher, who usually receives a good salary, should not pay for his poultices and pills. When he relieves cases of soul-sickness he does so "for the glory of God" and the long green. He expects to be paid twice for his services—once here and again in heaven. The doctor of medicine is not infrequently poorer in this world's goods than the preacher, and he looks forward to but one fee. He should not be deprived of that by men who sweetly sing:

> "I would not live always,
> I ask not to stay."

If the doctors treat the dominies gratis it follows as a matter of course that they must recoup themselves by adding to the bills of their lay brethren, just as railway companies which carry preachers at half-rate must saddle the loss upon their other patrons.

* * *

Mintonville, Ky., not only sticks to its gods, but insists on clinging with a death grip to its good old orthodox devil, horns, hoofs and tail. The Rev. Gilham of the Christian church of that city, who has doubtless discovered recently that that unimportant portion of the world which moves and has its being outside of Mintonville had several centuries back diplomatically dropped the devil question, undertook to inform his flock that he, too had arrived at the conclusion that his Satanic Majesty was a myth, a delusion and a snare, a howling farce. The reverend gentleman's intentions were good, but he had reckoned without his congregation. They had always had a devil who was responsible for their pecadilloes; he was a convenient little institution to have around when the pecadilloes were a little more numerous than was compatible with the moral standard of Mintonville, and they realized that if the devil were removed from the Mintonville directory they would have to reform or shoulder their own shortcomings. Either course was quite too sad to contemplate. In fact the Mintonvillians positively would not contemplate them. Give them their devil and they could safely straddle between the horns of their dilemma. Remove their devil and they were undone. But Parson Gilham asserted that there was no devil. Mintonville had consequently to choose between their devil and their parson. The world could furnish more parsons but it couldn't furnish more devils. It was the parson and the devil for it and the red downed the black—the parson had to go. The reverend gentleman was ejected from his sacred office with scorn and contumely and likewise a number of pistol shots. It is to be supposed that the devil now reigns triumphant in Mintonville, while Gilham smooths down his clerical coat-tails from the horizontal to the proper perpendicular and wonders if he has not, like the proverbial parrot, talked too damned much.

*   *   *   *   *

THE FOOTLIGHT FAVORITES.

BY ETHELYN LESLIE HUSTON.

In the December ICONOCLAST there appeared a tirade on "The Stage and Stage Degenerates" that was as sweeping in its assertions as it was narrow in its views. The writer revels in reminiscences of his newspaper associations with the cheap beer-drinking, sand-floor class, swings their vices and vulgarities before the public, describes them as garbed in "loud patterned" trousers and snow-white overcoats and epitomizes the whole thing as an Augean stable, impure, impossible, vile, vulgar and bad. He then tells us calmly that "these are the representatives of their profession, so far as America is concerned," and he gives them to us as the "middle class of the people of the footlights."

If these are the "middle class," what is the next grade below? Where does he place the dividing line? Does he make no distinction between the vaudeville, continuous performance buffoons and the thousands who are "not stars," but working well and perhaps hoping? Does he call our scullery-maids and stable-boys "representative American middle class?" Does he call Mable Strickland and other dainty little hard-workers in minor parts typical of the hideous coarseness and vice he has described? Does he bracket *them* with his beer-drunk, easy-virtue "chorus-girls?" Does he realize all he means when he says of those he depicts "there were no stars among them, and none of the lower stratum?" Briefly, did he know what he was writing about?

When a man sits down on a curb stone with his feet in the gutter to "study life" and imagines himself a philosopher, while he moralizes on the muddy feet that pass him, he would probably feel grieved if the strong hand of some clear-headed individual lifted him up out of the gutter's filth and he was informed that much depended upon one's view being from a level, not an incline. We do not Judge our middle-class citizens by our cooks, and it is apt to suggest unwisdom, to express it very mildly, to gauge the men and women workers of the stage by beer-hall habitues and fleshling courtesans.

This an age of work and a generation of workers. The times, the conditions, the needs of the century are driving women out into the world as never before in the world's history. They must work to live and to help others live and in every line of work possible is woman found. The stage gives employment to thousands of women eminently fitted to entertain and amuse the public. Under ordinary conditions the great army of players find its lot a not unpleasant one. Women bears its harness lightly, to whom manual labor would be a mental and physical crucifixion. It is a labor of brain as well as body, of the soul as well as the senses, of the artistic as well as the prosaic. Its temptations are many and its pitfalls are many, but they are little, if any, more than are the temptations in many other fields of self-support for women. And notwithstanding the gentleman's profound deductions, there are a number of good women on the American stage even if they are not "given credit for being so by their fellow professionals" — and iconoclastic writers. And by these I do not mean the weary females described by Lizzie Annandale as reclining on the shoulders of their men companions, in mal-adorous day coaches on cross-continent "jumps." These women, if he will pardon the contradiction, are not the "representative middle class of the American stage." They are the scullery-maid class, for they are on the lowest rung of the professional ladder and few ever ascend from that lowest rung. It is their native element.

But these women who are neither "stars or the lower stratum," who study and labor, even though the labor be light through being one of love for their profession, who give a refinement and a sweetness to the many little dramas that appeal to critique and common folk alike, who speak to us of wife and sister and mother and sweetheart, and whose voices are as sweet and gestures as gentle and personalities as refined as are those of our own home women nestling safe in the firelight of our ingle-nook — these women are not immoral in a ratio of "ten to one." And with them, as with our home women, it is not their sense of morality that is their greatest safe-guard. It is their sense of refinement. It is a mistake to think that only Christian and moral women are virtuous. "Passion leaps o'er cold decree," and Christian precepts and moral teaching are cold and distant things when the blood leaps like molton lava through heart and brain. With Marguerite telling her beads, the prayers become but a babble of empty sound on her lips when the sweet poison of her lover's teachings crept through ear and heart and opened to her wondering, frightened dreams a Paradise of sense and sound and sweetness and dreamy, swooning loveliness before which her pictured pearl and golden heaven waxed chill and distant and austere. Prayers did not save Francesca from the sweet torment of her Passion and her Purgatory. Prayers save but rarely, for they are to darkness and to mystery that give back only the awful weight of silence—silence under which the frantic heart struggles and stifles as beneath a pall. Prayers reach out to an infinity that is shrouded always, but the lover's lips are sweet and the caress is close and the arms are warm and human. What wonder if the brain forgets when the heart thirsts and pleads? What wonder if the reason waver and faint when the winged god nestles close in the breast? What woman if the woman wake and thrill and "answers to the touch of one musician's hand" as an instrument that is silent till the master touch sweep the strings? What wonder if the marble warm and waken and throb to quick life beneath the passion of Pygmalion's kiss? What wonder if women love with an answering love if their God have so created? And what wonder if their prayer to him faint on their lips beneath the surging diapason of the waking heart beneath? If he so created, what then? If he "saw them made and said 'twas good," what then? If he made love chief, to deity and then destroy, its ecstacy blending with agony "as swells and swoons, across the wold the tinkling of the camel's bell," what then? If he made the greatest thing in the world and life speaks to life as a magnet to the pole, what then? Can you break that strong, silent current by a breathed invocation? Did not the Man cry from the cross in his exquisite agony, "Eli, Eli, lama sabachthani!" And if his divine faith fainted on the threshold of his kingdom, is it strange if human faith sink beneath life's crucifixion and the babble of priest grow poor and harsh before the sweetness of "a little laughter and a little love"—the only hyssop in the sponge of vinegar? And we wander so far to find so little!

In Jean Paul's cry "How lonely is everyone in this wide charnal of the universe!"—is the explanation of—much.

We are as we are. And Allah is great.

And because we are as we are, it is fallacy to think that the good women, in the accepted sense of the term, are the only virtuous ones. Women of the stage and of the world ponder little on Moses and the prophets. Their lives are too full of grinding fact to reck much of unsubstantial fancies. And Prayer and Priest save women from little if Personality be not there. Teachings of virtue and morality are lip service and things of air. But when a woman's self rises to defend her honor—an honor that is a sacred thing in its own worth, not a question that will but win her reward in other life, then does true morality speak and then does woman find her greatest safeguard. A woman is but a weak thing who must cower behind the skirts of her religion to guard her purity. And these women of the stage who are its "middle class" are also its gentlewomen. For unfortunately its "stars" many of them but rival the other "stratum" in lawless infamy. In that, did the writer in December make his supreme mistake.

Temptation in the footlight world is strong, but a woman's pride is stronger. Under temptation's test, her religion might was dim, but her refinement would rise as a battlement in defense. Her church and creed might waver and sink, but that undefinable innocence which we call womanhood, would lead her, a Dian, through the fires of hell. In society and the slums a large percentage of women are courtesans by choice. The one has a refinement that is but a veneer, and the other has no refinement at all. And as with the world, so with the stage. In the middle class are found the truer gentlewomen. Women of the drama must of necessity be gentlewomen, the refinement must be innate, or they would fail utterly. An actress who is a gentlewoman can with her art stoop to portray sin, but an actress who is a common woman cannot rise to portray a refinement of which her coarse nature has no conception. Mrs. Kendal a woman who is as the wife of Caesar, can become a "Second Mrs. Tanguery" before the footlights. But Lizzie Annadale's chorus girl could never enact the role of a Mrs. Kendal on or off the stage. The former is a comparatively light task. The latter is an impossibility. And because they are refined women, though not necessarily "good" women, are they as a class virtuous women. Their instinctive womanhood would shrink from an impure life as quickly as they would lift their skirts from the mire of the gutter. The deadly chill of physical repulsion would be as strong in one case as in the other. In individual cases they have "sinned" as we term it, but qui voulez vous! The ratio on the stage is little larger than that of the world's middle class and not at all larger than that of the world's society women. I also object to those wild fanatics who would "elevate the stage," not because it would be Herculean labor, but because the aforesaid fanatics would find larger and more fruitful fields for their efforts in the shadow of their own church spire. Let them leave the women of the footlights alone and turn their attention to the women in the boxes. It would give a bored public relief and be distinctly and beautifully amusing—as an experiment.

Waco, Texas, December 11, 1897.

*   *   *   *   *

GINX'S BABY.

BY WILLIAM MARION REEDY.

In an old book store I found the other day, a little book that should not have been forgotten. It was written almost twenty-eight years ago by a man named Jenkins, an Englishman, born in India, and educated in part, in the United States. The name of the book is "Ginx's Baby; His Birth and Other Misfortunes."

With the remarkable growth of altruism or humanitarianism in the last thirty years, with the application of sincere sympathy as one of the possible solvents of the mystery of misery, it is strange that this book should have passed from the minds of men. The book is a true satire. That is to say its irony is excited for the benefit of mankind. The pessimism of the story, its note of despair, is in reality, a summons to man to do better by his brother. Underlying its bitterness there is such a gentleness of heart as must uplift the reader's own.

The author has the great gift of humor, which all true pessimists possess, and none more than Schopenhauer. He loves humanity though he scourges it. He loves, above all, the little children whom Christ loved, as typifying the heart perfect in innocence.

Somewhat the quality of Dickens is in his method of thought, and his turns of expression; but he is not the evident artist that Dickens is. He does not seek opportunity to revel in mere rhetoric. He goes for the heart of his subject and his literary charms are displayed quite incidentally to his progress thereto. His stylism does not clog his story or cumber his argument. The result is that he produced a tract of the Church of Man which is a powerful argument for a realization in Man of the Church of God. His book is superbly human and "Ginx's Baby" deserves immortality with other dream-children of good men's hearts and minds in story and in song.

Room for Ginx's Baby in the gallery of undying children; with Marjorie Fleming, Sir Walter's "Bonnie, Wee Coodlin' Doo," with Pater's "Child in the House," with Ouida's "Bebe," with Mrs. Burnett's "Fauntleroy," with Barrie's "Sentimental Tommy," with all the little ones in the books of Dickens and the poems and stories of Eugene Field.

The child in literature is something new, comparatively. We need more of the effort to understand the child mind, the child heart, the child point of view. It will aid us to develop the child, if once we can enter his world and come into sympathy with his impression. It will purify ourselves, this fresh, new, beautiful world of the child's; its clear, pure air will wash clean our souls; its innocence of doom will revive our hope. The child is a soul fresh from God's mint. If only we could study it more we might re-gain, from the contemplation, some of our own lost innocence, and, when we come to die, go to our Maker, like Thackery's immortal Col. Newcombe, with our hearts "as a little child's."

But "Ginx's Baby" is not an idyl. It is a tragedy. It breathes the spirit of Malthus, only the spirit is transformed into one of pity for the victim of life rather than one of preservation of the nation. We are not, in this book, the victim of the baby. The baby is our victim. His story will illustrate the philosophy better than any attempt at interpretation, and the humor of the telling only intensifies the tragedy. "The name of the father of Ginx's Baby was Ginx. By a not unexceptional coincidence, its mother was Mrs. Ginx. The gender of Ginx's Baby was masculine." That is the first paragraph of the book, and there you have a hint of the flippant flavor; also a very strong suggestion of Mr. Charles Dickens. The hero of the book was a thirteenth child. Ominously humorous! The mother previously had distinguished herself. On October 25th, one year after marriage, Mrs. Ginx was safely delivered of a girl. No announcement of this appeared in the papers. On April 10th, following, "the whole neighborhood, including Great Smith Street, Marsham Street, Great and Little Peter Street, Regent Street, Horseferry Road, and Strutton Ground, was convulsed by the report a woman named Ginx had given birth to "a triplet, consisting of two girls and a boy." The Queen heard of it, as this birth got into the papers, and sent the mother three pounds. Protecting infant industry! And protection, it seems, resulted in over-production for, in a twelvemonth, there were triplets again, two sons and a daughter. Her Majesty sent four pounds. The neighbors protested and began to manifest their displeasure uncouthly, so the Ginx family removed into Rosemary Street, where the tale of Mrs. Ginx's offspring reached one dozen. Then Ginx mildly entered protest. If there were any more, singles, twins or triplets, he would drown him, her or them, in the water-butt. This was immediately after the arrival of Number 12.

Here, under the chapter-heading of "Home, Sweet Home," the author, still reminiscent of Dickens, but delightfully compact and laconic, describes the miserable dwelling of the Ginx's with a bitterness of humor that mocks the sentiment of Howard Payne's song. As a specimen of clean realism, this description is more effective than anything of Zola's; for Zola's realism is idealism gone mad. The squalor of the slum is heightened by the associations that cling to the name Rosemary. A bit of sermonizing upon the responsibilities of landlords for the souls in that slum, and the author reverts to Ginx and his family.

"Ginx had an animal affection for his wife, that preserved her from unkindness even in his cups." You thank the author for not succumbing to realism and making Ginx a brute. Ginx worked hard and gave his wife his earnings, less sixpence, with which sum he retreated, on Sundays, from his twelve children, to the ale-house to listen sleepily while ale-house demagogues prescribed remedies for State abuses. He was ignorant of policies and issues; simply one of a million victims of the theories upon which statesmen experiment in legislation and taxation. He was one of the many dumb and almost unfeeling "chaotic fragments of humanity" to be hewn into shape in one of two ways; either by "coarse artists seeking only petty profit, unhandy, immeasurably impudent," or by instruction to be made "civic corner-stone polished after the similitude of a palace." He was appalled by the many mouths he had to feed. He was touched by his wife's continuous heroism of sacrifice for the children, and he felt, in a dim fashion, something of an intuition of "her unsatisfied cravings and the dense motherly horrors that sometimes brooded over her" as she nursed her infants. She believed that God sends food to fill the mouths He sends. She had been able to get along. She would be able to get along.

Ginx, feeling another infant straw would break his back. determined to drown the straw. Mrs. Ginx, clinging to No. Twelve, listened aghast. The stream of her affections, though divided into twelve rills, would not have been exhausted in twenty-four, and her soul, forecasting its sorrows, yearned after that nonentity Number Thirteen. Ginx sought to comfort her by the suggestion that she could not have any more. But she knew better.

After eighteen months the baby was born. Ginx thought it all out before the event. "He wouldn't go on the parish. He couldn't keep another youngster to save his life. He would not take charity. There was nothing to do but drown the baby." He must have talked his intentions at the ale-house, for the people in the neighborhood watched her "time" with interest. Going home one afternoon, he saws signs of excitement around his door. He entered. He took up the little stranger and bore it from the room. "His wife would have arisen but a strong power called weakness held her back." Out on the street, with the crowd following him, Ginx stopped to consider. "It is all very well to talk about drowning your baby, but to do it you need two things—water and opportunity. He turned toward Vauxhall Bridge. The crowd cried "Murder!"

"Leave me alone nabors," shouted Ginx; "this is my own baby and I'll do wot I likes with it. I kent keep it an' if I've got anythin' I can't keep, it's best to get rid of it, ain't it? This child's goining over Vauxhall Bridge."

The women clung to his arms and coat-tails. A man happened along. "A foundling? Confound the place, the very stones produce babies."

"It weren't found at all. It's Ginx's baby," cried the crowd.

"Ginx's baby. Who's Ginx?'

"I am," said Ginx.

"Well?"

"Well!"

"He's going to drown it!" came the chorus.

"Going to drown it? Nonsense!" said the officer.

"I am," said Ginx.

"But, bless my heart, that's murder!"

"No, 'tain't," said Ginx. "I've twelve already at home. Starvashon's shure to kill this 'un. Best save it the trouble."

The officer declares this is quite contrary to law and he recites the law, but that doesn't affect Ginx. He fails utterly to see why, if Parliament will not let him abandon the child, Parliament does not provide for the child; for all the other twelve. The officer declares that the parish has enough to do to take care of foundlings and children of parents who can't or won't work. Says Ginx: "Jest so. You'll bring up bastards and beggars' pups but you won't help an honest man keep his head above water. This child's head is goin' under water anyhow!" and he dashed for the bridge, with the screaming crowd at his heels.

A philosopher interposes at this stage with a query as to how Ginx came to have so many children. Of course Ginx had to laugh. The philosopher urges that Ginx had no right to bring children into the world unless he could feed, clothe and educate them, and Ginx replies that he's like to know how he could help it, as a married man. The philosopher goes over the old, old tale of rationalism in life. Ginx should not have married a poor woman, should not have gone on sub-dividing his resources by the increase of what must be a degenerate offspring, should not have married at all.

"Ginx's face grew dark. He was thinking of 'all those years' and the poor creature that, from morning to night and Sunday to Sunday, in calm and storm, had clung to his rough affections; and the bright eyes and the winding arms so often trellised over his tremendous form, and the coy tricks and laughter that had cheered so many tired hours. He may have been much of a brute, but he felt that, after all, that sort of thing was denied to dogs and pigs."

The philosopher could not answer these thoughts nor the rejoinder question to his own: what is a man or woman to do that doesn't marry?

And so the argument proceeds, the philosopher losing ground all the time because his rationality is based upon changing man's nature, not on making something out of "what's nateral to human beings." The act of parliament idea of solving the problem is riddled effectively by a stonemason, who points out that the head-citizen is not so worthy as the heart-citizen. In brief, the philosopher is rout-ed by the doctrine that love is better than law.

Ginx proceeds to the river again, but is stopped by a nun who asks for the child. She uncovers the queer ruby face and kisses it. After this Ginx could not have touched a hair of the child's head. His purpose dies but his perplexity is alive. The nun takes the child, and Ginx, in gratitude for her assurance that the child shall not be sent back to him, stands treat for the crowd. The child's life in the convent is material for some good satiric writing upon the question of his salvation. The picture is absurdly over-drawn so far as its effectiveness against conventional charity is concerned, but it touches the question of religious bigotry surely and strongly. Indeed the method of treatment here verges closely upon the Rabelaisian, as where the sisters want to make the sign of the cross upon Mrs. Ginx's breasts before allowing the baby to suck. Mrs. Ginx refused "the Papish idolaters" and the Protestant Detectoral Association is brought to the rescue of the child from superstition.

A little man with a keen Roman nose—he could scent Jesuits a mile off—took up the cause of the child and it got into court. The matter became a cause *celebré*. London was in a turmoil over "the Papal abduction." The author sketches it all graphically with a convincing fidelity of caricature. The "Sisters of Misery" triumphed. They retained the baby. Then after attempting to sanctify the baby—a ceremony wholly imaginary and described with a smutch of revolting coarseness—the sisters send the baby packing back to the Protestant Detectoral Association.

The Protestants had him, but the Dissenters protested against his being given to an Anglican refuge. The scene at the mass-meeting to celebrate young Ginx's rescue from the incubus of a delusive superstition is described with rare appreciation of the foibles of character. The bombast, the cant, the flapdoodle and flubdub, the silly unction of different kinds of preachers are "done to a hair." Five hours the meeting raged, and at last a resolution that the Metropolitan pulpit should take up the subject, and the churches take up a collection for the Baby on the next Sunday having been passed, the meeting adjourned—forgetting all about the Baby. A strange woman took the Baby "for the sake of the cause." He had been provided with a splendid layette by an enthusiastic Protestant Duchess.

"Some hours later Ginx's Baby, stripped of the Duchess' beautiful robes was found by a policeman, lying on a door step in one of the narrow streets not a hundred yards" from the meeting place. "By an ironical chance he was wrapped in a copy of the largest daily paper in the world."

"The Baby was recovered, the preachers "praught." The collections and the donations and subscriptions amounted to thirteen hundred and sixty pounds, ten shillings, and three and one-half pence. How the money was spent is shown in a deliciously absurd balance-sheet. Not quite 100 pounds were spent upon the Baby. The other money was wasted in various forms and styles of "guff." "In an age of luxury," says the Baby's biographer, "we are grown so luxurious as to be content to pay agents to do our good deeds, but they charge us three hundred per cent. for the privilege."

How the police found and treated the Baby is a chapter full of subtle sarcasm, leading up to the still more sarcastic portrayal of the way the Baby fared in the hands of the Committee appointed to take care of him. He was likely to be torn to pieces between contending divines. The debates in Committee are illuminating expositions of different varieties of bigotry. His body was almost forgotten, while the philanthropists were trying to decide what to do with his soul. Few of the reverend gentlemen "would be content unless they could seize him when his young nature was plastic and try to imprint on immortal clay the trade-mark of some human invention."

Twenty-three meetings of the Committee were held and unity was as far of at the last as at the first. The Secretary asked the Committee to provide money to meet the Baby's liabilities, but the Committee instantly adjourned and no effort afterwards could get a quorum together. The persons who had charge of the foundling began to dun the Secretary and to neglect the child, now thirteen months old. They sold his clothes and absconded from the place where they had been "framing him for Protestantism." As a Protestant question Ginx's Baby vanished from the world.

Wrapped in a potato sack, the baby was found one night, on the pavement exactly over a line dividing two parishes. The finder was a business man. He noted the exact spot where the child lay and took it to—the other parish. He would not be taxed for its support. The parish guardians would not accept the child. As the man who found the child was a guardian of the other parish, he was trying to foist a bastard,—perhaps his own—upon their parish. A motion was made to "get rid of the brat." "A church warden, who happened to be a gentleman," suggested the services of a lawyer. The brutality of the guardians as they examined and discussed the child is depicted with terrible power. The lawyer says the Board will have to take the Baby, *pro tem*, or "create an unhappy impression on the minds of the public."

"Damn the public!" said Mr. Stink, a dog-breeder member of the Board, thus antecedently plagiarizing an American millionaire. The parish accepts the Baby under protest, and a formal written protest addressed to the Baby, name unknown, is pinned on the potato sack. The two parishes go to law about the child. Neither wishes to take care of it. At Saint Bartemeus's workhouse, a notice was posted forbidding the officials, assistants and servants to enter the Baby's room, pendente lite, or to render it any service or assistance on pain of dismissal. The Baby was nigh starvation. The master of the work-house stealthily fed him on pap, saying in a loud voice as he did so, "Now youngster, this is without prejudice, remember! I give you due notice—without prejudice."

The Baby became ill. A nobleman discovered him and laid his case before a magistrate. The papers made a sensation on the Baby's case. There was a terrific hullabaloo. An inquiry was held. The guardians became furious. "The reports of their proceedings read like the vagaries of a lunatic asylum or the deliberations of the American Senate." They discharged the kindly master. The Baby was locked in a room. Food was passed to him on a stick. The inquiry was denounced and the bewildered public gnashed its teeth at everybody who had anything to do with, or say of, Ginx's Baby. "At last St. Bartemeus' parish had to keep him and the guardians, keeping carefully within the law, neglected nothing that could sap little Ginx's vitality, deaden his instincts, derange moral action, cause hope to die within his infant breast almost as soon as it was born." Every pauper was to them an obnoxious charge to be reduced to a *minimum* or *nil*. The Baby's constitution alone prevented his reduction to *nil*.

The bill of costs against St. Bartemeus was 1,600 pounds. Just as it was taxed, one of the persons who had deserted Ginx's Baby was arrested for theft. The Baby's clothes, given by the Duchess, were found in this person's possession. She confessed all about the Baby, and so the guardians traced the Baby's father and delivered to Ginx, through an agent, the famous child, with the benediction—"There he is; damn him!"

Mrs. Ginx couldn't recognize the Baby. His brothers and sisters would have nothing to do with him. Ginx took the Baby out one night, left it on the steps of a large building in Pall Mall, and slunk away out of the pages of "this strange, eventful history." The Baby piped. The door of the house, a club, opened and the baby was taken in. It was the Radical Club, but it was as conservative as it could be in its reception of the waif, and it was only in perfunctory kindness that the Club gave him shelter. The Fogey Club heard of the Baby and bethought itself of making campaign material of him. The Fogies instructed their "organs" to dilate upon the disgraceful apathy of the Radicals toward the foundling. The Fogies kidnapped the Baby; the Radicals stole him back. The Baby was again a great "question." However, other questions supervened, although it was understood that Sir Charles Sterling was "to get a night" to bring up the case of Ginx's Baby in Parliament. Associations were formed in the metropolis for disposing of Ginx's Baby by expatriation or otherwise. A peer suddenly sprung the matter by proposing to send the Baby to the Antipodes at the expense of the nation. The question was debated with elaborate stilted stultitude and the noble lord withdrew his motion.

The Baby tired of life at the clubs. He borrowed some clothes, some forks, some spoons, without leave, and then took his leave. No attempt was made to recover him. He was fifteen. "He pitted his wits against starvation." He found the world terribly full everywhere he went. He went through a career of penury, of honest and dishonest callings, of 'scapes and captures, imprisonments and other punishments.

Midnight on Vauxhall Bridge! The form of a man emerged from the dark and outlined itself against the haze of sky. There was a dull flash of a face in the gloom. The shadow leaped far out into the night. Splash! "Society, which, in the sacred names of Law and Charity, forbade the father to throw his child over Vauxhall Bridge, at a time when he was alike unconscious of life and death, has at last driven him over the parapet into the greedy waters."

The questions of the book I have condensed here are as alive to-day as are thousands of other Ginx's Babies in all our big cities. While philanthropists and politicians, priests and preachers, men and women theorize about the questions, the questions grow "more insoluble." What is to be done? is the first question.

How is it to be done is a question which is secondary and its discussion is useless until the first is settled. Too much State drove Ginx's Baby into the Thames. What's everybody's business is nobody's business. If the uncountable babies of innumerable Ginx's are to be aided, some one must aid them for the mere pleasure there is in loving-kindness.

A baby is a human being, not a problem. A baby can't be explained away by pure reason, because he didn't come by that route. Love brought him here and only Love can nourish him to the fullness of growth in soul and mind. True many come who, seemingly, were better drowned like surplus puppies or kittens. But who shall select those to survive? Grecian wisdom once attempted to improve on "natural selection" and Greece is the ghost of a vanished glory. Why shouldn't Ginx have drowned his Baby — or himself before the multiplication in the result of which the Baby was a unit?

I don't know why, unless because there is, in every life, even the most successful, apparently, enough of unhappiness and failure and emptiness to justify, at a given moment, a "leap in the dark." This logic of suicide would annihilate the race. The unwelcome Baby may be the best. Life must try us all. Those who do not stand the test disappear. Their own weakness eliminate them. Myriads must fail that a few may succeed a very little.

Ginx at least owed his Baby reparation for bringing about the first misfortune, his birth. Ginx was a sophist. His mercy of murder for the child was regard for himself. His reasoning was right. His heart was full of self and, ergo, wrong. Ginx surrendered before the fight was fought. So did the Baby. There is nothing for it, my good masters, but a fight to a finish. Yes, even though Birnam Wood come to Dunsinane, still must we fight, like Macbeth, and all the more valiantly for that we know our sins are heavy upon our heads and hearts. "Courage, my comrades, the devil is dead," said Denys of Burgundy. But there is a greater courage, my comrades: it is fighting the devil who never dies until the devil in us all shall die. This is not the courage of despair, but of hope and faith that by conquest of ourselves shall Evil be slain, though only in a fair, far time, and by scores of deaths of us and of our kind. That is why the book "Ginx's Baby" is false in its demonstration that it had been better if the "hero" had been thrown off the bridge at first. Its philosophy is the philosophy of the "quitter." The only courage is to endure.

And what shall we do for the Ginx's Babies so multitudinous in their misery? These, too, we must endure. It were well to love them a little, as babies, and not to discuss them so much as "questions." It were well if there were a little more individual charity; a good deal less of the kind described by Boyle O'Reilly as conducted "in the name of a cautious statistical Christ." If every one would do a little good for the poor, the unfortunate, the afflicted, the sum of all our doing would be a great deal of good. Take a penny from every person in the United States and give it to one man and he has seven hundred thousand dollars. Every Ginx's Baby in any land can be helped somewhat, and Ginx himself must do his share, to the full limit of his capacity for doing. We cannot save them all; cannot make their lives successes. Success is the sum of many failures. A million seeds must die that one rose may bloom. You or I may be the means, in part, of saving one child from the plunge of Vauxhall Bridge or through the gallows-trap. And one is worth while. That is the way to "look out for number one." Individual effort for individuals is the true humanitarianism. Lift up the person nearest you, who needs assistance. Bend to him and feel your own statue increase by so much as you uplift him. *Et voila tout.*

St. Louis, December 16th, 1897.

*   *   *   *   *

WHAT'S THE MATTER WITH MISSOURI?
BY WILLIAM MARION REEDY.

The art of politics in Missouri is not more depraved than in most other states, I imagine; but it seems that in Missouri the practitioners of that art are somewhat coarser-grained and smaller-minded than men in the like charlatanry elsewhere. I think I may write of them and their methods in the capacity of critic, without obtruding my prejudices as a gold-bug.

Missouri, like every other Western State, took kindly to the silver theory; indeed, possessing, as one of its chief citizens, Mr. Bland, a champion of silver for thirty years, Missouri was as ready for 16 to 1 as any silver producing State. "Coin's" book found welcome wide and warm when it appeared among a people who admired Mr. Bland, and who had equally admired "Farmer" Hatch.

But while the people of Missouri were for silver it was only partly in deference to popular opinion that the Democratic party declared for that doctrine.

When Col. Chas. H. Jones became editor of the Republic, coming from Jacksonville, Florida, he was taken up by the then Governor David R. Francis, a grain merchant, or speculator, a very rich man and an aristocrat. The two were fast friends until, Col. Jones having married, the wife of the governor, for reasons sufficient to herself, refused to receive Mrs. Jones. Out of this social episode grew a feud. As the first result of that feud Col. Jones was forced out of the Republic. He went to the New York World. Ad interim, however, he managed to defeat the plan of President Cleveland to name Mr. Francis as a member of his cabinet in 1893. When Col. Jones fell out with Mr. Francis, the editor made an alliance with Mr. Joel Stone, who succeeded Mr. Francis as governor of Missouri.

In course of time Col. Jones was sent West to take charge of the *Post-Dispatch.* When he arrived in St. Louis he conferred with Governor Stone. Col. Jones wanted to destroy Francis, who had control of the Democratic party machinery. Francis had been "mentioned" for president. He was the brilliant, if chilly, leader of the party. He had wealth and he and his friends could "take care of" the visiting rural committeeman. Col. Jones scented the silver sentiment in the State. That sentiment suggested, naturally, antipathy to wealthy bosses and "grain gamblers." Col. Jones declared that the way to destroy Francis was by "taking up silver." And Col. Jones "took it up" with a vengeance. The sentiment had been lurking among the people all the time. For years the party committees warned the speakers to "steer clear of the money question." Col. Jones in print and Governor Stone on the stump, appealed to the people on the very thing the old rulers of the party had hedged on, and the battle was on.

Mr. Francis evaded the fight. He wanted harmony. He was suave and clammy but non-committal. He did not wish to come out for silver. He did not wish to oppose the silver people. Once or twice he threatened to fight and then he threw up his hands. Missouri declared for silver at 16 to 1, without a dissenting voice in the convention. The State committee was enlarged to render Mr. Francis' friends innocuous. Col. Jones and Governor Stone voted to support Bland for President at the Chicago convention and the National battle was precipitated. When Missouri declared for silver, with a candidate who represented the silver issue wholly and whose character endeared him especially to the bucolics everywhere, the silver sentiment became a political force to reckon with the stampede that ended with the nomination of Mr. Bryan was started.

So it seems to me that if Mrs. Francis had swallowed her prejudices and received Mrs. Jones there might have been a great deal of different history. Mrs. Jones was the Helen of the Siege of Wall Street. This incident is important only as showing, once again, how trifling things affect the destinies of Nations.

Had Mr. Francis and Col. Jones never disagreed, Col. Jones never would have left the "Republic." Col. Jones would have stood by Francis' interests as a banker and monied man. Col. Jones never would have obtained control of the *"Post-Dispatch."* Silver sentiment would have been smothered by the politicians of Missouri and Bland never would have been a candidate. There would have been no Missouri alliance with Mr. Altgeld and the combination of peculiar political ability that was attracted to Stone. Jones and Altgeld never would have dominated the Chicago convention as wholly as they did. To resent an affront to Mrs. Jones the Democratic party was rent asunder. Mr. Bland was taken up to destroy Mr. Francis and was himself destroyed in due time. The senators from Missouri, Messrs. Vest and Cockrell, were forced into the anti-Francis movement under threat of defeat by the men who had identified themselves with the popular feeling for their own purposes.

The late Mr. McCullagh of the *Globe-Democrat,* told me, when Vest became a silver champion that it was because he had to do so to retain his seat, and that Mr. McCullagh was a friend and extravagant admirer of Mr. Vest and his abilities.

Whatever one may think of silver he must admit that the turning down of Mr. Francis was a good thing. Mr. Francis represented the dodging Democracy. He stood for the evasion of a great issue; for intellectual and moral cowardice, for nauseous neutralism. Mr. Francis was the impersonation of political insincerity. He thought of the party—of keeping the party together, with himself on top—and his stand for what the opponents of silver call "sound money" was a very perfunctory performance. He never declared himself against the Chicago platform until he was offered the Secretaryship of the Interior, vice Hoke Smith, resigned.

In this we have a picture of the man whom I saw alluded to the other day as "the leader of the sound money forces in Missouri." A leader! Why, he couldn't be induced to come within the borders of the State, during the fight, nor did he come until he came home to vote, when, under the inspiration of a stupendous sound money parade, he declared himself.

When silver was the cry every spoilsman took it up, and the fact is that some of the loudest shouting was done by men who cared not at all for the doctrine. All the politicians got on the popular side. Every fellow that wanted an office became a shrieker for silver. All the men who had truckled to Francis while he was in power left him and went with the crowd. The party in Missouri had been in power for years and the same old gang had controlled the offices. They stayed together and they still retained their grip upon the offices. The gang got together on silver as upon everything else. The elimination of Francis carried out of the party no politicians of note. They remained. The corporation "attorneys" or lobbyists stood by the regulars. The fine workers of the Missouri Pacific, the 'Frisco, the Burlington roads were hand in glove with the party which was making war on corporations, with its mouth. Some of the railroads contributed to the support of the men who were "denouncing them in unmeasured terms." No one was more regular than "Bill" Phelps, the Missouri Pacific lobbyist, against whom Governor Stone and Col. Jones made war in connection with the enactment of a fellow-servant law. Col. Spencer of the Burlington was with the regulars too. All the party hacks, the caucus bosses, the township and country and congressional district leaders who had made the ticket for years fell in line. There was made no real change in party management. Mr. Francis and his lieutenant, Mr. Maffitt, were turned down, but the crowd that had trained with them went over to the opposition. I am not aspersing the silver cause. I mean to say only that the gang that ran things joined the silver cause in order to stay in power. There were no politicians at all in the ranks of the Missouri Gold Democrats. The politicians seized upon silver, which represented a general desire for change, in order to fasten themselves more thoroughly upon the party.

The result was that the nominations for State offices went to the same old crowd. Mr. Sesueur was nominated for Secretary of State. Mr. Siebert, who had been auditor, was nominated again. Frank Pitts, an ex-Confederate, who had been a candidate for a dozen things, but who, when defeated, never had done aught but "take his medicine," was nominated for Treasurer. Mr. Lon V. Stephens, who had been Treasurer was nominated for Governor and elected. He had been appointed Treasurer by Francis after the Noland defalcation, had been elected and had changed his allegiance from Francis to Stone. Mr. Stone, a man with somewhat of the scholarly taint to him, inclined to think, but prone to machination, ambitious, vindictive, able, elusive, made Stephens the nominee, and has been "sore at himself" ever since.

Stephens is a National banker. His family is wealthy and his wife's family is said to be the wealthiest in the State. It was the belief that when he was nominated he would "cough up" large "chunks of dough." But he didn't. The necessity for "dough" was evident to the managers of the party. There was no hope for funds from the interests that feared free silver. They wanted an "angel" candidate. Stephens failed to contribute. As an "angel" he was a "frost."

This National banker made a campaign of extreme rabidity. When Debs was managing the big Chicago strike this man wrote a letter to the *Mirror* in which he advocated Gatling guns for the suppression of Debs and his like. When he wanted to be Comptroller of the Currency under Cleveland he declared in an interview that Cleveland was "the greatest man since Jesus Christ." He denied that he was a National banker with his name on the bank's stationery. He denounced Cleveland for calling out the troops to suppress Debs. And while in the country he was posing as the enemy of the plutocrats, he was "tipping" them the wink in the cities, that they needn't be afraid he would hurt their interests. This candidate, who was proclaiming honesty had to suppress in Col. Jones' paper, a sensation dealing with his own alleged irregularities in the settlement of his father's estate. This personal-liberty Democrat had written a letter in favor of Prohibition. Mr. Stephens proclaimed that he was going to purify politics. When elected he appointed as Election Commissioner a man against whom there was a tremendous protest upon the part of the best element of the party. This man was accused of taking $1,200 from Ed Butler, the St. Louis "boss," to give to the members of the St. Louis city committee to boom the charter amendment providing for capital removal, and of putting the money in his own pocket. Ed. Butler entered suit for the money against this man Brady and his friend Higgins, appointed Excise Commissioner by Stephens. The suit was dismissed at Brady's expense. Then the capital movers at Sedalia sued for the money on the ground that the contract was against public polity. In other words he took the money to do something illegal, and, therefore, was entitled to keep it after failing to do the wrong. As a result of my comment upon this, Mr. Brady and I had a passage at fisticuffs on the street the other day, and the day following the Circuit Court here decided that the contract was valid and the suit for $1,200 would have to be tried on the issue of fact.

Mr. Brady was appointed Election Commissioner at the instigation of Mr. Louis C. Nelson, a St. Louis banker, brother-in-law of Governor Stephens. Mr. Brady is interested in a wholesale liquor store. His company rents a building from Mr. Nelson. Mr. Nelson is said to be interested in the company.

Mr. Higgins, the Excise Commissioner, was appointed at Mr. Nelson's instigation. The Excise Commissioner has charge of the issuance of all saloon licenses in St. Louis, Mr. Higgins is a good friend of Brady's and a protege of Nelson. A whisky drummer told me, and it is a common report around St. Louis, that the relationship of the man controlling the saloon licenses to Brady and Nelson is taken advantage of by the saloon men to ingratiate themselves by buying supplies at Brady's liquor store. I am not adding a word of color to the aspect of the case. The saloons are under tribute to Stephens' brother-in-law and his appointees. These people may not hold up the saloons, but the saloonists know that it is good policy to stand in with "the powers that be." A daily paper, the "Star," asserts that one of the Police Commissioners, a brewer, uses his position as controller of the police to protect dive-keepers who sell his beer. The paper has not been sued for libel. All this has been done in the name of silver and friendship for the people.

A brother of "Silver Dick" Bland was nominated for Judge of the Court of Appeals. The Populists had nominated a candidate named North for the same place. It is in evidence in Mr. Bland's own letters that he gave $1,000 to the Chairman of the Democratic State Central Committee to get North of the track. North withdrew. Afterwards he was reported reporter of the Court of Judge Bland. He denied that he had received $1,000. The Chairman of the State Democratic Committee then said he gave the money to the chairman of the Populist committee. The chairman of the populist committee denies that he got the $1,000. And so the matter stands. The Judge bought off the Populist candidate. The $1,000 is unaccounted for. The $1,000 does not appear in the Judge's statement of expenses as required by law. This "boodle" deal evokes the query whether if a candidate for Judge will buy his election he will not sell his justice. This deal, too, was consummated in the name of the masses.

I am told that the Governor has given the best places within his gift to his relatives, or the men selected by his relatives. I know that he appointed a man manager of the Nevada asylum on condition that he would vote out the Superintendent. The Superintendent showed the manager a letter from the Governor in which he declared that the Superintendent's retention was his dearest wish. The manager voted for the retention of the Superintendent and the Governor promptly removed the manager. This illustrates the gubernatorial character beautifully. The Governor of Missouri was receiver of the Fifth National Bank of St. Louis. He gave out that the bank would not pay more than 50 cents on the dollar in all. Therefore, his brother-in-law and other relatives bought up outstanding claims at that figure and below it. They bought up at least $30,000 worth. The bank paid 50 per cent. in sixty days. It has paid ninety-six per cent. in ten years. The question is, how could a receiver say a bank, that was in position to pay 50 per cent. in sixty days, would only pay that much in all? The receiver's relatives made 46 per cent. on their speculation. This is one of the performances characteristic of this kind of "friends of the people." The popular cause of silver, with all its generous enthusiasm for the rights of the poor, all its just resentment against oligarchies, political bosses, gangs of "grafters," combinations of the few for the plucking of the many, was taken charge of, in Missouri, by politicians of the type which can be imagined from what I have stated here of simple fact and conservative deduction. The cause of silver may be my "pet aversion" as a political theory, but I have all respect for the honest multitude who espoused it. I am convinced that what there is of good in that theory of reform of our evils is not advanced toward embodiment in our law by the character of the men who make the Chicago platform an excuse to get the public confidence and carry out schemes of public plunder, political corruption and miscellaneous incivism.

A few days ago Judge Klein in our Circuit Court uncovered what we call "a graft" in the matter of building association receiverships. It was discovered that politics stepped into these affairs to get for certain political lawyers, good fees. There was a ring in the receiverships of these concerns. The commissioner in one case would be attorney in another. The attorney in one case would be receiver in another with the commissioner as attorney and receiver as Commissioner. There were fees for all. No duty in connection with winding up the associations, to which there attached any compensation, was ever given outside the "charmed circle." Political attorneys got large fees for only going into court and asking that building associations be wound up. All these fees came out of the money of the poor people, which happened to be left after the looting or failure of the concerns. Those whose savings were invested in the concerns had little coming to them after the failures. The fees of the ring left little of that. All this "grinding of the faces of the poor" is being accomplished by those politicians who were most vocal in proclaiming their allegiance to the Chicago platform as a new "Magna Charta of Mankind."

These facts have nothing to do with the righteousness or wrongfulness of the Chicago platform. The suggestion that a good cause may be advanced by bad men and mean methods, it may be retorted that such men are calculated rather to injure the cause by their prominence than to help it by their unique idea of practical politics. People are apt to believe that the New Democracy is the outgrowth of such men, or that such men are the outgrowth of New Democracy, when, in fact, the men have attached themselves to the movement only for their own selfishness. When we think that the men who are doing the things I have pictured are engaged in an effort to make Stephens the next Senator from Missouri, it is plain that the character of the organization and its purpose will react dangerously against whatever there may be of genuine merit in the propositions of the Chicago platform.

And all this is being done in Missouri and the rural press connives at it. To criticize the administration is sacrilege. The papers are slavering over the Governor. They declare that he is "the champion of the people" next to Bryan. They identify him with the ideal that Mr. Bryan gave voice for in his Chicago speech. Nothing is to be said of any administration peccadilloes or crookedness, for fear of hurting the party and delaying the triumph of the great cause. All the political corruption of the party when it was dominated by plutocrats is condoned because its perpetrators shout "sixteen to one!" The administration, at a breath of criticism, has its subsidized organs—subsidized by anything from two to ten dollars—declare that the critic is a traitor to the cause, that he is a gold-bug or a republican in disguise. The people seem to respond to all this and the honest country editor dares not express himself for fear of losing subscribers or advertisers. The party cry drowns the criticism of acts that impeach the party. Submission to the party fetich makes every and any deed acceptable because it is done by the party's men. Nepotism, falsity to pledges, the plundering of the poor, the squeezing of the saloon interests, the "skinning" of depositors in banks, the records of violation of trust,—all these things are jammed down the throats of the Democracy of Missouri, and if the faithful dare to gag at the dose they are told "You traitor, you don't believe in Bryan, or 16 to 1!" And they swallow it all. The papers are slaves of the administration. They vie with each other in printing stomach-turning gush about these leaders. The country editors are forced into a conspiracy of silence and of support of a "machine" as vile as ever was worked under plutocratic auspices. The gang cries "silver, silver, silver," and so their jobs and schemes of personal profit are allowed to go on uncriticized. They have the faith. Damn the good works! The "push" in control of things in Missouri are Silver men, with about the same exalted purpose as Chilo, the Greek charlatan in "Quo Vadis" had in aligning himself with the Christians. It is a combination that is ready at any time to desert the cause of silver. It has been stated in Missouri time and again that the administration wants to "heal the breach" with the gold Democrats, that Governor Stephens has made overtures to ex-Governor Francis who, fortunately, is not much more of a gold bug than Stephens is a silver Democrat. The new party faith means nothing to the men in power and warfare upon them is not, in any sense, a warfare upon the principles they profess to represent, unless it may happen that the character of the men shall become confused with the principles. But these men were "in the push" before the Chicago platform was an issue. They are what they were before. The new principles have made them no better. They are worse because they plot their infamy in the name of a political purification and a humanizing of economy.

In view of the almost unparalleled lack of independence in the Missouri rural press there does not seem much hope of reaching the people with a statement of the truth about conditions. The country editor in Missouri insults his subscribers by taking for granted that they are so prejudiced they will not take a paper that criticizes the man who sneaked into power as a bogus silver man. By keeping their readers in ignorance of the deeds of their officers and servants, by suppressing all unfavorable comment, the newspapers block the way to reform. There is no way to reach the people. They are kept in ignorance. They are fed upon "plate" fake puffs of the administration prepared by the Governor's "literary bureau." Whatever he prepares is printed, and nothing else. The people are stuffed upon "taffy" and the men in power are thus enabled to deceive the people and strengthen themselves for the tightening of their grip upon the offices. The subserviency of the rural press in Missouri is something slavish beyond imagination heretofore. The papers, in the main, are edited by the political machine. The press, that engine of enlightenment, is industriously engaged in clouding the intelligence of the people and identifying a cause which in its abstract intention is good, with the selfishness of bad men. Reform cannot come from the politicians. It cannot come from the people kept in ignorance of the need of it by prostitutes of the press.

The matter with Missouri is that there is too much idolization of the party. There is no partisan independence. There is no courage in the Democratic press. The truth is suppressed rather than the evil about which a truth is told. The worship of party goes to the extreme of worship of all the moral ugliness of partisanism. The men who know what is wrong, who know that the leaders of the New Democracy are in harmony with it only for their own ends, who know that in the name of political purity and economic honesty a lot of political jobbers and crooks are continuing the evils of the old political regime, remain silent. The St. Louis *Republic* shifts and shuffles and maintains a neutral attitude. It is suspected of gold bugism and it dares not criticize the Governor that it scourged in cartoon and comment. The *Post-Dispatch*, that was the greatest silver daily and is owned by the millionaire Pulitzer, is now suspected of gold bugism. It makes war upon the Governor, but its position robs its criticism of effectiveness. The Kansas City Times scores the Governor but its opposition is believed to be based upon the refusal of the Governor to appoint its owners' candidate to a position of importance. My criticism is denounced as the criticism of a gold-bug. But I am not criticizing the party policy s I am writing here about the men. They would disgrace any principles they might profess. I am not opposing anyone because he was for Bryan. I am pointing out conditions and circumstances that are matters of public record, of common talk among silver men, of wide-open notoriety, that are flourishing in Missouri, under the cloak of a bogus devotion to Mr. Bryan and the Chicago platform. These things are true. If the people knew them, if the fact of the existence of these things were not suppressed, the fact that the men who are working the evil are silver shouters would not save them from the popular wrath.

"O Liberty," said Madam Roland on the steps of the guillotine,"what crimes are committed in thy name!" In the name of Silver, too, crimes are committed and the criminals flourish as prophets of a new and better time. Silver will have a better chance when the crooks who have identified themselves with it, in Missouri and other States, are repudiated. If free coinage be a good thing, it will never be believed while bad men conspicuously stand for it. If education will develop the mind to the destruction of our political and economic miseries, a gagged press is not the means to such education. How can a press be trusted in its assaults on the old order when it suppresses the truth that the men and methods of the old regime are flourishing to the profit of the former under the new? What use is any platform, however noble in its aspirations or purposes, if the men who attain to power upon it continue all the meanness and nefariousness of the men who flourished under the old domination of the bosses, the corporations and the trusts?

The altruism of the Chicago platform—which I think mistaken—is admirable in so far as so many millions of people honestly believe its principles are for the benefit of the oppressed and unfortunate of the earth. This altruism is knocked and blasphemed by being made the means to the entrenchment in power in Missouri, of self-and-pelf seekers. The people are deceived. The press keeps them deceived. The Chicago principles are betrayed into the hands of men who have no principle but profit. A reform movement is turned over to the men against whom the movement is directed. The cause of free coinage is committed to a national banker. The cause of honest elections is committed to the care of a professional ballot-eater. The cause of the people is made the means to build up a machine. The liberty of the press is advocated by paper subsidized by political pap. The "friends of the people" in Missouri, are "grafters." The "foes of the corporations" are the tools of these institutions. The "enemies of corruption" are themselves corruptionists. The people are kept ignorant of all this under a false impression that the eradication of evil will injure the cause of Silver, under cover of which these men grasped power.

And that's what's the matter with Missouri.

St. Louis, December 16, 1897.

Lector House believes that a society develops through a two-fold approach of continuous learning and adaptation, which is derived from the study of classic literary works spread across the historic timeline of literature records. Therefore, we aim at reviving, repairing and redeveloping all those inaccessible or damaged but historically as well as culturally important literature across subjects so that the future generations may have an opportunity to study and learn from past works to embark upon a journey of creating a better future.

This book is a result of an effort made by Lector House towards making a contribution to the preservation and repair of original ancient works which might hold historical significance to the approach of continuous learning across subjects.

HAPPY READING & LEARNING!

LECTOR HOUSE LLP
E-MAIL: lectorpublishing@gmail.com